Horses and wagons wait [...]
passengers and cargo (Joh[...]

W. Ahhem
Falconer Phaoc
Leominster

CHANNEL ISLANDS' RAILWAY STEAMERS

The Outer Dock at Southampton with, from left to right, Normannia in Berth 9, Isle of Guernsey in Berth 8, and Isle of Sark in Berth 7 (British Railways).

CHANNEL ISLANDS' RAILWAY STEAMERS

KEVIN LE SCELLEUR

PSL

Patrick Stephens, Wellingborough

First published in 1985

British Library Cataloguing in Publication Data

Le Scelleur, Kevin
    Channel Islands' railway steamers.
    1. Ferries—Channel Islands—History
    I. Title
    386'.6'094234   HE5813.C4/

ISBN 0-85059-707-2

Photoset in 10pt Baskerville by MJL Typesetting,
Hitchin, Herts. Printed in Great Britain on 115 gsm
Fineblade coated cartridge, and bound, by The
Garden City Press, Letchworth, Herts, for the
publishers, Patrick Stephens Limited, Denington
Estate, Wellingborough, Northants, NN8 2QD,
England.

Contents

Dedication

On May 9 1945 a small boy was taken by his parents to St Helier Harbour, Jersey, to watch the British forces as they arrived to liberate the island after five years of occupation by the German army.

Six weeks later a second journey was made, this time to watch the arrival of the first mailboat from England since June 1940. That ship, the *Isle of* *Guernsey*, painted grey apart from her yellow funnels with black tops, inspired the boy's interest in the mailboats, an interest which has never waned. This book is dedicted to my late father for passing on to me his love of the sea and ships.

To the memory of A.W.J. Le S.

The Isle of Guernsey *arrives in St Helier Harbour on June 26 1945, re-opening the mail service to the islands. This was the occasion that inspired the author's lifelong love of the Channel Island railway steamers (Author).*

Introduction

Over the past forty-five years a number of books and articles have been published devoted to or including coverage of the shipping services to the Channel Islands and north-west France. Reading these it becomes apparent that each is a re-write, taken from previous re-writes, whose origins can all be traced back to a series of articles which appeared in the magazine *The Engineer* in the first half of 1902. Articles on the London and South Western Railway (L & SWR) shipping services written by Mr T.C. Orme, a company official, appeared in magazines in 1907 and 1912, and views expressed in these have been taken as fact in later works; this has led to inaccuracies being perpetuated. In an endeavour to shed more light on the subject I have drawn up a day-by-day chart of shipping arrivals in Jersey, from the time the railway companies first became involved in the services on May 1 1842. My research has extended back as far as 1823 to when steam ships first commenced on the routes, so as to give as full a history as possible.

Information culled from the newspapers of Jersey, Guernsey and Southampton is combined with that from the minute books of the railway companies held in the Public Record Office at Kew and with that from the Customs Registers held at the same place. Added to this is the data gained from an inspection of the records held in the Harbour Offices of St Helier and St Peter Port and the result is a book which I hope will shed new light on the subject.

The book was only intended initially to cover the Southampton–Channel Islands route but, as the research progressed, so much information on the other routes came to light, that I extended the work to cover these. It must be emphasised, however, that the routes to the Channel Islands are the main subject of this work.

Illustrations

In selecting the illustrations for this work, I have tried to choose those which depict the ships in the areas and ports where they operated; others are included purely because they are unique.

The early vessels are portrayed from paintings or watercolours by the Jersey artist P.J. Ouless (1817–1885), a prolific painter of both sailing ships and steamers, without whom the maritime heritage of the area would be much the poorer.

I have tried to provide two illustrations if a vessel has undergone major alterations during her life and, in the case of sister ships, many are shown in differing colour schemes, to give a more varied coverage.

The credit for each illustration is given to the collection from which it came except where the photographer is known, in which case his name is given. The Southampton City Museums now house a number of maritime collections which form their Historical Ports Collection.

Chapter 1

Evolution of the steamer services

The origins of the railway-steamer service to the Channel Islands may be traced back to 1823 when, for the first time, a steamer, the *Triton*, operated a short summer season sailing from Southampton to Havre de Grace (Le Havre). In the same year the *Medina*, a vessel used on the Isle of Wight route, was hired for a trip to Guernsey and from there made an excursion to Jersey.

From these humble beginnings, the service rapidly expanded and, only one year later, there were no less than three ships operating a regular service on these routes. As might be expected, in these early days 'a regular service' only applied to the summer months. The *Lord Beresford* and the *Ariadne* sailed to the Channel Islands from Portsmouth and Southampton, respectively, while the *Camilla* took over the service to Le Havre though, due to the late arrival of the last ship, *Medina* ran the service for the first few weeks of the season. After her first season the *Lord Beresford* moved her English terminal to Southampton and ran in direct opposition to *Ariadne*. In 1827 competition began on the Le Havre route, when the *St David* commenced service; she ran for one season, being replaced in 1828 by the *George IV*.

At first the steamers were owned by partnerships, with frequent changes in share ownership (this explains the mistaken assumption in previous works, whereby the names of major shareholders were taken to be those of the owners). This all changed in 1834 when the steamer *Apollo* replaced the *George IV* on the Le Havre route. Her significance lies in the fact that she was the first ship we shall encounter to be registered to a company, the Apollo Steam Packet Company. The following year, a London firm, which wished to enter the passenger trade to the Channel Islands, chartered the Glasgow steamer *Liverpool* and placed her on a service from London to the Channel Islands via Southampton. She was a much larger vessel than those trading to the islands, offering a superior service, and it was not long before the London calls were dropped and she operated in direct competition from Southampton. A price-cutting war then ensued, the result of which was the withdrawal of the *Liverpool* from the islands on August 20 1835. The vessel then went on the Spanish route and was sold in November to owners in Dublin, and in early 1842 she passed to the Peninsular and Orient (P&O) Company of London.

The higher standard of accommodation that the *Liverpool* offered, as compared with the ships already on the route, meant that her withdrawal caused letters to appear in the Channel Islands press calling for a stock company to be set up in order to improve the service. Soon after these letters, a prospectus for the South of England Steam Packet Company appeared in the Jersey press on September 8 1835. The company was to have a capital of £200,000 though, in the event, it was not formed—a point which has caused confusion to many historians. Its principals, however, joined with others and came forward on November 17 with a prospectus for the formation of the South of England Steam Navigation Company,* in which it was stated that agreement had been reached for the company to purchase the *Ariadne* and *Camilla*. Slightly earlier, on November 2 1835 a prospectus had been published for the formation of the British & Foreign SN Company, to be based in London, whose share issue was fully subscribed within two weeks according to the local Channel Island press.

The British and Foreign SN Co did not purchase the *Lord Beresford* as many works have claimed, advertising instead that its service between Southampton and the Channel Islands would commence on December 8 1835 using the newly acquired *Byron*. She, too, was not purchased, nor did the service start on that date, as the company had decided to purchase a brand-new vessel from the builders. This ship, the *Lady de Saumarez*, had arrived at Southampton on January 4 1836 and completed her

*Henceforth, the initials 'SN' are used to represent 'Steam Navigation' in company titles.

maiden voyage to the Channel Islands on January 8 1836. The South of England SN Co had meanwhile ordered two new ships for their services; the first, the *Atalanta*, was built at Cowes and arrived in the Channel Islands for the first time on August 24 1836. The *Monarch* was launched on May 1 1836, but did not enter service on the Le Havre route until April 4 1837.

With *Atalanta* in service, *Ariadne* took up the summer service between Jersey and St Malo, being replaced on July 30 1837 by *Camilla*.

During the winter of 1835–36, the *Lord Beresford* was given a thorough overhaul, which included new engines and conversion into a passenger-only ship. She re-entered service to the Channel Islands on August 23 1836 but, being no match for the new steamers mentioned above, was withdrawn after only one voyage and placed on the Le Havre route. She was no more successful on this route and was put up for sale. The British & Foreign SN Co also acquired a share of the Le Havre route in 1836, when they purchased the *Apollo*, a vessel already on the service.

The service given by the British & Foreign SN Co did not last long, finishing on July 29 1837 when the *Lady de Saumarez* arrived in the Channel Islands and fired her signalling gun to announce the transfer of the service to the Commercial Steam Packet Company* of London. The latter company had been in existence since at least May 1834, and had gradually taken over the vessels of the British & Foreign SN Co. The Commercial SP Co was engaged in the Spanish trade, as is shown by an advertisement in the press on September 4 1837 announcing that 'the *Calpe* would leave the Tower (London) on 6th September and would call the following day at Southampton, leaving as soon as Her Majesty's Mail arrived from London, for Lisbon, Cadiz, Gibraltar and Malaga. The vessel would in future not call at Falmouth, but Southampton instead.' The vessels used on this service were the *Calpe, Chieftain* and *Transit*.

The following year the Peninsular SN Co (later P&O) also commenced calling at Southampton on its service to Spain. The *Liverpool* made the first such arrival on August 25 1838, followed by the *Royal Tar* on September 8. Within a few weeks the Commercial SP Co withdrew from the Spanish trade and concentrated on coastal and cross-Channel trade. The vessels which had been on the Spanish trade were dispersed on the company's other routes. One such vessel which appeared on the London–Southampton–Weymouth route in October 1838

was the *Grand Turk*, a vessel which was later to feature greatly in services from Southampton. An advertisement in a Southampton paper for April 13 1839 indicates that the Channel Islands service was maintained by the *Lady de Saumarez* and that to Le Havre by *Grand Turk*. The paper also stated that the service from London to Weymouth, maintained by the *City of Glasgow* for the preceding two months, would no longer call at Southampton, but would route direct.

* * *

Southampton at this time was a fast-growing port due both to its tidal advantages and to the fact that the railway line from London was nearing completion. The first section from Nine Elms to Woking was opened in May 1838, while two more sections, from Southampton to Winchester and from Winchfield to Basingstoke, were opened in August 1839. The complete line was opened on May 11 1840 and Southampton became a terminal for rail passengers who wanted to travel to the south-west of England. Shipping services then took passengers onwards to Weymouth, Torquay, Dartmouth and Plymouth. It was on this latter service that the *Robert Burns* first came to Southampton, calling on December 9 1841, while our old friend *Lord Beresford* had been acquired by the Falmouth & Southampton SP Co, which commenced operations between the two ports named in its title in September 1841.

1841 also saw more competition on both the Le Havre route, with *Calpe* and *Monarch* being opposed by the *Hamburg*, and on the Channel Islands route, where the Commercial SP Co used the *Lady de Saumarez* and *Transit* while the South of England SN Co relied on the *Atalanta*. Towards the end of 1841, the Commercial SP Co found itself in financial difficulties, which should logically have resulted in the merger of the two companies in the area, but this was not to be the case.

The steamers from Southampton were viewed by the proprietors of the London & South Western Railway (L & SWR) as a natural extension of the railway service, and, hence, they entered negotiations for the purchase of the vessels based at Southampton.

The terms of the (private member's) Railway Act did not allow the railway company to own or operate steamships and, to circumvent this, a separate company was set up called the South Western SP Co, which had virtually the same shareholders as its parent railway company. Apart from taking over the Southampton operation of the Commercial SP Co, the new company also acquired two vessels owned by a Mr Frewn of Rye. Contrary to the statements of earlier works, no trace of these

---

*'Steam Packet' is denoted by 'SP' in the remainder of this book.

vessels having operated to the Channel Islands can be found and therefore they are not featured in this book. The new company took over the Commercial SP Co's services on May 1 1842, having acquired the following vessels: *Calpe, Grand Turk, Lady de Saumarez, Robert Burns* and *Transit.* On the same day the directors of the railway company agreed to loan the packet company £20,000 to put the shipping services in proper order. The loan also financed the building of two new ships as was announced in September 1842. The newly acquired ships were re-located so that *Robert Burns* moved from the Plymouth run to join the *Grand Turk* on the Le Havre service, *Calpe* took up the Plymouth station, while the Channel Islands service was maintained by *Lady de Saumarez* and *Transit.*

Both the Channel Islands and Le Havre services were operated once a week in the winter, with the vessel on the islands service making a trip to St Malo during her stay-over in Jersey. During the shoulder months of the season, both services operated twice a week, this being stepped up to three times a week during the summer. To maintain these services, which took approximately 14 hours each way, one ship was placed on each route while a third vessel made one trip per week on each route. The first of the new ships, the *South Western,* was launched on May 15 1843, and took the company directors on a trial trip from Southampton on July 10 before taking up the duties of third vessel, arriving in the Channel Islands on her maiden voyage on August 1 1843. In October 1844 the second of the new ships, the *Wonder,* arrived at Southampton. She was to prove an outstanding vessel, remaining in the fleet until December 1873.

The two new ships had been built mainly to improve the service to Le Havre as the Directors regarded the opening of the railway line between Paris and Rouen in May 1843 as a major boost to the cross-Channel traffic; it was not until the line was extended to Le Havre in March 1847, however, that the full potential of this line could be realised.

For the winter of 1844–45, an agreement was reached between the South Western SP Co and their rivals, the South of England SN Co, for the operation of a joint service on both routes, though it was only the name of the former Company that appeared on the advertisements. These announced that *Grand Turk* and *Calpe* would operate on the Le Havre route, while *Atalanta* and *Transit* would maintain the Channel Islands service. This arrangement did not last very long. Before 18 months had expired, on April 16 1846, a newspaper reported that differences had arisen between the two companies and that, henceforth, both would operate on their own account. One of the reasons for this could

have been the talks taking place between the South Western SP Co and the Post Office, regarding the carriage of mail to the islands by the packet company.

Since 1794 the Royal Mail had been conveyed to the Channel Islands in sailing cutters based at Weymouth, but with the introduction of passenger steamers in 1824 there was mounting pressure for steamers to take over this service and they did so in 1827. Control of the steamers passed from the GPO to the Admiralty in January 1837. However, they were no match for the privately owned steamers, and with the South Western SP Co acquiring ever faster vessels some action was called for.

Such action was taken when, in April 1845, a contract was entered into between the company and the GPO for the transportation of mail to and from the Channel Islands from April 26 at a cost of £2,000 per year. The contract called for three round voyages to the islands each week throughout the year, which, with the breaking of the agreement with the South of England SN Co, stretched the South Western SP Co to the limits. Initially the service was operated by the *South Western,* the *Wonder* (making her first call to the islands) and the *Transit,* the latter being replaced after a few weeks by the *Calpe.* It was normal for the Le Havre steamer to make a call off Portsmouth to pick up passengers and mail; in late 1845 this call was re-placed by a separate service, operated by *Grand Turk.* She was replaced in 1846 by *Transit* and, in May 1846, *Robert Burns* reappeared in the company's advertisements after a four-year absence.

With two new ships and the mail contract, the South Western SP Co was in a very strong position, and the question was raised of how long the South of England SN Co could continue to compete against the might of the railway-backed company. The question was answered in July 1846, when talks were held between the two parties and it was announced, on August 1, that they would merge on October 1 1846.

Developments after the merger

The merger was effected by the formation of a new company, named the New South Western SN Co, which purchased the South Western SP Co and its effects for £56,623 and the South of England SN Co and its effects for £29,500. The last advertisement for the South of England SN Co was on September 30 1846. The demise of the company also brought about the end of the Torquay–Channel Islands service which it had operated since 1843 using the *Ariadne;* she departed for the last time from the Channel Islands on September 25. The *Atalanta* and *Monarch,* both former South of England SN Co

Ships, were laid up, leaving the winter service in the hands of the former packets company's vessel.

The new fleet totalled eleven vessels, of which only two were modern ships, the remainder being well over ten years old, two of them being twenty-two years of age! This led, on December 11 1846, to the directors of the L & SWR agreeing a loan of £50,000 for the new company, which allowed three new ships to be built and the services to be put on a more economic footing.

With competition at an end, services were reduced to a realistic level and the direct Portsmouth–Le Havre service was discontinued and replaced by a call from the Southampton steamer in October 1846. After their winter lay-up the *Atalanta* made her first call with mail to the Channel Islands on April 20 1847, being followed by the *Monarch* on June 8. They were not used long as mailboats due to the construction of the new vessels, *Atalanta* spending only two months as a carrier of the mail until June 23 and *Monarch* lasting until November 18. *Atalanta* then commenced a cargo service to the islands and Le Havre.

The first of the new vessels, the *Express,* was commissioned in July 1847 and placed on the Le Havre route. A virtual sister to the *Wonder* with the exception that she had two funnels, her arrival released the *Grand Turk,* which opened a new service between Southampton and Penzance that was maintained until the end of the year. The service was operated again the following year, but that is the last trace that can be found of it. *Camilla* had continued to maintain the Jersey–France services between May and October each year but, upon the completion of her 1847 season, she was withdrawn and not seen in Jersey again.

The first of the new ships for the Channel Islands route was the *Courier,* which was completed in October 1847 and made her maiden voyage to the islands on November 12. (It should be noted that the ship was registered as *Courrier* but was never referred to as such.) She was joined by her sister, the *Dispatch,* in May 1848, which made her maiden voyage to the islands from the port of Poole on May 2. Poole was being hailed as the new cross-Channel packet port, but the service to the islands lasted only one season. The *Dispatch* in fact made only two trips from the port before taking up service from Southampton, leaving the route in the hands of the *South Western.* The service from Poole went to Jersey and then continued to St Malo, thereby providing a French link. On the last sailing of the season on September 30, the *South Western* ran aground when leaving Poole, the passengers being taken off by the *Monarch,* while, the *South Western* waited for the next spring tides to refloat her.

The loans made by the railway company resulted in the mortgage of most of the fleet to the railway in November 1847, though with the entry into service of the new ships there must have been little value left in the older members of the fleet. At a meeting of the company in February 1848 this was clearly shown when it was decided to sell off these older units and no buyers could be found. Only *Grand Turk* found employment, being chartered to run the mail from Alexandria to Jaffa and Beirut in connection with the P & O company.

In 1848 the L & SWR presented a private bill to Parliament which requested, among other things, the right to operate steamship services. This request was granted on August 14 1848, but only for a period of fourteen years. The railway company then sought a lease of the steamship company, and this was discussed at the latter's meeting held on February 15 1849. After a stormy debate the meeting was adjourned until the 18th, on which date the lease was approved by 1673 votes to 829. The lease was deemed to have come into effect on January 1 1849, and a special committee was set up by the railway company to run the Steam Packet Department, as it became known. The services continued to be advertised in the Channel Islands under the name of the 'New South Western Steam Navigation Company' until May 1851, after which the shipping advertisement appeared under the L & SWR company title, which had already been in use in Southampton in September 1849.

The new, L & SWR-dominated company now began to dispose of surplus tonnage. In August 1849 it sold the *Monarch,* which was converted into a barque and sailed out to Australia via New Zealand. In November 1849 the newspapers informed the public 'that four of the older wooden vessels were to have their machinery removed and the hulls broken up, the vessels being *Camilla, Ariadne, Calpe* and one other'. The other vessel was presumably the *Robert Burns* and, despite the report, *Calpe* was not broken up but sold and converted into a sailing ship, being lost on the coast near Tangiers in April 1852.

By 1850 the re-organised services had settled into a regular pattern, with *Courier* and *Dispatch* on the Channel Islands route, *Express* and *Wonder* on the Le Havre route, and *South Western* acting as relief. The Channel Islands route, with its mail contract, was now the senior route and commanded the best vessels, and when either of the regular ships were off service the *Express* came from the Le Havre route, which would be covered by the *South Western;* in reserve were the *Atalanta, Transit* and *Lady de Saumarez.* During the summer of 1850, the *South Western* was stationed in Jersey and maintained a service to St Malo and Granville, and also made ex-

Alliance disembarking passengers in St Malo—a scene that gives
some idea of the scale of operations in the early days (*J.Mc David*).

cursions to Sark, Alderney and Cherbourg. On
August 14 1850 she began a service from the islands
to Weymouth; this service was terminated in
December.

Atalanta introduced a short-lived cargo service in
1850, but this only operated to Jersey on a few
occasions. In February 1851, the cargo service was
reintroduced, now advertised as a 'Cheap Boat' service and was maintained on a regular basis by the
Transit. The *Grand Turk* returned to L & SWR

service and was used to open a new route from
Southampton to Morlaix, calling en route at
Guernsey. She first made this trip on May 12 1851,
but the service was not a success and was
discontinued in the December.

A major development occurred in 1852 when the

L & SWR introduced the first screw steamer to its services. For a ten week period, in May–July, they chartered the *Lady Seale* to operate the cheap-boat service. On July 6 1852 the *Courier* re-entered service after a major overhaul, which included installing new boilers, a ventilation system and new davits, and the raking of the masts and funnels. The ship was also painted in the new colour scheme, adopted by the L & SWR, of all-black funnels, and white paddle boxes and lifeboats. In November of the same year, the *Dispatch* went into the repair yard to have similar work carried out on her, returning to service on April 25 1853.

On account of the Crimean War, the Le Havre route was carrying much more traffic than previously and so the *Express* was kept on this route while the *Wonder* was used to undertake relief duties to the Channel Islands. By 1854 the *Grand Turk* had reached the end of her useful life and a new vessel was built for the Le Havre route. She was named the *Alliance* to commemorate the end of hostilities and entered service in July 1855. October 31 1855 saw the last trip of the *Transit* on the cheap-boat service to the Channel Islands, her place being taken for a short time by the *South Western* and then by the *Atalanta*. A further new ship was built for the Havre service in 1856, named *Havre*; with her began the tradition of naming the ships after the ports served by the L & SWR, a practice which lasted until 1877.

A challenge to the L & SWR

In 1857 the L & SWR found that after an eleven-year monopoly they again had competition on the Channel Islands route. For many years the Channel Islanders had campaigned for a passenger service from the port of Weymouth, as this route had a much shorter sea crossing than that from Southampton and also did not suffer as greatly from the menace of fog, which often delayed the Southampton boats. The disadvantage of Weymouth had been the lack of rail communication; with the line's arrival at Weymouth in January 1857, this obstacle was removed.

The islanders had never liked the idea of the railway company operating services on which they depended and could easily recall the fact that the early steam ships had had owners in the islands. Now as the L & SWR appeared not to want to operate from Weymouth, an opportunity presented itself to the islanders to operate their own service, and the Weymouth & Channel Islands SP Co was set up with money from Jersey, Guernsey and Weymouth.

The L & SWR had let it be known earlier that they intended to introduce a service to the Channel Islands from the Dorset port, but it took the an-

nouncement of the Weymouth and Channel Island SP Co that it too intended to commence a service in April to spur the L & SWR into action and they set the date of their first such service as May 1 1857. The L & SWR was actually ready to start before that date, as it turned out, and placed an advertisement in the papers on March 31 giving the starting date of the service as April 13. On the same day, the Weymouth & Channel Island SP Co had announced that their service would commence on April 11. In the event, the Weymouth company were not ready for the 11th, and so it was the L & SWR that reaped the glory, with the *Express* opening the service on the appointed day.

The Weymouth & Channel Island SP Co began its operation very quickly; to ensure as short a delay as possible two ships had been chartered, the *Aquila* and *Cygnus,* which commenced service on April 17, the former from Jersey and the latter from Weymouth. *Express* maintained the L & SWR service alone, being relieved mainly by *Wonder,* though *South Western* did spend occasional periods on the route.

In September 1858, the Weymouth & Channel Islands SP Co attempted to take a share of Continental traffic by opening a service between Weymouth and Cherbourg. The steamer *Brighton* was purchased from a Mr H. Maple of Newhaven, for the route; *Brighton* also made calls at Alderney. The venture was not, however, a success and was withdrawn in June 1859.

Express made only a few trips on the Weymouth–Channel Islands route in the summer of 1859, on the last of which she was wrecked (see Ship Histories entry for details). *Wonder* maintained the Weymouth service until December 12 1859, after which the service was suspended as the *Wonder* was needed in Southampton and, indeed, the service was never resumed—the L & SWR simply left it to the Weymouth & Channel Islands SP Co. The *Express* was replaced by the *Southampton* which arrived in the islands on October 13 1860.

By 1860, eleven years of the 14-year lease of the New South Western SN Co had passed, and the L & SWR went back to Parliament seeking permanent steamship powers. These were granted on August 6 1860 and talks then commenced between the two companies. Agreement could not be reached, however, and the matter went to arbitration.

The L & SWR officially took over the New South Western SN Co when the lease terminated on June 30 1862. From that date their shipping services expanded at a hitherto unprecedented rate and Southampton became the hub of a large holiday trade to the Channel Islands and France, carrying in addition most of the cargo on the routes.

Chapter 2

L & SWR operates in its own right

With the shipping services now firmly under their control, the L & SWR set about improving both the services and the ships. *Atalanta* was given a complete refit to allow her to continue the cheap-boat service to Jersey, while the *Southampton* was also given a thorough overhaul with the object of improving her speed, running trials on February 24 1863. A large new paddle-steamer was also ordered, being launched as the *Normandy* on June 17 1863, which underwent trials on September 12 and arrived in the islands on her maiden voyage a week later on the 19th.

Expansion of services

On July 11 1863 the L & SWR took over the Jersey–St Malo route which had been previously operated by the Jersey SP Co and the *Wonder* was stationed at Jersey to maintain the route. The *Dumfries*—which had maintained the service—remained idle at Jersey until November, when she proceeded to Southampton and was then used on a cargo service to Le Havre and later Honfleur.

The bye-laws of the Port of Southampton required that all passengers should embark from the Royal Pier (to help repay its building costs) and thus the steamers loaded cargo in the docks, then proceeded to the Royal Pier for their passengers before sailing. This was most inconvenient and, in May 1864, talks were held, which resulted in the termination of this requirement.

A large new paddle-steamer was built for the fleet in 1864, being launched on August 8 as *Brittany*, and arriving in the islands on her maiden voyage on November 17. This allowed *Southampton* to move to the Le Havre route until 1870 when, due to the loss of *Normandy,* she again took up the islands service. 1864 also saw the completion of the railway line between Paris and St Malo, with the opening taking place on June 27. The Brittany port was then seen as an attractive alternative to the Normandy ports already served and a new direct service from Southampton commenced. The following year, a screw steamer, the *Griffin*, was purchased for the service,

while a new screw vessel was built. Named the *Saint Malo* this latter ship entered service early in October 1865, which allowed the *Griffin* to have improvements carried out, including the building of a poop to provide extra covered accommodation.

Earlier the same year a new service to Honfleur had been opened and, after a short period, the *Dumfries* was placed on the route, remaining linked with it until she was sold. On January 7 1867 the *Caesarea* was launched for the St Malo route and entered service on March 22, replacing the *Griffin.* A further expansion of the L & SWR routes took place later in the year, when in December the Jersey–Granville route was taken over from the French company which operated it, together with the vessel *Comète*. The ship left Jersey on January 1 1868 for a refit at Southampton, returning on May 28 as the *Granville*. At this time the L & SWR ventured into the second-hand market, and the first large paddle steamer so purchased was the *Waverley* which, after a refit, arrived in the Channel Islands on December 23 1868, having been delayed by bad weather. In April the following year the *Alice* was also purchased, arriving in Southampton on May 3; after a refit, she ran trials on June 22 and was then placed on the St Malo route.

New ground was broken in May 1869 when, on May 10 the *Dispatch* opened a new service between Southampton and Cherbourg. On the day that the *Alice* ran her trials, it was announced that her sister ship, the *Fannie,* had also been acquired; in July *Fannie* commenced on the Honfleur service, though it was not until after a refit and official trials in March 1870 that she entered full passenger service.

With the fleet increasing in size, it was time for the older vessels to bow out and, in September 1869, the *Atalanta* was towed to Jersey and converted into a coal hulk to supply the needs of the two ships based in the island (for the Jersey–St Malo and Jersey–Granville services).

On January 1 1870, the Channel Islands service was increased from thrice weekly to daily (except Sunday), the alteration being made to provide a better mail service to the islands. The extra three services were operated by the smaller units of the fleet, which also carried some passengers, though the majority of passengers still preferred to travel by the larger paddle-steamers. It was, therefore, a major disaster when the *Normandy* was lost due to a collision on March 17 1870. The ship was bound from Southampton to the islands when, 25 miles south of the Needles in poor visibility, she collided with the steamer *Mary*. The speed of the *Normandy* caused the bow of the other ship to cut deep into her hull just aft of the paddle box on the starboard side, causing her to sink quickly with the loss of 33 lives.

By late 1870, the Franco–Prussian War was at its height and the L & SWR fleet was extended to its limits, carrying thousands of people fleeing from France, while in the other direction they carried foodstuffs and materials of war. On May 5 1871, there arrived at Southampton the last paddle-steamer to be acquired by the L & SWR. Named *Wolf*, she was initially placed on the St Malo service, but later moved to the Le Havre route. In early 1872 the L & SWR replaced the *Dumfries* on the Honfleur service with the *Maria*, which they had just purchased from her Liverpool owners, the vessel having been completed as late as October 1871.

The first chartering of a ship to carry the ever increasing volume of produce from the Channel Islands took place in 1873, and from that time it was an annual practice for the bulk of the islands' crops to be carried in chartered ships. In November of the same year the daily mail service reverted to a thrice-weekly timetable and the cheap-boat service was re-introduced to run twice a week and carry mail to the islands. The cheap-boat service was, in the main, operated by the *Caesarea* and the *Honfleur,* and for both vessels it was the first time that they saw regular service to the islands, even if the service was only operated during the winter.

New generation of steamers

The 1870s was a period of major improvement in the steam engine, with the basic engine being compounded and superheaters being applied to the steam supply. This helped to make the vessels more economic, though it was not worth spending money on the very old units in the fleet, which were gradually withdrawn. These improvements allowed the screw-propelled ship to come into its own and, between 1873 and mid-1875, five new screw steamers were built.

On June 5 1873 the *Waverley* was lost on the Platte Boue off the north-east coast of Guernsey. Soon after, in late 1873, the first of the new vessels was launched. Named *Cherbourg,* she was followed early

the following year by *Honfleur* and then *Guernsey,* the latter being placed on the St Malo route. The next new ship, the *South Western,* ran trials on December 28 1874 and joined the *Guernsey* on the St Malo station, but in March 1875 ran for a period on the Channel Islands mail service, and as a result an order for a slightly larger screw-propelled vessel for the Channel Islands service was placed. The last of the five new vessels, the *Alderney,* ran trials in May 1875. In the meantime, another paddle steamer, the *Havre* which had helped on the islands route since 1869, was lost on February 16, also on the Platte Boue.

A new steamer for the Channel Islands route, the *Diana,* was launched by Aitken & Mansel of White-inch, Glasgow, on November 30 1876 and, after trials on February 9 1877, was placed on the St Malo service from February 14, after which she made her maiden voyage to the Channel Islands on April 7 1877. From this ship developed the line of mailboats that culminated in the *Caesarea* in 1960, that is, passenger ships offering cargo facilities. Further tonnage was added in 1878 when, after a period of charter, the Aberdeen vessel *Hogarth* was acquired and renamed *Caledonia.* She was bought for the St Malo trade but did not have a long career as, when replacing the *Fannie* on the Channel Islands mail service, she struck the Oyster Rock outside St Helier Harbour on February 19 1881 and became a total loss.

In 1880 the *Southampton* was lengthened and given new engines and boilers, and a year later the L & SWR had a new screw-propelled mail steamer, the *Ella,* built. She entered service on the Channel Islands route, arriving on her maiden voyage on July 31 1881. In July 1882 a sister ship, the *Hilda,* was launched by the same builders but, due to a strike at the yard, it was not until January 19 1883 that the ship arrived in the islands on her maiden voyage.

In 1883 the L & SWR improved the *Brittany,* to bring her in line with the *Southampton,* and the ship re-entered service on the Channel Islands route, arriving on September 19. The additional vessels on the islands route allowed the *Fannie* to move and join her sister on the Le Havre route in late 1880, where they were joined in August 1883 by the *Southampton.* This allowed *Alliance* to be moved to the Jersey station to replace the old *Dispatch,* which was withdrawn and converted into a hulk. The L & SWR fleet suffered a further loss, when on June 27 1884, the *Caesarea,* on passage to St Malo, was in collision with a Jersey potato boat, the *Strathesk.* The railway company's ship sank and to replace her the *Laura* was built; the latter entered service on May 18 1885 to St Malo.

Revival of competition

In 1878, a second railway company commenced operating steamship services in the area covered by this book, when the Great Western Railway (GWR), which had been granted steamship powers in 1871, re-opened the Weymouth–Cherbourg route, using two ships from their Irish Sea services. The service opened on August 1 1878 with the *Great Western* and the *South of Ireland,* which were occasionally relieved by Weymouth and Channel Islands SP Co vessels. On Christmas Day 1883, the GWR service to Cherbourg suffered a setback when *South of Ireland,* inward bound to the Dorset port, went ashore and was lost. She was replaced in April 1884 by the *Gael.* Early in 1885, the *Gael* suffered boiler trouble and was replaced from early March by the *St Andrew.* The route was not, however, a success and was withdrawn on June 30 1885.

At this time there seemed little competition to trouble the shipping services of the L & SWR, which had kept pace with improvements in design, while the Weymouth & Channel Island SP Co were still using old outdated paddle-steamers. The Weymouth company had received limited financial help from the GWR, but there was no control or lease as there had been in the case of the L & SWR and the South Western SP Co in 1842. The Weymouth & Channel Islands SP Co was made even weaker when, on January 29 1887, the *Brighton,* approaching Guernsey from the north, struck rocks and was lost. The *Great Western* was chartered during the following summers to take her place.

The position was to change in 1889, due to a decision made the previous year by the GWR to cease giving financial support to the Weymouth company and operate the service in their own right. Three twin-screw vessels were ordered from Lairds at Birkenhead and the commencement date for their service was set as July 1 1889. Meanwhile the L & SWR had ordered a further vessel of the *Diana* class, this time from R. Napier of Glasgow. The ship, named *Dora,* was launched on March 2 1889 and, after the fitting of electric light, arrived on her maiden voyage to the Channel Islands on May 26. She was to have a very short life as a mail steamer, being first eclipsed by the GWR steamers and then replaced by newer L & SWR vessels.

The L & SWR had been aware that the GWR intended to take over the Weymouth–Channel Islands service, but it must have been a shock when it was found that three fast twin-screw vessels were to maintain the service, as little information had leaked out of the GWR's preparations.

The process of winding up the Weymouth & Channel Islands SP Co was set in motion in June 1889. The *Great Western* came on service to help the Weymouth & Channel Islands SP Co through its last month, providing a service on six days of the week. The *Cygnus* arrived in the islands for the last time on Thursday June 27, sailing the following day in ballast for Southampton. *Aquila* arrived for the last time on Saturday the 29th and took the return 5:00 pm sailing to Weymouth, while the last arrival on Sunday the 30th was that of the *Great Western,* which then remained in harbour, ready to take the first GWR sailing on Monday July 1.

Chapter 3

Great Western provides a challenge

The new GWR ships were not ready to take up the service on July 1 and thus two old paddle-steamers had to fill the gap. As already mentioned, the *Great Western* was already on the route and took the first sailing on July 1 1889, which was from the Channel Islands to Weymouth. She was joined by the *Gael,* which arrived at Jersey in ballast on Sunday June 30, ready to take the Tuesday sailing from the islands. The two ships then maintained the service for just over a month, by which time the new steamers were ready.

The first two of the new ships entered service over the August Bank Holiday weekend. The *Lynx* arrived in the islands on Sunday August 4, while the *Antelope* had arrived in Jersey from Milford the day before. On the Bank Holiday Monday there was an outing of the Jersey Foresters to Guernsey and, while *Antelope* took the Weymouth sailing, *Lynx* operated an excursion. The L & SWR did the same using the *Dora* and *Ella,* and this gave the GWR's ships a marvellous opportunity to show their paces, which they accordingly did. With the GWR timetable giving the Weymouth departure at 2:10 am and that from Jersey at 8:00 am, coupled with faster ships, the GWR ended for ever the virtual monopoly which the L & SWR had enjoyed on travel to the Channel Islands for so long.

The success of the GWR's entry into the Channel Islands service is dramatically illustrated by the fact that, within the short period of two months, the ratio of passengers transported from Southampton and Weymouth had changed from being 3:1 in Southampton's favour to virtually 1:1 by the end of September, with the ratio now marginally in Weymouth's favour (September figures: 2136 passengers from Southampton; 2314 from Weymouth). Exacerbating the effect of declining passenger figures was the ignominy of the GWR ships catching and overtaking those of the L & SWR, even their latest, the *Dora.*

L & SWR picks up the gauntlet

In an effort to improve the speed of the *Dora,* forced draught to the stoke-hold was fitted, together with a new propeller, but she was still no match for the new GWR ships, the last of which, the *Gazelle,* entered service on September 8 1889. Even before the *Dora* was modified, however, the directors of the L & SWR had decided to match the GWR by ordering from J. & G. Thomson Ltd of Clydebank, three ships with a speed of 18½ knots under natural draught and 19½ knots under forced draught, plus a premium for every knot in excess of these speeds. The first of the new ships, the *Frederica,* was launched on June 5 1890, entering service on July 31, being followed by the *Lydia* on October 7 and the *Stella* on November 6. All three ships made their speeds with ease and, with their entry into service, the L & SWR regained their position as regards superior vessels, too late, however, to regain their dominant position in the number of passengers carried.

Battle was now joined and, not to be outdone, the GWR ordered one further ship from Lairds; she was larger than the previous trio and was intended for the operation of a new 'daylight' service to the Channel Islands. This was not, however, introduced at this time, and she took her place alongside the other ships plying standard routes. Named *Ibex* she made a VIP call to the Channel Islands over September 5–7 1891, before making her maiden voyage proper on the 9th. With her entry into service there commenced an era which has been described as the 'Race to the Islands', of which more shall be written later.

When the *Frederica* and her sisters had entered service, they displaced three single-screw vessels and a paddle steamer, leaving only the *Dora* out of the previous vessels to act as relief. Of the ships displaced, the *Brittany* moved to the Le Havre route, replacing the *Fannie,* which was withdrawn and broken up. *Hilda* also helped out on the Havre route for a time, before taking up her regular station on the St Malo route. *Ella* and *Diana* went straight to the St Malo route, but the latter was lost off Cap de la Hague on June 21 1895.

With the sudden surplus of vessels in the L & SWR fleet, the opportunity was taken to install triple-expansion machinery in those vessels thought worthy of the expense, as and when such vessels came up for major overhaul.

In 1892 the L & SWR took the bold step of acquiring the Southampton Docks Company and pressed ahead with the development of the port to allow the largest liners in the world to call. This development together with the port's unique double high waters saw Southampton become the terminal for most of the Atlantic liners and many of those serving other parts of the world.

The first of the Atlantic lines to use Southampton was the Allan Line, in 1893; immediately, there was a great increase in traffic on the L & SWR's Le Havre route, which put pressure on the ships serving that route. To help relieve this pressure, the *Frederica* was drafted in to provide an extra service once a week from September 6 1893 and, in December 1893, was transferred permanently to help operate a service running on six days a week, a task in which she was joined by the reboilered *Brittany*. Another consequence of the arrival of liners in Southampton, was the realisation that the cabin accommodation on the cross-Channel steamers was thoroughly inadequate. Passengers who had just crossed the Atlantic in luxurious splendour on a

Passengers embarking on Roebuck *at Weymouth straight off the train—clearly an excellent connecting service (John Attwood).*

liner were then subjected to crossing the Channel in outmoded 30-year old paddle-steamers. The L & SWR, in view of the facts above, ordered two new ships from J. & G. Thompson Ltd.

The *Columbia* was delivered at Southampton on October 19 1894, entering service on December 1 while here sister *Alma* was delivered on December 10. They were splendid vessels and had been given cabin accommodation, much of which was positioned amidships between the two boiler rooms which allowed for the greatest comfort, and the ships were also the first to have flush decks.

On June 21 1895, the L & SWR lost the *Diana* when she grounded on rocks under the light at Cap de la Hague in thick fog, on a voyage from St Malo. All the passengers were landed safely, but the ship broke up and sank two days later. One year later Thompsons completed a smaller version of the *Columbia* for the service between Jersey and France. Named *Victoria* she took up duties on August 1 1896 and replaced the two ships which had maintained the services to St Malo and Granville. One of these ships was the *Alliance* which had been on the Jersey station since 1879 and was therefore the last of the L & SWR's paddle-steamers in regular service, though *Southampton* and *Brittany* were yet to make excursions round the British fleet at Spithead in June 1897.

Returning now to the GWR, it had been their intention in 1891 to introduce a daylight service, and, as may be recalled, the *Ibex* had been specially built for that purpose. Although in the event this service had been shelved, six years later the GWR had two new vessels built by the Naval Construction & Armaments Co Ltd at Barrow and commenced with them the daylight service. Named *Roebuck* and *Reindeer* they were the largest and fastest vessels on the Channel Islands route, being some twenty feet longer than the *Frederica* class and having a speed of 19 knots, and these ships gave the initiative back to the GWR. The *Roebuck* entered service on July 1 1897, being followed on August 2 by the *Reindeer*. One drawback to these large vessels was that they were heavy users of coal; thus they were only operated in the summer, leaving the winter running in the hands of the *Ibex* or one of the *Lynx*-class ships, as these were more economical.

Era of the 'race'

All the ports used by the railway companies, except Southampton, suffered from an insufficient depth of water to allow ships to arrive and leave on any tide. St Helier harbour was the worst and thus there was always a rush to arrive as early as possible on the mornings of spring tides as otherwise a ship had to stay in the Small Roads and discharge all its passengers via small boats. With both the Southampton and Weymouth overnight boats due to arrive at the same time, the importance of being the first boat in can be seen, as otherwise it could mean a day in the Roads. This and the prestige involved, for both company and ship's master, led to many risks being taken and, allegedly, racing, which both company and masters denied, insisting that catching the tide was their only concern.

The inevitable happened on April 16 1897, when the *Ibex* and the *Frederica* were on passage to the islands, each under the command of the most respected captain in their respective company. The *Ibex* left St Peter Port first, being followed ten minutes later by the *Frederica* which gradually overhauled the GWR ship. As Corbière drew near, the ships were neck-and-neck, each seeking the inside berth in order to take the Inner Passage and thus arrive at St Helier first. The *Ibex* misjudged her position and hit the Normontaise rock, losing most of the blades of her propellers and putting a hole in her hull bottom. She managed to make Portelet Bay where, with her decks awash, she put her passengers ashore by boat. The ship was refloated in the evening and, after a great struggle lasting all night, was put ashore in St Aubin's Bay. This minor disaster brought home to both the railway companies the fact that some sort of restraint on 'racing' would have to be applied and, consultative meetings took place. Tragically, however, before any agreement could be reached, a major disaster befell the L & SWR ship *Stella*.

On Maundy Thursday, April 30 1899, the ship was operating on the 'daylight' service from Southampton to the islands, a similar service to that operated by the GWR from Weymouth. The *Stella* steamed across the Channel at full speed; she encountered fog on the way but did not reduce speed. When she had run the estimated distance to the Casquets, nothing could be seen of the Lighthouse, but when rocks did become visible there was no time either to stop or alter course and she struck at full speed. Of the passengers and crew, 105 lost their lives (112 were saved), and at the Board of Trade Inquiry that followed the question of racing between the two companies was raised. Both companies denied the existence of racing.

It was fortunate, so far as the L & SWR was concerned, that it had built a new ship the previous year to act as relief vessel on the Channel Islands and Le Havre routes. Launched on July 4 1898, the *Vera* took over the islands route for the summer after the loss of the *Stella*.

Chapter 4

Working partnership between L & SWR and GWR

Agreement was finally reached between the L & SWR and GWR for the operation of an amalgamated steamer service to the Channel Islands from October 1 1899, with receipts being pooled and any profit being shared in the ratio of the receipts for 1897 and 1898. Each company would operate three services a week during the winter, and during the summer the GWR would run daylight services only, while the L & SWR would run overnight to the islands and return by day, with the departure times from the islands staggered to prevent any racing. The introduction of the new working had a dramatically beneficial effect on the running expenses of the service, with, however, the unfortunate corollary that it also caused the laying off of many crew at Weymouth.

The new agreement was but a few months old when trouble struck the GWR with the sinking of the *Ibex*. She was bound from Weymouth to Guernsey when, early on January 5 1900, she struck rocks off the north-east coast of the island and sank in the Little Russel, just outside St Peter Port. The middle of the winter was not considered the right time to try and raise the vessel, and salvage operations did not commence until late spring, with the ship being raised on July 21. She was towed to Birkenhead for repairs and did not return to service until April 23 1901.

The L & SWR meanwhile had a permanent replacement for the *Stella* built. They had returned to the same builders, who had again changed their name, now being called John Brown & Co Ltd. The ship, named *Alberta*, was on the same hull as the *Vera* with similar layout but with the addition of a bridge deck. Launched on April 3 1900, she entered service to the Channel Islands on June 2. With better accommodation being provided on the ships, the islands and the north-western coast of France were becoming very popular as holiday resorts, and increasing numbers used the services in the summer months. The French privateer port of St Malo and the town of Dinard just across the river were very popular with the English, and many took up

residence there, the casinos proving especially popular! Following the loss of the *Diana* in 1895, the *Ella* and *Hilda* had maintained the service, but the ships were not up to the required standard, and thus the *Vera* was tried on the route in the summer of 1902 and altered to give better facilities in time for the following season.

With the ever growing number of liners using the port of Southampton there was another trade building up, but instead at the port of Plymouth, where the liners called to discharge urgent mail and those passengers who wished to reach London without delay. The reverse applied on the outward voyages and, to cater for this trade, tenders operated from the port. With the *Lynx*-class not being required much at Weymouth due to the companies' agreement, outlined above, the *Lynx* and the *Antelope* were dispatched in January 1903 to take up tender duties at Plymouth. The L & SWR saw the traffic developing and, in late 1903, withdrew the *Victoria* from the Jersey station and, after altering her, sent her to Plymouth in May 1904. The ships not only acted as tenders, but also operated excursions from the port. *Victoria* was replaced at Jersey by *Laura*. Even with their tender duties at Plymouth, the *Lynx*-class vessels were still not overworked and the GWR looked at the possibilities of operating a service between Weymouth and Nantes in the autumn of 1903, though the idea came to nothing.

With the advent of ships with private cabins, the older units of the L & SWR fleet were withdrawn so that their accommodation could be modernised. *Lydia* returned to do service on June 16 1904 after a complete rebuild of the first-class accommodation, which was placed aft in these vessels, and much improvement in the rest of the ship. The most noticeable outward change was the removal of the mainmast, and the erection of a large cabin on the aft promenade deck which contained the ladies' lounges. In May 1905, the *Frederica* underwent similar improvement to the *Lydia*, having in addition a new boiler and funnel. She had already had a nine-foot extension fitted to her old funnel in 1903, in an unsuccessful effort to improve performance under natural draught and reduce coal consumption.

On November 18 1905, the *Hilda* was lost when entering St Malo in a snowstorm, 128 of the 133 on board not surviving. To replace the *Hilda,* the company went to the builders of the two cargo boats, Gourlay Brothers of Dundee, and had the *Princess Ena* built. The building time was very short and the ship entered service on July 16 1906. Althought the *Lynx*-class ships had found work elsewhere, the *Lynx* herself spent the summer of 1906 on charter to a group of Jersey businessmen, who operated her on a series of excursions from the island to a variety of places, including the French island of Chausey.

On January 1906, the new Aliens Law came into force. Due to the controls this placed on the movement of individuals between France and England, there was a marked drop in the number of passengers carried on the French routes.

In response to the constantly increasing elegance of transatlantic liners, the L & SWR decided to update two ships on the Le Havre route. They started with the *Columbia* which, when she returned to service in April 1906, was a very different vessel.

She had been reboilered, with the forward boiler-room moved aft into the area previously occupied by the first-class accommodation. The accommodation was then rebuilt into the space of the former forward boiler. Clearly this work must have been quite costly, as it was not repeated when her sister underwent similar work.

The L & SWR then decided that a purpose-built tender was required at Plymouth as well, and ordered a new ship, which was to be named the *Atalanta*, from Gourlay Bros Ltd of Dundee. She ran trials on May 9 1907 and took up duties at Plymouth on May 27. On her arrival, the *Victoria* returned to the Jersey–France service, after conversion back from a tender, which included the restoration of her mainmast. Apart from normal tender duties at Plymouth, the vessels undertook other work as required; thus, in March 1907, the *Antelope* worked on the White Star liner *Suevic*, which had gone ashore at the Lizard. The following year, the GWR had two new tenders built for service at Plymouth and the *Lynx*-class ships were again out of work, though not for long.

Expansion of cargo services

During the early years of this century, cargo traffic increased greatly and, to help cater for this, the L &

Busy port scene with horse-drawn carts and wicker trunks giving the flavour of the period. Alberta *is in the background (Author).*

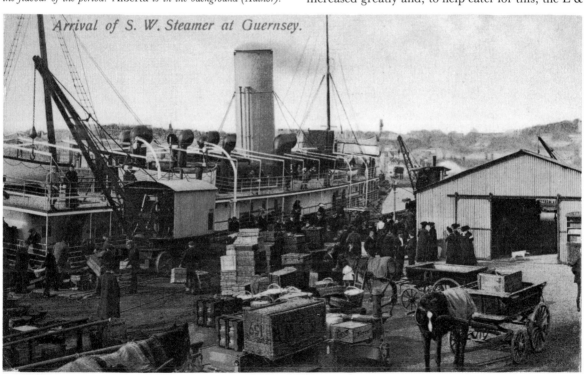

Arrival of S. W. Steamer at Guernsey.

SWR had the *Ada* built at Dundee; the vessel ran trials on April 20 1905.

In May 1905 the GWR also acquired a ship for the Channel Islands cargo traffic when they bought the *Melmore*, with the intention of using her mainly to carry the Jersey potato traffic. Meanwhile, the L & SWR had been so pleased with the *Ada* that they requested her builders to provide a sister ship, which became the *Bertha* and was delivered in December 1905. The GWR cargo traffic had been closely identified with the transport of the Guernsey tomato and grape crops and, to cater in a better way for this trade, the *Gazelle* was converted into a pure cargo vessel, and as such entered service in May 1908.

Apart from the tender duties at Plymouth the ships of the *Lynx*-class were also chartered to transport French produce from Brest to Plymouth; following this charter the GWR went to Parliament seeking powers to operate a proper service on this route, which were granted in August 1909, and the *Melmore* was then put on this route. Meanwhile the L & SWR had seen the expanding GWR French traffic as a threat to their own St Malo service and, on July 1 1909, inaugurated a new route to Roscoff in an attempt to retain the produce traffic.

Technical developments

The turbine had by now been installed in many of the new passenger vessels being built for cross-Channel work, and indeed the L & SWR had evaluated its potential employment before ordering the *Princess Ena*. With replacement ships being required, the matter was again looked at in 1909. Two new ships were ordered in October of that year from Cammell Laird of Birkenhead, to be propelled by three direct-drive turbines. They were to prove the worst purchase the company ever made. Their triple screws and the way the steam was fed to the turbines made them difficult and slow to manoeuvre, and a handful to their masters.

Due to an upsurge in traffic on the Le Havre route in the summer of 1910, the L & SWR decided to operate a new 'daylight' service, using the *Lydia*, which was due to be replaced on the islands route by the two new vessels. As it turned out the *Caesarea* and *Sarnia*, as the new ships were named, were late from the builders; the former arrived in the Channel Islands on her maiden voyage on September 24 1910, and her sister ship arrived the following year. Because of the gap in service due to the tardy delivery of the new ships, the *Frederica* was retained on the islands route, while *Lydia* went off to commence the 'daylight' Le Havre service on July 22.

Although perhaps daunted by its early experience of turbine-driven vessels the L & SWR went ahead, in 1911, and ordered two further turbine ships, but this time from Fairfield Shipbuilding & Engineering Co Ltd, Glasgow. These ships were to have the first geared turbines in the world. The L & SWR had already found itself at the leading edge of contemporary technology when, in late 1910, the *South Western*, which was on the Cherbourg service was used to carry out trials with a new invention called radio, at that time of course only the dots and dashes kind!

The first of the new geared-turbine steamers on the Le Havre service, the *Normannia* arrived at Southampton on February 26 1912 and entered service after the fitting of radio on April 2, her maiden voyage having been delayed by the coal strike. Her sister was launched as the *Louvima*, but this was changed to *Hantonia* before she entered service on May 7 1912.

The only other change of any importance occurred in 1913 when, because of the *Titanic* disaster of 1912, lifesaving equipment was improved; most vessels had their cutters replaced by large new lifeboats and, at the same time, a new type of liferaft was introduced.

Rationalisation and growth

In May 1910, an agreement was reached between the L & SWR and the GWR, covering mainly general railway-related items in the west of England, but which included as well the transfer of all liner-tender duties at Plymouth to the GWR and the withdrawal of the Southampton–Roscoff cargo service of the L & SWR. The Plymouth tender *Atalanta* was sold to the GWR and sailed from Southampton on June 10 and was delivered at Fishguard three days later. In June the GWR bought the *Chelmsford* for their Brest service, which was operated from Plymouth during the summer and Weymouth in the winter. The service had been maintained mainly by the *Lynx* class, but at peak periods *Ibex* and *Reindeer* had also helped out. The *Chelmsford* was renamed *Bretonne* but had a very short life with the GWR.

This agreement was followed up two years later when, in May 1912, the L & SWR purchased from the London Brighton & South Coast Railway both the 'goodwill' and the ships, which operated the latter's service between Newhaven and Caen. The ships taken over were the *Normandy* and the *Brittany*, which were delivered to Southampton on May 31 and June 3 respectively. They were not good-looking ships and, to try and improve this, the funnels were shortened and the masts raked, but to little effect.

During the summer of 1911 it had become clear

to the GWR that its services to Brest and Nantes did not carry the required amount of traffic, and both routes closed at the end of September that year. Having withdrawn their French services, the GWR had the *Lynx* converted into a cargo vessel, while the other ships were put up for sale; *Melmore* and *Bretonne* were sold in June 1912, and *Antelope* was sold the following year. The L & SWR, which had withdrawn its Roscoff service in 1910 after the agreement with the GWR, decided, on the GWR terminating its French services, to recommence operating the route and did so in December 1912.

1913 proved to be even more successful—on all routes—and even the *Victoria* on the Jersey–France routes had on many occasions to turn away hundreds of would-be passengers, who wanted to take advantage of the day trips which were being offered. With a further increase in trade forecast for 1914, the L & SWR went for the first time to Wm Denny & Bros of Dumbarton with a requirement for two vessels, one large and one small. The large ship was to replace the *Lydia* which, in turn, would replace the *Victoria* on the Jersey station, while the small ship was to replace the *South Western* on the Cherbourg route. In the event, after a month of discussion, Denny only tendered for the larger vessel, which was to be delivered in June 1915. However, all the forecasts and plans became valueless when war was declared on August 4 1914. Many ships of both the GWR and the L & SWR were taken over for military service, and some never returned.

Chapter 5

The Great War and its aftermath

Naturally, after war had been declared, there was a sharp decline in the numbers of civilians travelling and consequently the Channel Islands services were put on the winter timetable from August 24. Of the two companies, the GWR was the worst affected, as all their Weymouth vessels were taken over by the Government with the exception of the *Ibex*. The L & SWR also had a number of ships taken over, but were left with a selection from which they managed to maintain their services. As the German forces pushed into France and it looked as if Le Havre might fall, the service was moved on September 16 1914 to St Nazaire for a period before returning to Le Havre.

Of the GWR's ships, *Reindeer* made her last mail crossing from the Channel Islands on August 6 1914, while her sister *Roebuck* left on October 1 and was in Portland as HMS Roedean on November 25. *Roedean* then proceeded north to Scapa Flow, where she was lost on January 13 1915 when, while at anchor, she fell across the bow of HMS *Imperieuse*, was holed and sunk. The two cargo ships were also taken over, the *Lynx* being renamed HMS *Lynn*. In October 1914 *Caesarea* was converted into an Armed Boarding Vessel, as was her sister *Sarnia* after her last voyage from the islands on November 20. On November 28 the *Victoria* sailed from Jersey bound for Portsmouth, it being stated in the papers that she was to be used as a pilots' accommodation vessel, but in fact she became a 'Q' ship for a couple of months before returning to Jersey on January 11 1915.

On March 12 1915, the *Lydia* sailed from the Channel Islands for the last time as a mailboat, being taken over to become Admiralty Transport No 280 and returned to Jersey a week later bringing POW's for detention; she then spent the rest of the war on military service between Southampton and Le Havre.

The first ship that the L & SWR lost during the war was the *Guernsey* which went ashore on Cap de la Hague on the night of April 9th 1915 with the loss of seven crew. Only three weeks later, the *South*

Western went ashore in the same place, but managed to refloat herself and reach Cherbourg.

On April 27 1915, the *Princess Ena* was taken over for special services and she operated as a 'Q' ship in the south-west approaches under the command of Commander F.M. Simon RN, a Jerseyman. As mentioned, *Ibex* was left to maintain the Weymouth–Channel Islands service alone, and when she was off service for boiler cleaning or overhaul another ship had to be found; thus *Vera*, *Galtee More* and *Mellifont* all had spells on the route during 1914–1915.

Towards the end of 1915, the *Caesarea* and *Sarnia* were no longer required as Armed Boarding Vessels and the former took up duties on the military service between Southampton and Le Havre, while *Sarnia* went out to the Mediterranean, where on October 29 1915 she sank the railway cargo vessel *Hythe* off Cape Helles. She carried out duties between Mudros and the Peninsula and her Commanding Officer, Commander H.G. Muir was mentioned in despatches for his efforts.

Princess Ena was later converted into a troopship and sailed from Southampton on October 18 1915 for the Mediterranean, where she maintained a service between Mudros and Salonica. The L & SWR had retained four of the large passenger ships in their fleet, the *Normannia* and *Hantonia* to operate the Le Havre service, the *Alberta* to maintain the Channel Islands route and the *Vera* to act as relief on both routes. All went well until November 19 1915, when *Vera* hit the quay on entering Southampton, sustaining bow damage. With *Alberta* off service, the *South Western* was put on the islands mail service for a month to cover. By 1916 the GWR was having great difficulty in obtaining a ship to cover for the *Ibex* when required and thus the old *Pembroke* was brought round from the Irish Sea and put on the islands cargo and mail service; she arrived for the first time on March 30 1916.

By May 1916 the state of the war was such that by the 25th, the Government had closed all cross-Channel routes for civil use except for Southampton–Le Havre, which accordingly attracted extra traffic that was catered for by an increased number of sailings. Late in 1916 the Channel Islands mail service was without its regular vessels and both *South Western* and *Laura* spent brief spells on the route.

1917 was remarkably free of incident; the only major one was the running down and sinking of the GWR-chartered cargo vessel *Aletta* on September 19 by none other than the GWR's own *Ibex*!

Another development in 1917 was the arming of the cross-Channel vessels in the early part of the year, effected in response to the ever increasing menace of German U-boats. This menace was brought home early in 1918 when two L & SWR vessels were lost in quick succession. The first loss was the *Normandy* which, while on a voyage from Southampton to Cherbourg on January 25, was torpedoed eight miles from the Cherbourg breakwater. Only 13 out of 55 passengers and crew were saved. Less than two months later, on March 16, the *South Western* was lost on a voyage to St Malo sixteen miles from the Isle of Wight. The loss of these two vessels caused the suspension of the service to Cherbourg, as out of the smaller passenger-cargo vessels, only *Laura* survived.

With a major offensive taking place at the front, the Government chartered the four remaining large passenger ships for the period March 28 1918 to April 9, but could only enjoy the services of three as *Alberta*, while leaving Southampton on the 29th, broke her starboard crankshaft and was thus out of commission. For the duration of this charter, the L & SWR services to the Channel Islands and to Havre were suspended.

Work on the ship being built by Wm Denny Bros for the L & SWR had been suspended in August 1915, but with an urgent requirement for vessels of this type, work resumed n December 1917, and the *Lorina*, as she was known, was launched on August 12 1918.

U-boats continued to menace shipping in the Channel and as a precaution, in September 1918, all the ships were painted in the camouflage dazzle-paint system required by the Government. The same month also saw the loss of another of the L & SWR's vessels. The *Sarnia*, serving in the Mediterranean, was torpedoed soon after leaving Alexandria in the afternoon of September 12.

The Armistice was declared on November 11 1918 and, although the fighting ceased, the armies stayed in position. Not until the peace treaty was signed in June the following year was the task of bringing back British and colonial forces commenced. The new *Lorina* was fitted out as an Admiralty Transport, and arrived at Southampton on Decem-

ber 30 1918, and took up duties on the military service to Havre four days later.

On March 27 1919, the service between Jersey and France was discontinued, the service having suffered heavy losses during the war. The route was maintained by the *Victoria* up until September 18 1918 when, due to the Government requiring her, she was replaced by the *Laura* which remained until the last sailing on March 27 1919. Although the service finished on the March 27, occasional sailings continued until mid-May. The *Victoria* had been renamed *Surf II* and conversion work started on her, but it was not completed before the end of the war, and she was handed back to the L & SWR. With the Jersey–France routes abandoned, there was no service for which the *Victoria* was suited and in April 1919 the company attempted to sell her at a Baltic Exchange auction, but she did not reach the reserve price. She found a buyer the following month, being sold to James Dredging Towage & Transport Co Ltd, for £16,500.

The return of the forces from France continued through 1919 with the military service between Southampton and Le Havre being placed under the control of the L & SWR on June 8. The service finished in the last week in October when the last two ships in Government employ, the *Caesarea* and the *Lydia*, were handed back to the L & SWR. The *Lydia* had visited Guernsey on September 21, when she took returning troops to the island, and the *Caesarea* arrived in Jersey on October 16 with the King's Regiment.

Lydia was not considered worthy of repair and, in a deal conducted by James Dredging, she was sold to a Mr T.R. Sales, who sold to the L & SWR an escort vessel, ex-HMS *Peony*, which was then at Malta. The deal was agreed on December 18 1919 and by mid-January 1920 the *Peony* had arrived at Southampton, been accepted by the L & SWR and sent to Dundee for conversion by the Caledon ship-building firm, which was also refurbishing the *Caesarea* and *Lorina* (the latter because Denny were unable to handle the work).

Reindeer was overhauled by Thornycroft's at Southampton and returned to the Channel Islands service on Sunday, February 8 1920. The next ship to return was the small *Lynx*, which made her first call at Jersey on March 12; one of the first persons to go on board the ship was Captain H. Bond, a Jerseyman, who had commanded the ship while she was in the Mediterranean and he confirmed that the story of the ship capturing her old sister, the *Atromitos*, was untrue.

Lorina arrived at Southampton, from fitting out, on March 28 1920, and her maiden voyage was to the Channel Islands where she arrived on April 1.

She made only a few trips, then relieved on the Le Havre route for a short time before taking up her intended station between Southampton and St Malo on July 31. When the *Lorina* entered service, the *Vera* was sent to Birkenhead for a complete overhaul, which included new boilers and a nearly completely new bottom.

In May 1920, the GWR sent the Irish Sea vessel *Waterford* to Weymouth to help out with the cargo traffic, but on May 22, while in Jersey waiting to load potatoes, she was suddenly dispatched back to Fishguard and in her place came the *Great Southern*. She not only carried cargo but helped out as relief passenger ship as required, and from thenceforth either she, or her sister the *Great Western* (nearly always the latter), came round to Weymouth every summer to help out. *Gazelle* arrived back in Jersey for the first time in May 1, and on June 7 the *Caesarea* returned to Southampton and again took up the Channel Islands service.

The sale of the *Lydia* to Mr Sales cannot have been completed, as on June 14 1920 the ship was registered to James Dredging Towage and Transport Co Ltd; two days later she was moved out from Southampton Docks (where she had been shown, with James as agents, since the beginning of the year) into Southampton Water, no doubt to take the place of the *Victoria*. The *Princess Ena* arrived back at Southampton, after being refitted by the Admiralty at Devonport on July 7, and took up the St Malo service, where she was joined by the *Lorina*. By this time the services were now virtually back to normal pre-war levels, though there was a shortage of vessels, as is shown by the fact that when the *Alberta* hit rocks off Guernsey on July 21, the L & SWR had to charter the LNWR's *Rathmore* to maintain the summer service.

The *Vera* arrived back at Southampton in early November and became a permanent vessel on the Channel Islands station. Her arrival released the *Alberta*, which proceeded to Dundee for modernisation. The crew of the *Alberta* returned from Dundee with the *Peony*, which by this time had been renamed *Ardena*, and arrived with her at her new home port on November 29. *Ardena* then made her maiden voyage on the St Malo route, on December 6. She spent most of her winters on the St Malo service, while in the summer she operated the route for which she had been purchased, that to Cherbourg, which she re-opened on July 6 1921.

At this time, both new and second-hand tonnage was very expensive and difficult to obtain, so the L & SWR took the decision to extend the life of the older units of their fleet. The *Cherbourg* was taken in hand by the company's own yard and her compound machinery was replaced by a triple expansion engine which had been built by J.P. Rennoldson at South Sheilds in 1897.

Although she had by then left the L & SWR fleet, a few words about the *Lydia* would not be out of place at this point, as in most histories these years are not recorded. On March 28 1921 she sailed from Southampton bound for the Mediterranean to commence a service between Malta and Syracuse having been purchased by a Captain Montague Yates. It was an ill-fated venture, and in September he was arrested in Syracuse after a two-day siege by Italian police. The ship returned to James' possession and was sold on September 30 1922 to Coast Lines Ltd, but she did not remain with them long, being resold to Greek owners on May 14 1923.

The Channel Islands were garrisoned by troops from England and, in addition, there was a local militia which, during the First World War, had been called up for active service and sent to France. After the cessation of hostilities, as a mark of respect, the islands received a visit from the King and Queen in July 1921 and, in keeping with custom, one of the mailboat masters acted as pilot on board the royal yacht; on this occasion the honour went to Captain William Mulhall of the GWR.

The *Alberta* had been due back in service in time for the 1921 summer season but, due to industrial action at the yard, the work was delayed and to fill the gap so caused during the height of the summer period, the *Galtee More* was chartered from July 11 for two months, though this was extended due to a mishap occurring to the *Hantonia*. Early 1922 saw an increase in the cargo fleet of the L & SWR when first the *Laura* was converted into a purely cargo vessel and then two ships were purchased from R. Penny of Shoreham and renamed *Rina* and *Vena*.

By the middle of 1922, all the ships had been overhauled, and most war losses made good, with the exception of the *Roebuck*. Nearly all the ships, however were over ten years old and the railway companies, due to the war, were virtually bankrupt. To strengthen the railway companies, the Railway Bill of 1921 was enacted, coming into effect on January 1 1923; this reorganised all the railway companies into four large groups.

Chapter 6

Southern Railway comes into being

The grouping scheme had no effect as far as the Channel Islands were concered on the title or services of the GWR, but the L & SWR became part of the Southern Railway (SR), as did the London, Brighton & South Coast Railway and the South Eastern & Chatham Railway, both of which had operated cross-Channel shipping services. The SR thus had a considerable fleet of vessels and Southampton, with its workshop and dry-dock facilities, became the headquarters of the marine section under the Docks & Marine Manager; this section lasted at the port until 1956.

The GWR embarked on a programme of refurbishment and, early in 1923, the *Reindeer* was sent to Liverpool for a major overhaul, which included the addition of a shelter deck aft of the bridge, returning to service on March 11. Even with such work, however, the ships on the Weymouth route were nearing the end of their life-span. In the summer of 1923 the directors of the GWR made a tour of all the ports involved in their shipping services. The result of their visit to the Channel Islands was a decision to replace all the vessels then serving the islands.

Bertha working cargo in Honfleur, with staff and early motorlorries proudly posed in the left centre distance; note that her mainmast is missing (John Attwood).

The SR was also faced with an aging fleet, and the *Caesarea* was looked at with a view to converting her to burn oil fuel, but before any decision could be taken fate intervened. Shortly after leaving St Helier harbour on July 7 1923, the ship struck rocks off Noirmont Point causing severe bottom damage and the loss of her port propeller and shaft. The ship turned round and headed back to harbour, touching more rocks on the way, before taking the ground outside the harbour. She was covered by each tide, but was refloated and later towed to Southampton where she was sold to the Isle of Man SP Co, being renamed *Manx Maid* before entering service the following year. To cover the departure of the *Caesarea*, the *Hantonia* was moved from the Le Havre route, and the *St Patrick* was chartered from the GWR to take *Hantonia*'s place.

After the sale of the *Caesarea*, the SR ordered two new ships from Wm Denny & Bros, announcing that they were for cross-Channel services from Southampton to the Channel Islands. At functions held in the islands in the latter part of 1923, however, various railway officials referred to the new ships that were being built and stated that if the islands did not improve their harbour facilities then the new ships would be placed on another service. In the event there was no time for the required work

to be carried out and the ships did not serve the islands.

The first of the new SR ships was named *Dinard* and made her maiden voyage to St Malo on July 22 1924. Her sister, the *St Briac*, was delivered in September and made her maiden voyage on the Le Havre route on October 3. The *Dinard* was the main St Malo vessel, while the *St Briac* operated only at the height of the summer, spending much of her time as relief ship on the Le Havre route and later, as we shall see, operating cruises. With the entry into service of the *Dinard*, the *Lorina* moved to the Channel Islands station to replace the *Caesarea*. A summer service to Cherbourg was not a success and for 1925 the French terminal was moved to Caen, with the *Ardena* making the pleasant trip up the canal from Ouistreham.

Apart from ordering new passenger ships, the SR commenced replacing their cargo ships, building the same type of ship for both Dover and Southampton. The first of the Southampton vessels was the *Haslemere*, which ran trials on the Clyde on July 3 1925, and the second was the *Fratton*, which was delivered at Southampton on September 27. A further ship, the *Ringwood* was added in 1926 and at the same time some older units of the fleet were disposed of.

During this period the GWR had not been standing idle and an order for two new passenger vessels was placed with John Brown & Co at Clydebank, while two cargo ships were built on the Tyne. The first of the new passenger ships, the *St Julien*, arrived in the islands for the first time on Sunday May 24 1925, being followed by her sister, the *St Helier* on June 17. The new cargo ships *Sambur* and *Roebuck* entered service in May and, of the older ships, only the *Reindeer* remained to act as relief cover and to carry out day excursions. Her career ended three years later, her last mail run being on February 23 1928, after which she was withdrawn and sent to Briton Ferry where she was broken up on November 30 1928.

Improving the facilities

To cater for an increasing number of cross-Channel passengers using the port of Southampton, the facilities at the Outer Dock were remodelled in

A panoramic view of St Helier Harbour in 1933. Berthed at the Albert Pier may be seen Brittany, Essonite *(on charter to the SR),* Isle of Sark *and* Isle of Jersey. *Close examination of the latter two will show a difference in the way white paint was applied to their superstructures (A. Smith).*

1923–24. Berths 7 and 8 were rebuilt and a Marine Station built adjacent to them; from these berths were to sail the expanding numbers of passengers that made the late 1920s and 1930s the golden era of cross-Channel travel. In June 1924 came the unveiling of the SR's new colours for their fleet. This meant major repainting for most railway ships, apart from the L & SWR's; the yellow funnels of the old L & SWR were simply given black tops. On June 27 the Prince of Wales visited Southampton to open the new floating dock and, on the same day, the new SR house flag was first broken out.

Later, due to the growing number of passengers travelling to the islands, coupled with the introduction of the new GWR ships and the requirement to replace the *Alberta* and *Vera*, pressure was applied by the two companies on the island authorities and also on Weymouth Corporation to improve their harbour facilities. The result was that Guernsey built a new jetty and dredged the harbour during the period 1926–1929, while Jersey carried out major works during 1928–1931 and Weymouth did the same in 1931–1933. Meanwhile, at St Malo, the lock which the SR had expected to be in use for 1925 took until 1931 to complete.

Once both Guernsey and Jersey were committed to improving their harbour facilities, the SR commenced talks with Wm Denny concerning the construction of two more ships for the Channel Islands route, to replace the *Alberta* and *Vera*. The first of the new ships, the *Isle of Jersey* was launched on October 22 1929, being followed by her sister the *Isle of Guernsey* on December 17. With the new ships under construction, the faithful *Alberta* made her last crossing from the islands on December 13 1929, having steamed 750,000 miles and carried 700,000 passengers for the Railways. Her career ended sadly on April 23 1941, when she was bombed and sunk by German aircraft when at Punta (Salamis). The *Isle of Jersey* arrived on her maiden voyage to the islands on March 13 1930, being followed by her sister on April 5. These two ships were not, however, the only new ships to enter service, as the GWR had also had a new passenger ship built.

Following the withdrawal of the *Reindeer*, the *Great Western* had been covering a few sailings in the summer, as there was no official stand-by vessel. The loss by fire of the Fishguard vessel, *St Patrick*, in 1929, gave the GWR an opportunity to build a ship which would be able to operate on both routes. The new *St Patrick* was built by Alexander Stephen & Co on the Clyde and made her maiden voyage to the Channel Islands on April 18 1930. She then spent the summers on the Channel Islands route, while the winters were spent on the Irish Sea. She was the first ship operating to the islands to be owned by the

Fishguard & Rosslare Railway & Harbour Company, a joint company owned by the GWR and the Great Southern Railway of Ireland. Following her introduction, the GWR altered the departure time from Jersey from 07:30 to 08:30 and, at the same time, withdrew the facility for passengers to sleep on board overnight.

Improving the services

The summer service to Caen in 1930 saw an increase in capacity at weekends, with the introduction of the *Princess Ena* to cover the Friday nightsailing, but the ship only ran to Ouistreham, which is at the seaward end of the Caen canal, to a specially constructed landing-place. The move did little to increase the number of passengers using the service, and it was withdrawn at the end of the 1931 season. It was the intention to revert to Cherbourg for the 1932 season but this did not occur and, thus, the *Ardena* remained laid up in Southampton until July 1934, when she was sold to Greek buyers. The success of the new *Isle*-class vessels on the islands route resulted in the ordering of a third ship, which was stated to be a replacement for the *Vera*, which had not been sold as expected in 1930. The new ship, named *Isle of Sark* was launched on November 12 1931 and arrived in the islands on her maiden voyage on March 19 the following year.

The *Vera* should then have been disposed of, but instead the ship was used to re-open the service between Jersey and St Malo which the L & SWR had given up in 1919. In the intervening years, French companies had maintained a service but with slow small vessels; the opening of the new St Malo lock was seen as an opportunity for the railway company to put a larger vessel on the service. The SR paid the French company compensation and the *Vera* took up service on June 1 1932. It was intended that the *Ardena* would cover the winter period and that one of the Newhaven steamers would take over from 1933, but in the event a new ship was built, and the *Vera* continued until she was delivered.

1932 also saw the SR enter the cruise market, when the *St Briac* undertook a series of cruises which took in the French ports of Rouen, Havre, Cherbourg and St Malo, and calls were also made to the Channel Islands, the harbours now being able to accommodate a vessel of this size. Later Flushing and Antwerp were added to the programme. These were not the only cruises that the SR operated as the *Isles*, in early and late summer, made trips from the islands to Dartmouth, Newhaven, Cherbourg, Le Havre and Rouen.

At the same time the GWR used their vessels to

the full, calling at Dartmouth, Plymouth, Alderney and Cherbourg, plus one special annual trip when the *St Patrick* returned from Weymouth to Fishguard and undertook a cruise which called in at the Scilly Islands on the way. In the same period, the day-excursion traffic from Weymouth and Torquay to Guernsey built up, and calls were also made to Cherbourg and Alderney.

The *St Patrick* had a lucky escape on Friday August 5 1932, while on the direct Weymouth–Jersey sailing with 314 passengers on board. Approaching Jersey in thick fog, she struck rocks off Corbière, which caused damage along the port side as well as to the propeller. The boiler-room flooded and thus, with no power, the ship anchored off the Kaines reef. The passengers were taken off by the *Isle of Sark*, which came out from St Helier, and the local tug *Duke of Normandy*, while the *St Julien*, which had left Weymouth at the same time for both islands and which was anchored off the Brayes, got under way and went to stand by the crippled ship. The fog did not lift and the ships, with the exception of the tug, were forced to spend the night at anchor; it was not until 7:00 am on the Saturday that the *St Julien* was able to commence towing the *St Patrick* towards St Aubin's Bay where she remained until the evening when she was towed into St Helier Harbour by the *Princess Ena* assisted by the *Duke of Normandy*. Temporary repairs were carried out and the ship left in tow of the tug *Seaman*, bound for inspection at Plymouth. Every one was full of praise for the way in which the incident had been handled, for many recalled the fate of the *Stella*, *Ibex* and *Hilda* in similar circumstances.

Up to this time the two railway companies had each maintained its own staff in the islands but following the grouping scheme of 1923 the companies had come closer together and, from November 2 1932, a joint working scheme came into operation in both islands.

New Board of Trade Load Line requirements came into effect in 1932, which a number of the older units of the SR fleet could not meet and as two of these ships, the *Ada* and *Bertha*, maintained the Honfleur cargo service, the decision was taken to give up the route as it was already a loss maker, and this was done in September 1932. The *Vera* was another ship affected by the new regulations, but as already mentioned, a new ship was being built to replace her, which was launched as the *Brittany* on April 12 1933 and made her maiden voyage from Jersey on June 18. The official party which travelled to Jersey for the occasion returned the same night in the *Vera*, which then remained at Southampton until October 28 when she was towed away to Pembroke by the tug *Seaman* to be broken up.

With the arrival of the *Brittany*, both the railway companies had up-to-date fleets and with the ever increasing number of visitors travelling to the Channel Islands and France, the railway companies' shipping services enjoyed a boom period. Even then, however, the seeds of their decline were being sown.

The year 1935 proved to be the last year in which a railway steamer was lost while on service from Southampton or Weymouth. The *Princess Ena*, which by now only operated as a relief ship, conveyed a party of Scouts from Southampton to Jersey and, after they had disembarked on August 3, the ship sailed 'light' to St Malo. When about six miles south of Corbière, she caught fire and, despite all efforts to save her, she sank 24 hours later.

Threat of the aeroplane

Soon after *Vera* was towed away, a company was set up in Jersey called Jersey Airways Ltd, which on December 18 1933 commenced a service between the island and Southampton. By the summer of 1934 the company had six planes in its fleet. The services were operated from the beach at West Park near St Helier Harbour and though, due to this, they could only operate when the tide was down, air travel quickly gathered momentum.

The four railway companies were quick to react to the many companies that were being set up to operate air services and, in March 1934, Railway Air Services Ltd was set up in conjunction with Imperial Airways. In January the following year, the GWR and the SR took a third share in Channel Islands Airways Ltd, which was set up as a holding company for the operations of Jersey Airways Ltd and Guernsey Airways Ltd.

From small beginnings, Jersey Airways rapidly expanded, carrying ever greater numbers of passengers. In March 1937, the new airport at St Peters was opened in Jersey and, on June 1, the first regular air-mail was carried to the island. From this time onward, all urgent mail has been carried by aircraft and the morning arrival of the mailboat has ceased to be of much significance to the islanders. Two years later Guernsey Airport was opened, but by this time the clouds of war again loomed on the horizon.

Threat of war

It could have been these rumblings which caused an increase in the passenger carryings for 1938, the most marked being a 77 per cent rise in the figures on the St Malo route. With the forecast of a further increase on the route for the 1939 season, the *Isle of Thanet* came to join the Southampton fleet for the summer to provide extra sailings from July 22. Even the *Brittany* was drafted in to help out, but, before the season could end, war had been declared and services curtailed.

The *Isle of Jersey* was withdrawn after leaving the islands on August 24 1939, and by mid-September the *Isle of Guernsey, St Helier, St Julien, St Patrick* and *Lorina* had all been withdrawn from the Channel Islands route, and the Weymouth route suspended. The *Isle of Sark* and *Normannia* were left to maintain a service to the islands, while *Brittany* continued to run from Jersey to St Malo and the *St Briac* took over the Le Havre route after *Hantonia* went to the Straits of Dover to supplement services there.

When the mailboat arrived in the islands on September 8, she had donned war-paint, as did the *Britanny* during the Christmas holiday, when she was in St Malo. She was withdrawn from that service on December 27 and was sent to the Straits of Dover to replace the *Hantonia*. The latter relieved the *Isle of Sark* for three trips in February 1940 and took the place of the *Normannia* on the islands route from early May.

German forces had by this time begun a rapid advance across France, with the result that the Le Havre route was closed by the *St Briac* on May 19 1940, after which the service was routed through St Malo until May 28. Following this, the Jersey–St Malo service (which was fortnightly by mailboat) was operated twice as frequently, that is, became weekly, and was routed direct from St Malo to Southampton; the last sailing on this route was the *Hantonia*'s, leaving St Malo on June 16. The service to the islands continued till June 28 1940, on which day the *Isle of Sark* made the final run from the islands, which were then left open for the German forces to invade on July 1 1940.

During the time the army was 'de-storing' the islands some unusual railway company ships called, the most notable being the SR's *Shepperton Ferry*, and the LNER's *Train Ferry No 1* and *Train Ferry No 3*. Railway company services to the Channel Islands and Northern France then ceased and their fleets went to war, some never to return. Details of the vessels' war service can be found in the Ships' History section.

Chapter 7

Services restored and nationalisation

The first civilian route to be restored between England and France was that from Newhaven to Dieppe. It fell to the *Isle of Guernsey* to inaugurate the resuscitated service on January 15 1945 and also to re-open the railway companies' service to the Channel Islands.

The Channel Islands had been liberated on May 9 1945 and on June 26 the *Isle of Guernsey*, still painted grey, arrived in the islands, proudly flying both the SR and GWR house flags. The *Isle of Guernsey* was not the first railway company ship to visit the islands after the war, as the *Haslemere* had arrived in Jersey three days before. After only five trips, the *Isle of Guernsey* was replaced by the *Hantonia*, which had just been returned to the SR after overhaul, and she maintained the service alone until October 1945 when she was joined by the *Isle of Jersey*, which arrived in the islands on the 10th.

To replace war losses at Southampton, the SR moved the *Whitstable* from Dover, the ship making her first call at Jersey on July 23 1945, and ordered two new ships from Wm Denny & Bros, one a cargo vessel and the other a passenger ship that was declared to be for use on the Channel Islands route. In the event the ship was placed on the St Malo route to cover the loss of the *St Briac* and the transfer of the *Dinard* to Dover.

The first GWR vessel to call at Jersey after the war was the *Sambur*, which arrived on September 19 1945, being followed by her sister, the *Roebuck*, on October 17. To replace their war losses, the GWR ordered two passenger ships from Cammell Laird at Birkenhead, one of which was to become the extra seasonal ship for the Weymouth–Channel Islands service.

As the islands had been occupied, there were two main sources of traffic travelling to the islands, those who had been evacuated at the start of the war and were now returning, and the armed forces, which had the task of returning the islands to a peaceful state. The limited service that the SR could operate did not satisfy demand and therefore a Military Corvette service was commenced on January 1 1946. This lasted until October 5 1946, by which time more of the cross-Channel fleet had been released by the government. The ships used were the *Empire Lifeguard*, the *Empire Rest* and the *Empire Peacemaker*, vessels which had started out as *Castle*-class frigates but had been converted into ocean-rescue ships. The service operated from Southampton, being managed by the SR which also supplied commanders and many other personnel for the ships; Captains Durley, Trout, Pearce, Light, Breuilly and Abbey had spells in command.

To help out at Southampton came the *Autocarrier*, which was used to re-open the Jersey–France service on January 15 1946. Due to St Malo not yet being ready, Granville was used as the port of call. On April 16 1946 the *Autocarrier* made the first trip to St Malo and the ship was also used to re-establish the community on the island of Alderney, making her first call on December 15 1945. The GWR also helped to revive life on the island by introducing from June 14 1946 a once-weekly call by their cargo boats en route to Guernsey; this service lasted until the end of March the following year.

Before the war all railway company shipping services at Southampton used the Inner and Outer Docks but on April 10 1946 the *Whitstable* docked at Berth 32, Itchen Quays, and shortly afterwards the cargo services moved to Berths 20–23 in the Empress Dock, where they remained.

The *Brittany* returned to Jersey on June 5 1946 and, the following day, took up the service to St Malo, which she operated once a week, while at weekends she helped out on the cross-Channel service. The GWR re-opened the Weymouth–Channel Islands service on June 16 1946 using the *St Helier*, which had received a very quick refit, and she maintained the service until December 1, when the *St Julien* took over the service for a month, before going to help out at Fishguard.

The 1946 summer service of the SR was covered by the *Hantonia, Isle of Jersey* and the *Isle of Sark*, which had also returned to the islands on June 25 1946.

The *Dinard* was released from war service in July 1946 and the SR decided to have her converted into a car carrier to replace the *Autocarrier*. Thus on August 8 she left Southampton bound for the Tyne to be overhauled and refitted for her new life at Dover, where she took up her new duties on July 1 1947. The French routes to Le Havre and St Malo were restored in 1947, the former started up again on January 13 by *Autocarrier*, which operated a fortnightly schedule until the *Brittany* took over on March 10. On June 2 1947 all the flags were out when the old faithful, *Hantonia*, took over the service.

The following month on July 14, the new *Falaise* sailed from Southampton on her maiden voyage to St Malo and thus, with this journey, all the pre-war SR passenger services were restored. Due to the lock at St Malo having been destroyed by retreating Allied forces in 1940, the ship was unable to enter the port and had to remain at anchor in the River Rance, with the passengers being ferried ashore by vedettes. The service was operated twice a week, which allowed the ship to provide a direct service to Jersey at weekends, her first call there being on Saturday July 19. At the end of the summer, the ship took the mail sailing from Jersey on the Saturdays, and thus she made her first call at St Peter Port on September 6 1947. On June 5 1947, the *Brittany* took up her Jersey station for the summer, and again offered excursions as in pre-war years.

The first of the new ships for the GWR had entered service on the Irish Sea during the summer, and to find out how the vessel would handle in Channel Island waters, she was sent there for a trial period in September 1947. The *St David* arrived on her maiden voyage on the 4th of the month and remained on service for four weeks, but this was the only time that the ship was seen in the islands. In December 1947, a new cargo ship entered SR service. Named *Winchester,* she made her first call at Jersey on December 2 and, with her distinctive appearance and the sound of her two Sulzer engines, she became a notable member of the fleet.

British Railways take over

If the railway companies had found themselves in a poor financial state at the end of the First World War, then the position at the end of the Second World War was even worse. This and the election of a Labour government led to the nationalisation of the four railway companies as from January 1 1948. The airlines had also been nationalised, with Channel Islands Airways, in which the SR and GWR had increased their holding to 50 per cent in 1942, becoming part of British European Airways on April 1 1947. Thus the railway companies lost

any chance of the profits which might have come from the explosion in air travel which took place in the 1950s.

On January 1 1948 all the assets of the four railway companies were taken over by the British Transport Commission (BTC) which, under the title British Railways, operated the railway system, with the network being divided into six regions. The SR became part of the Southern Region, while the GWR became part of the Western Region, and thus the Channel Islands were served by two Regions. Common sense did prevail, however, and on November 1 1948 the shipping services based at Weymouth were put under the control of the Southern Region.

British Railways were only a month old when their first new ship was delivered and placed on the Channel Islands route. The *St Patrick* was a sister of the *St David*, but with a slightly different internal layout. Her maiden voyage was on February 4 and she arrived in the islands resplendent in the colours of the GWR, and flying their house flag, as the new colours of BR had not yet been decided. The ship stayed on the service until October 26 1948. She then went to Fishguard to act as a relief vessel, but she returned to Weymouth every summer for the Channel Islands service. The addition of a third ship at Weymouth allowed the cross-Channel day excursions to be reintroduced, the first being from Weymouth to Guernsey on July 21. At Southampton the *Falaise* had taken over the role of the old *St Briac* by making long weekend cruises to the French ports and the Channel Islands, both before and after the summer season.

The end of the independent railway companies was symbolically marked when, at 10:00 am on April 4 1949, all ships of the British Railways fleet hauled down for the last time the house flags of their old companies and hoisted the new BR flag, which was dominated by a golden lion astride a railway wheel. The ships had the previous year been painted in the new colours, which were mainly those of the old Southern Railway, but with the removal of the white line between the black hull and the red boot-top. The new flag and hull colours did not apply to the *St Patrick* which was owned by the Fishguard & Rosslare Railway & Harbour Co, a company owned jointly with Irish Railways. She kept her original colours and, in the place of the GWR flag which she had worn, wore the flag of her owning company.

Two strangers came to the islands in 1949, the first being the *Worthing*, which made an excursion between the islands on April 28 and then, the following day, took a party of Channel Islanders to Southampton for an excursion to the Cup Final.

The other stranger, the *Isle of Thanet* eventually became a regular visitor, as due to the St Malo service being increased to three trips a week, the *Falaise* could no longer fit in a trip to Jersey and to make up for this the *Isle of Thanet* came round from the Straits of Dover each weekend to operate the Friday night-service to Guernsey, as she was considered too long to enter St Helier Harbour.

Another Dover ship was put on the Southampton strength in May 1949, when the *Hythe* was transferred. She had been on the service temporarily the previous year, but she now became a permanent member, though she was loaned out during the winter as required to other ports.

On August 31 1949 the press in the islands reported that a new ship of 4,000 tons was to be built for service to the islands; this was inaccurate, however, as the ship was destined for the Le Havre route to replace the *Hantonia*. This was the second time that the islands had expected a new vessel, as when the order for the *Falaise* has been announced, it had been stated that she was for the Channel Islands route.

The formation of British Railways allowed an easy transfer of ships from one Region to another. Thus for the 1950 season the *Duke of York* spent the summer at Southampton and opened a twice-weekly service to Cherbourg, and also covered the weekend sailing to Guernsey. The Cherbourg service was not any more of a success than it had been in pre-war days, and the ship did not return.

The railway companies had owned many ports around Great Britain, but with the formation of the BTC it was decided that the port installations should be placed under a separate body and, on September 1 1950, the Southampton Docks were transferred to the Docks & Inland Waterways Board, though control and operation remained in the hands of the BR Docks and Marine Manager. From late October 1950 improvements were made to Berths 7, 8 and 9 in the Outer Docks in Southampton and this resulted in the passenger steamers using Berth 46 in the Ocean Dock for about five months.

From January 14 1951 the berths used by BR vessels at Jersey were altered for easier operation. The Weymouth mailboat was moved across the harbour from the New North Quay to a berth astern of the Southampton ship, while the Southampton cargo ships took the place of the Weymouth steamer. The new lock at St Malo was open in time for the 1951 season and, with an expected increase in the number of passengers who would use the service, an extra ship was placed on the route. The *Princess Maud* came south from Holyhead to operate two trips each week to St Malo and to cover the weekend service to Guernsey. The new ship for the

Le Havre route was launched as the *Normannia* on July 19, and sailed from Southampton on her maiden voyage on March 3 1952, taking over from the forty-year old *Hantonia*.

The *Dinard* returned in 1952 to Southampton, when she came round from Dover each weekend in the summer to operate sailings to St Malo. She was not the only Dover ship to come round that year, as the *Isle of Thanet* also made the weekly voyage to operate the Friday night-sailing to St Peter Port. She then came every summer up to 1958 to make that sailing; 1958 was the last season that an extra ship operated from Southampton.

By this time the tourist trade to the Channel Islands had increased considerably; the following table shows the Jersey arrivals.

	By Sea	*By Air*
1951	159,792	95,289
1952	178,824	119,745
1953	170,803	138,770
1954	172,163	161,375
1955	181,383	188,079

As can be seen, the major increase occured in 1952, when a hard runway was laid at Jersey Airport, allowing larger aircraft to operate, and within four years the air-passenger arrival figures had overtaken the figures for those arriving by boat. The comfort offered by the aeroplane caused complaints to be voiced about the facilities on the boats, as the *St Patrick* was the only modern ship on the Channel Islands service and the conditions on the pre-war vessels left much to be desired. Talks were held between BR and Channel Island officials and, on January 27 1953, the States of Jersey (the island's legislative body) agreed in principle to the deepening of St Helier Harbour, if British Railways went ahead with their plans to build three ships of the *St Patrick* type. BR invited tenders, but in July it was stated that no decision had been taken and nothing more was heard on the matter for some time.

By 1955 the ever increasing number of passengers travelling to the islands was causing distress to many of those using the cramped overnight sailings. On August 19 the *Daily Mirror* published a feature article with the headline 'Eight hours of misery on a cross-Channel trip to the Channel Islands' which gave a graphic account of conditions on board. It is not known whether this article was the root cause of ensuing events, but on November 8 1955 a meeting was held in Jersey between the island officials and those of BR, where it was agreed that St Helier Harbour would be deepened and that the approval of the British Transport Commission would be sought for the replacement of the *St Helier* and *St*

Julien. In Guernsey the following day, at a similar meeting, it was stated that two new cargo ships would also be bought.

The cargo side of the operation had seen a general decline over the last few years, as more direct services were opened by motor ships which operated at much lower cost than the coal-fired steamers in the old railway companies' fleet and the only profitable line was the carriage of Guernsey flowers and tomatoes, which were shipped to both Southampton and Weymouth, the latter having a new cargo stage opened in May 1954. The *Hythe* made her last call at Jersey on August 23 1955, being replaced by the *Brest* from the Newhaven–Dieppe route. On December 2, the *Winchester* and *Haslemere* were in collision in the Solent, which led to the *Pentland Firth* being chartered to cover.

The following year, 1956, was to prove to be the start of the decline, too, of the port of Southampton, as far as railway-owned shipping was concerned. On September 30 1956, Mr R.P. Biddle, a Jersey-man, who was a considerable figure exerting a great deal of influence over BR policy, retired as Docks & Marine Manager of the Southern Region. With his departure the control of the Docks went to Mr Finnis of the British Transport Docks, while control of the SR-fleet passed to Mr R.E. Sinfield who adopted the title Shipping & Continental Manager and was based at Victoria Station in London.

On November 9 came the announcement that the BTC had agreed to the building of four new ships and it was speculated that one passenger ship would operate from Southampton and the other from Weymouth; in the event this turned out to be no more than speculation. This decision to build new ships was followed on November 30 by the States of Jersey agreeing to spend £280,000 on the deepening of St Helier Harbour. The deal was described as 'An act of faith' on the part of both sides, as there was never any formal agreement in writing between them. On April 17 1957 the *St Julien* entered St Helier Harbour dressed overall to mark the 100 years of service between Weymouth and the islands. Within three years of this historic visit, Weymouth would be the only mainland terminal used for railway-passenger services to the Channel Islands.

Chapter 8

Wind of change

In 1955 'No Passport' day-excursions had again been allowed, after agreement between the French and British Governments, and on the Dover Straits' route these were mainly operated by the *Isle of Thanet*. Coupled with the steady increase in the numbers of passengers travelling by air, this meant that 1958 was the last summer that the ship operated the Friday night sailing to Guernsey. If the summer traffic was suffering a decline, then the winter figures were even worse, and in August 1958 came the news that both the Southampton–Le Havre and Southampton–Channel Islands routes were to be reduced by one sailing each week. This would allow the *Falaise* and *Normannia* to cover both routes for the winter and, because of this, *Normannia* made her first call in the islands on November 13 1958. The *Brittany* was also withdrawn for the winter, leaving the Jersey–St Malo sailing to be covered by the mailboat, in this case the *Normannia*, which arrived in Jersey every Thursday. The Weymouth–Channel Islands route was also reduced by one trip per week and with these cuts it was hoped to make substantial savings in the overall costs of the shipping services.

With four new ships for the service being built, early 1959 saw the first withdrawals of the old steamers. *Whitstable* was the first to go, being followed by the *Haslemere* and, during the interval before the arrival of the new ships, chartered tonnage was used. *Elk* made her maiden voyage on August 6, which allowed *Ringwood* to make her last voyage on October 9 1959. *Moose* paid her first call to Jersey on October 31 1959, the day on which the *Isle of Jersey* made her last call to the island after which she was named. There had been rumours that the ship was to be withdrawn, but these were denied by BR. This did not stop a crowd gathering to see the ship off and, as events turned out, she did not return. Although no mention was made in the papers of the fact, the *St Patrick* formed part of the re-organisation of the Channel Island services, and did not return to Fishguard at the end of the 1959 season, but remained at Weymouth to undertake the winter ser-

vice, being officially taken over by BR on December 17 1959.

The 1959–1960 winter service from Southampton to the islands was further reduced to only one round-trip each week and, as the new cargo vessels did not have any passenger accommodation—something that was always full in the old steamers—nearly all the passenger traffic was forced to use Weymouth. Even the new cargo vessels started to run from Weymouth to cover the overhauls of the two Weymouth ships, with the *Winchester* also taking her turn. The other major change which occurred at the start of the winter timetable was the transfer of the Weymouth boat-train from Paddington to Waterloo, which was no doubt done to stop the confusion that occurred due to the change in the shipping schedule. The move also broke one of the remaining GWR ties with the services and a further one took place early in 1960 when, after being relieved for overhaul by the *Normannia*, the *St Patrick* returned to service on February 27, painted in the full BR livery—gone forever was the old red funnel of the GWR.

With only two new passenger ships being built for the Channel Islands service, there was debate as to BR's intentions. These were revealed on June 4 1960, as follows: (i) to use fewer but bigger ships to run the service; (ii) to concentrate all the ships on the shortest sea route, using only one mainland port, namely Weymouth; (iii) to introduce a one-class, comfortable standard for all services; and (iv) not to carry cargo on passenger ships, something which had caused delays in the past. As can be imagined, these proposals were not well received in Southampton, where not only were the port's links with the islands threatened, but the city's airport was also threatened—by the Ministry of Aviation—with closure, thus severing all links with the Channel Islands. With the proposals only a month old, the shipping services were dealt a further blow in July, when it was announced that to improve the mail services to the islands, all mail except printed material and parcels would from July 18 be transported to the islands by air. Although the first-class mail had for years been carried by air, this transfer removed the last real importance of the mailboat's arrival and though the ships continued to fly the Royal Mail pennant, even this was allowed to lapse in the next few years.

On September 14 1960 the South Eastern Area Transport Users Consultative Committee held an enquiry at Southampton into the proposed closure of the Southampton–Channel Islands service, during which it was stated that the hoped-for savings from using Weymouth alone would be £209,000 annually. The most salient advantage was the shorter sea journey and the Committee ultimately gave its blessing to the transfer.

At the end of the 1960 summer service, three more of the older ships were withdrawn; *St Helier* after an excursion to Guernsey on September 14, *St Julien* after her trip from the Channel Islands on September 27 and the *Isle of Sark* after her arrival in the islands on Saturday, October 29, after which she sailed light back to Southampton. The new *Caesarea* was delivered to her owners on November 5 1960 and arrived in Jersey on a VIP call on November 18, during which the bell of the *St Helier* was presented to the town after which the ship had been named. On the 21st the ship proceeded to Guernsey, before returning to the mainland and making her maiden voyage proper on Saturday, December 3. The entry into service of the new ship allowed the *St Patrick* to be converted into a one-class ship, and she returned to service as such on April 21 1961.

By this time the *Isle of Guernsey* was again on the Southampton service, and on May 11 a farewell gathering was held on board to mark the termination of the passenger service. The last sailing arrived in the islands on May 13 and, after the passengers had disembarked and the cargo had been unloaded, the ship sailed light back to her home port, thus ending a railway company passenger-ship link that had existed since May 1 1842. Symbolically, on the same day, the new one-class service was inaugurated from Weymouth by the *Caesarea* and *St Patrick*, being helped out until June 10 by the *Isle of Guernsey*. Soon afterwards, on June 14 1961, the *Sarnia* appeared at St Peter Port, on a 'show-the-flag' call, before entering service on June 17. Her arrival meant the relegation of *St Patrick* to duties as third ship.

In the winter of 1960–61, the Guernsey Tomato Marketing Board was set up to handle the packing, shipping and marketing of the entire Guernsey crop. A large new labour-saving packing shed was built, where the trays of fruit were placed directly on to pallet boards on which they remained until reaching English markets. A three-year contract was signed with BR for the transportation of the crop and Weymouth was chosen as the English terminal for this service. The Southampton-based *Elk*, *Moose* and *Winchester* were used exclusively on this contract; and thus the Weymouth-based *Sambur* and *Roebuck*, filling the gap, saw much service into Southampton, being joined by chartered tonnage at peak times during these three years. The success of palletisation for the Guernsey crop led to its adoption for exports from Jersey and, with the reduced rates that this offered, BR increased its share of the trade.

In April 1962, the *Sarnia* moved up to Folkestone for a short spell to cover for the *Canterbury*, during which time she was very well received by the passengers. She was back in time for the start of the summer service on May 12, the timings of which were eased to allow more time in Guernsey. Towards the end of the summer, there were rumours that the *Brittany* was to be withdrawn and either replaced by the *Brighton* from Newhaven, or not at all. This was denied by BR and little did people realise when the ship closed her 1962 season on November 29 that she was not to return. It was the intention of BR to withdraw from the service completely but the Jersey authorities persuaded them to operate a limited service between St Malo and Jersey using the *St Patrick;* this in turn reduced the number of day trips she made to Guernsey.

The whole structure of the nationalised transport system changed on January 1 1963, when the BTC was disbanded and responsibility for the railway system was vested in the British Railways Board. Within the BTC had been the posts of Chief Shipping & International Services Officer and Shipbuilding & Marine Engineering Officer, and these were now placed within the Shipping & International Services Department for which a board member was made responsible. The day-to-day operation of the shipping services remained with the Regions, but with the board introducing a more commercial approach in all areas the Department became more involved in operations until, as we shall see later, all shipping was placed directly under its control on January 1 1968.

Even before the formation of the British Railways Board in January 1963 there was a design panel working on producing a new image for BR and in March 1963 one idea for the ships was for light blue hulls, buff boot-topping, cheat-line and funnel with much more of the superstructure being painted white. This was altered, however, before the new image was launched in January 1965.

As already indicated, the Le Havre service was under threat and a survey that BR carried out showed that there was no demand for a car-ferry service on this route. Another significant event occurred, early in February 1963, when a consortium headed by the Norwegian, Otto Thoresen, announced plans to commence a car-ferry service between Southampton and Cherbourg in 1964 using a purpose-built vessel. With the decision not to build the Channel Tunnel, BR saw that car-ferry services across the Straits of Dover would be in demand and the quickest way to provide them would be to convert existing passenger vessels. The *Falaise* and *Normannia* were the chosen ships and at the end of 1963 they were sent to the north-east coast for alteration.

To cover the Le Havre service, the *St Patrick* was transferred from Weymouth after her last trip from the islands on October 10 and, after a refit, took up the Le Havre route on December 5 1963, maintaining it until the route was closed on May 10 1964. The ship then opened the summer service to St Malo and, in addition, maintained the service to Jersey from St Malo and also carried out Weymouth–Guernsey day-trips. The season finished on September 27 1964 and on that day the railway-company passenger services from Southampton ended. The *St Patrick* sailed the next day for Newhaven where she was overhauled before a new life at Dover.

The departure of the last railway-company passenger vessel from Southampton also marked the closure of the marine workshops in the port. The facility had in fact been run down from the end of the previous winter's overhaul programme; the last Channel Islands passenger vessel to leave the yard was the *Sarnia* on February 26, while the *Hampton Ferry* was the last big ship to leave, on May 15 1964.

In 1964 the cargo services suffered a setback when the three-year contract with the Guernsey Tomato Marketing Board was not renewed. Instead the transportation of the crop was shared with the Commodore Shipping Company, a Guernsey firm which was just starting to become involved in cross-Channel traffic after years of inter-island shipping. This reduced the number of ships required to maintain the services and thus *Sambur* made her last trip from the islands on March 29 1964.

Although the passenger service between Jersey and St Malo had been terminated by the *St Patrick* in September 1964, the cargo service continued until December 19 when the *Moose* arrived in Jersey from St Malo for the last time.

In January 1965 a new corporate image was introduced, the logo 'British Rail' replaced the full title, and a new double-arrow symbol was teamed with house colours of monastral blue, pearl grey and flame red. Ships hulls were painted blue, with a thin white dividing line above the light brown bottom, while the superstructure was grey, and the funnel red with a white double arrow thereon and a thin black top. The *Winchester* was the first ship to be seen in the islands in the new colours when she returned from overhaul in December 1964. The grey superstructure was, however, deemed a hazard in foggy conditions, and by February 1965 those ships already in the new colours had had their superstructures repainted white. The new image was first seen in the Jersey press on January 16, when British Railways Southern Region became British Rail Shipping Services on all the advertisements regarding shipping matters.

January 1965 also saw the introduction of a simplified timetable, giving an 8:15 departure throughout the year from Jersey, with the winter service being overnight and the summer service a daylight operation.

The last of the old cargo steamers, the *Roebuck*, was withdrawn after her final crossing from Guernsey to Weymouth on February 27 1965 and, to replace her on the Weymouth station, the *Winchester* was transferred from Southampton on March 1. The *Roebuck* had at the end of 1964 been diverted from her normal duties, when she was used at Poole and in Weymouth Bay in the filming of the World War 2 epic, the *Heroes of Telemark*.

The manning of the vessels based at Southampton and Weymouth had always been on a separate basis, but the two stations were amalgamated in 1966, and on July 7 the *Caesarea* arrived in the islands under the command of Captain B.A. Caws, a Southampton master.

Though passenger figures were still in decline, the number of people wishing to take their cars with them on holiday was increasing sharply and, to cater for this, a special cargo boat service was operated between July 10 and September 10 1966 to coincide with the passenger ships. 'Cheap-weekend specials' were introduced in the autumn to help boost winter traffic. In December, the *Caesarea* went to Dover to cover the *Invicta* on the Golden Arrow service, this following two previous stints in the area by the *Sarnia*. The success of the car-ferry service in 1966 cause BR to step up the operation for the following year, with a ship being specially chartered to do nothing else but transport cars from July 3 to September 10 and the service was then extended until November 7. A new £250,000 customs hall at Weymouth was officially opened on July 31 1967, which greatly eased the processing of inward passengers, while its first-floor offices gave some welcome relief from the previous cramped conditions to shipping employees. The passenger figures had remained almost static since the basing of all the Channel Islands services at Weymouth in 1961 but, with the completion of the electrification of the railway line to Bournemouth in mid-1967 and the announcement in August of a 16 per cent increase in air fares, the pendulum was about to swing back towards sea travel.

Cargo traffic was also about to undergo some major changes with BR making proposals in October 1967 for the introduction of a containerised service, a new concept, which required new containers, new ships and new port facilities to handle. Thus at the end of 1967 the BR services to the islands could again look forward to a bright future. Before any of these alterations could take place, however, the control of the Southern Region's shipping services was to pass to the newly created Shipping & International Services Division which, from January 1 1968, assumed control for all the shipping activities of the British Railways Board.

Chapter 9

Revival

The electrification of the railway line from London to Bournemouth greatly reduced the journey time, which meant that the departure time of the boat-train from London could be put back to 9:55 am, thus allowing passengers from outside London more opportunity to connect with the train. The ship departure from Weymouth was retimed at 1:30 pm and though the 8:00 pm arrival time at Jersey brought initial opposition from hoteliers due to late evening meals, the 'new look' service which commenced on Easter Monday, April 15 1968 was an immediate success, the overall increase in traffic to Jersey being 25 per cent, while that to Guernsey was up by no less than 37 per cent. Such was the increase in traffic that passenger numbers on the peak summer sailings had to be restricted by the issue of sailing tickets and, on a number of occasions, passengers were turned away.

This increase led to a study of how best to overcome this welcome problem and one option considered was the introduction of the *St David* as a third ship on the service, but nothing came of the idea, and instead the two existing vessels provided extra sailings.

Traffic figures for the first season of this 'new-look' service showed an increase of 80,897 passengers to a total of 382,224, while accompanied cars increased by 2,468 to 12,287.

Progress towards containerisation was slower than had been expected, partly due to the Channel Islands' reluctance to install the facilities required to handle large containers. In June 1969 it was announced that BR had come to an agreement with the Commodore Shipping Co to share the equipment required in the islands. To acquaint themselves with the problems of the islands the Executive of the Shipping & International Services Division visited their outposts in October 1970, after which events moved more swiftly.

The *Winchester* was not suitable for the transport of containers and made her farewell visit to the islands on December 29 1970, being replaced two days laters by the *Selby* which operated mainly out of Southampton. The *Winchester* had spent most of her time on the 'flower' service between Guernsey and Weymouth, the flowers being charged by weight, but for the 1971 season BR altered this system to one charged for by volume. This brought the costing into line with that of the airlines and had the effect of increasing some rates by as much as 156 per cent and, as might be expected, it brought about the end of the special 'flower' boats.

Full details for the planned container service were announced in February 1971; the service was to operate from Southampton with only the Guernsey tomato traffic remaining at Weymouth. Two new ships were to be built and these would be joined by either the *Container Venturer* or *Container Enterprise* with only *Elk* or *Moose* being retained for the tomato trade. Six weeks later a further announcement stated that the English terminal would be Portsmouth and not Southampton, and thus the last link the islands had with Southampton was to be broken.

The growth of passenger traffic during the summer months entailed many more overnight crossings. To improve passenger comfort, extra seating was installed in the ships early in 1971, providing 870 numbered seats under cover, and in May of that year a reservation system was introduced, which prevented the scramble which normally occurred as the passengers boarded the ships. At the same time a limit of 1,000 passengers on night crossings was introduced, thus ensuring every passenger a seat or berth for the journey.

With two new container ships already launched, British Rail caused something of a shock in December 1971 when they announced the pooling of their cargo services to the islands with those of the Commodore Shipping Co Ltd of Guernsey. The new service under the title of Brit–Comm would give a daily service to both islands and be maintained by four ships, with Portsmouth as their English terminal. The two new BR cargo ships, the *Guernsey Fisher* and the *Jersey Fisher* entered service early in 1972; as the names imply, they were owned by James Fisher & Sons Ltd of Barrow and were time-chartered for five years to BR. In April the general-cargo service from Weymouth ended, though Guernsey tomatoes continued to be shipped through the Dorset port.

April 28 1972 will go down in Channel Islands history as the date which was to bring about the transformation of sea travel to and from the islands for, on that day, BR announced the introduction of a roll-on/roll-off (ro/ro) car-ferry service that would commence operation in 1973, using either the *Falaise* or the *Normannia*. The service was to be only between Weymouth and Jersey as the States of Guernsey decided not to install a ramp.

The introduction of the Brit–Comm agreement should have occurred on May 1 1972 but, due to the port facilities not being ready, it was not until October 1 that it took place. It fell to the *Elk* to make the final sailing of a railway-company ship from Southampton, when she left port in the evening of September 29 1972 bound for the islands. That same evening, the *Guernsey Fisher* sailed from Jersey bound for Portsmouth, ready for the first sailing of the new service on Monday, October 2. The *Elk* and the *Moose* were withdrawn from service over the weekend of October 7–8, while the *Selby* was kept in service until October 21. All three ships were sold before the end of the month. It was rare for the islands to see any 'foreign' BR ships on the service to the islands, but in 1972, the cargo ship *Isle of Ely* made three trips, as did the *Maid of Orleans*, which covered for the damage *Caesarea*, on her last trip taking her passengers to Newhaven so that she could arrive earlier at Folkestone.

Early in 1973 Guernsey had a taste of things to come when the *Holyhead Ferry I*, a purpose-built car ferry, called at the island when she replaced the *Caesarea*, but she did not continue to Jersey, as at the time she was considered too large to enter the harbour.

The *Falaise* was replaced at Newhaven by the new ship *Senlac*, after which she proceeded to Holyhead for alterations and a refit, to ready her for new duties. She made a trial run to Jersey on May 25 1973, followed by an inaugural voyage on May 30, before her first scheduled crossing on June 1 1973, an event from which was to stem a complete reorganisation of sea transport to the islands. The *Falaise* made one round trip a day, leaving Jersey at 7:30 am and Weymouth at 3:30 pm, and such was the success of the summer-only service that it was extended to cover the winter period. The car-ferry took two of each week's winter schedule, leaving the mailboat to operate the weekend sailing. As Guernsey had no ramp, the cars had to be craned off the ship from the stern ramp and, seeing this, Guernsey lost no time and ordered a ramp.

As the car-ferries had no provision for the carriage of mail, their introduction to the winter timetable caused the mail to be routed via the container service, and thus the passenger ships lost the title Royal Mail Steamer, and no longer flew the distinctive Royal Mail pennant. It fell to the *Caesarea* to carry the last of the regular mail to the islands on Friday, October 5 1973, and the same ship took the last outward mail on Monday, October 8.

Southampton again forged railway links with the islands in December 1973 when a new Operations Headquarters was set up in the old South Western Hotel to control the services to the islands, as well as the new service between Weymouth and Cherbourg which was to commence in April 1974. This service was to be operated by the *Maid of Kent*, which was no longer required at Dover as, due to the lack of height in her car deck, she was unable to carry commercial traffic. A familiarisation trip to Cherbourg was made on March 27 1974, returning the next day, and the service commenced on April 6 leaving Weymouth at 9:45 am and returning from Cherbourg at 3:00 pm, with a return overnight trip being made at the height of the summer. The ramp at Guernsey was installed in time for the 1974 summer season; the *Falaise* made her first call on June 26 and from then on called twice a week, the other days remaining on the direct Weymouth–Jersey route.

Although the service to the Channel Islands had been advertised as being a *car* ferry only, it was not long before commercial traffic started to be carried and, with the inclusion of Guernsey in the schedule, the need to replace the aging *Falaise* became urgent. The ship had been given an extended refit early in 1974, after which it had been hoped that she would continue until the end of the year. She was being run hard, however, and boiler troubles caused her to be withdrawn after a very late arrival at Weymouth on August 14, the same day that it was announced that the *Caledonian Princess* would replace the *Falaise* on the service in 1975. At very short notice, the Swedish ferry *Svea Drott* was chartered for the route, being replaced in late September by the *Caledonian Princess* which operated until the *Normannia* came on service in late October for the winter of 1975 during which the ferry had to operate alone on the route as the two passenger ships were laid up for the winter. The *Svea Drott* so impressed BR while on charter that she was purchased in December 1974, being renamed *Earl Godwin*. It was hoped that she would be converted in time for the 1975 summer season, but this was not to be the case, and the *Caledonian Princess* replaced the *Normannia* on July 15 1975.

The car-ferry now made three calls per week at

Guernsey, and such was the demand for vehicle space that it was decided to combine the passenger service and the car-ferry service into a multi-purpose operation for the 1976 season, using the *Earl Godwin* and the *Caledonian Princess*, with the *Sarnia* being retained to provide extra passenger capacity at peak times. The *Caesarea* made her last voyage from the islands on October 6 1975, moving to Dover in time for the next season, where she replaced the *Maid of Orleans*. The *Earl Godwin* made her maiden voyage from the Channel Islands to Weymouth on February 2 1976—something not done since 1897—and her arrival allowed the *Caledonian Princess* to be withdrawn to be altered for the multi-purpose service.

The new multi-purpose service commenced on May 12 1976 and, although the timings of the previous 'classic' (foot passenger) service were almost entirely retained, there was one noticeable change in that the evening sailing from Jersey did not call at Guernsey, but went direct to Weymouth. The *Earl Godwin* always took the 1:30 pm sailing from Weymouth, while the *Caledonian Princess* took the 12:30 am sailing, which routed direct to Jersey, and sailed at 8:00 am to Guernsey and Weymouth. Extra mid-week trips to Guernsey and a weekend service to both islands was provided by the *Sarnia* during the summer. Although still advertised as a cary-ferry service, freight traffic quickly took advantage of the service offered, to such an extent that a third ferry, the *Viking II*, was purchased in December 1976. Renamed the *Earl William*, the ship was to commence a new multi-purpose service from Portsmouth to the Channel Islands in late 1977, replacing the existing container service and removing the need for the services provided by the 'classic' ships at Weymouth. Thus the *Sarnia* made her last regular call to the islands on Sunday,

September 4 1977, while her last voyage was a special excursion on September 10, when, during her time in port, various items from the ship were presented to the Maritime Museum at Castle Cornet.

The *Jersey Fisher* made her last call in the Islands as a BR ship on September 29, and was then handed over to the Commodore Shipping Co Ltd, which renamed her *Commodore Challenger* for use on their services. Her sister, the *Guernsey Fisher* remained in service until October 27 1977 when she sailed from St Peter Port and thus closed the BR cargo service, though a cargo ship was chartered each season to carry Guernsey tomatoes to Weymouth. With the ending of the cargo service the Brit–Comm Agreement was dissolved and, with it, any need in the Channel Islands for the name British Rail, as by now 'Sealink' had become the brand name for the BR Shipping Services.

Sealink had been launched in November 1969 as a brand name for the joint shipping fleets of British Rail, SNCF and the Zeeland SS Co. The Belgian Maritime Transport Authority joined the Sealink banner in 1971 and, a year later, the first two ships appeared with the word 'Sealink' in huge white letters on their hull sides, with the rest of the fleet also adopting it in 1973.

In the islands, though 'British Rail' continued to be used in the press, much of the publicity for the car-ferry service carried the Sealink title and the way was now clear for the full adoption of the title Sealink.

The ending of the BR container service also brought about the end of the Royal Mail contact, as although trials using trailers were made, it was found that transport of parcels by containers best suited the needs of the Post Office and, early in 1978, the 137-year old contract was terminated.

Chapter 10

Full ahead with Sealink

The new multi-purpose Portsmouth service was due to commence on October 31 1977, but a pay dispute delayed this until November 8. The *Earl William* was not yet ready and thus it fell to the *Earl Godwin* to provide the initial service which left Portsmouth at 11:00 pm, five nights a week, bound for Guernsey and Jersey where she arrived at 8:30 am. She left on the return trip at 9:50 am, again calling at Guernsey, and arrived back at Portsmouth at 6:50 pm. The Friday night-sailing routed to Jersey first, so that the ship could spend the weekend in Guernsey, as the Weymouth vessels took up the space in St Helier Harbour.

The *Earl William* entered service with the 11:00 pm sailing on January 16 1978 and, with her arrival, the reorganisation of the Channel Islands service was complete, although minor alterations were still to come. The new service was an immediate success with loadings 100 per cent above expectations and the result of this was that from April 1 1978 the service was increased to six sailings a week, and it has remained at this level even during the winter months ever since. To ensure that the extra day's service is kept on time, the Weymouth service on a Saturday is routed to Jersey first and then on to Guernsey, the ship returning light to Jersey after discharge.

The spring of 1978 caused a few headaches at Weymouth, as the *Earl Godwin* was held up at Immingham, due to a labour dispute at the repair yard, while the *Maid of Kent* took longer than expected on overhaul and the *Lord Warden* had to be brought in to open the Cherbourg route. The *Normannia* was the first ship to cover for the *Earl Godwin*, but as the traffic built up the *Viking Victory* was chartered. Then, to allow the *Caledonian Princess* to be withdrawn from service for overhaul, the *Normannia* was brought back and to help out on the passenger side, the *Caesarea* came down from Dover.

The 1978 summer timetable gave the islands a service never seen before, with three multi-purpose sailings each day, seven days a week — something else not seen before and a distinct change from the

days of cutbacks in the late 1950s. Thus five short years had seen the complete reorganisation of the Channel Islands railway company shipping services, the pattern of which had developed over a period of 150 years. A further break was made on January 1 1979 when the British Railway Board's shipping division was transferred to the ownership of Sealink UK Ltd, a wholly-owned but completely autonomous subsidiary of the Board.

Another, less pleasing break with tradition took place in April 1979 when the timetable of the Weymouth service was altered so that the vessel arriving in Jersey on Saturday morning no longer remained over the weekend, but operated a return sailing to Weymouth. During the traditional weekends in port many friendships had developed between the crew and the locals but with the ships now making quick turn-arounds, much of the *entente cordiale* has been lost.

The ever increasing cost of fuel made the operation of steamers uneconomic and, to replace the *Caledonian Princess*, the Finnish ferry *Viking 4* was acquired, and after being re-engined and modified at a total cost of about £10 million she was renamed *Earl Granville*, entering service on March 29 1981 on the Portsmouth route. This allowed the *Earl William* to undergo refit, after which she was transferred to the Weymouth route which she took up on May 3, the day after the *Caledonian Princess* had made her last departure from the islands amidst much blowing of her steam whistle.

On June 22 1981, a fire broke out on the *Earl Granville* in the domestic boiler room when south of the Isle of Wight and she had to be replaced for a time by the *Caledonian Princess*, hot-foot from Dover. During the time she was on the service, the *Earl William* suffered a mishap in St Helier Harbour and, to help out, the freight-only *Viking Trader* was chartered, while *Earl Siward* was brought in to help out with three trips over the weekend of July 11–13. The latter made the record books at the time as the largest ship ever to have entered St Helier Harbour.

The *Maid of Kent* enjoyed a much-publicised final

season on the Cherbourg service and was given a great send-off at both ports on Friday, October 2, 1981, when she made her final sailing. Not only was it supposed to be her final voyage, but it was also supposed to be the final sailing of a steamship in the service of Sealink; however, events were to prove otherwise.

The *Maid* was only allowed a brief respite, as on October 5 the *Earl William* ran into difficulties at Jersey for a second time that season and had to be withdrawn from service; the *Maid* was then called in to help out at weekends by operating services to Guernsey. Thus it was in fact October 30, at 7:04 pm, that the ship commenced her last voyage when she left St Peter Port bound for Weymouth. With her went the last of 'railway' steam.

The Guernsey tomato industry was another victim of the ever increasing cost of oil and with less tonnage to be transported, and the ferries taking a growing share of the trade, Sealink decided that there was no need for a charter vessel any longer and 1981 was the last year it operated.

Various ships were rumoured to be the replacement for the *Maid of Kent*, but in the end it was the *Ailsa Princess* which opened the Cherbourg service on April 2 1982. Before the ship came into service she was converted into a one-class vessel, with extra accommodation being built aft to provide more seating and, at the same time, the ship was converted to burn heavy-grade fuel. The Cherbourg route is very popular during the summer months, and in 1983, an extra afternoon sailing was introduced on Saturday and Sunday during July and August by retiming some of the Channel Islands services, which allowed the *Earl Granville* to take the Saturday sailing and the *Earl William* the Sunday.

Railway finale

Although all the services were now operated by motorships, one was already 20 years old and in January 1981 plans were announced for the building of two new ships for the Channel Islands services, with work due to start in 1985, but these proposals were overtaken by other events.

On July 14 1980 it had been announced in the House of Commons that some British Rail's interests were to be de-nationalised, including Sealink Ltd. It took time to disentangle Sealink from its ties with British Rail, but by July 1983 the management was able to set out to the staff the progress that had been made and the various options as to how privatisation might be achieved. The target date was set for mid-1984.

The first outward sign of the move towards privatisation was seen in the Channel Islands on Wednesday, February 22 1984, when the *Earl Granville* arrived back in service after overhaul without the white BR emblem on her funnel. On March 27 1984 Sealink unveiled their new image to the press, this giving ships a white hull with two-tone blue trim and a gold SL insignia on the funnel, coupled with re-styled lettering. This was only applied to four ships for the 1984 season, none being on the routes covered in this book, but the new house flag was hoisted by all the ships in the fleet.

A number of companies made a bid for Sealink, and on Wednesday, July 19 1984, it was announced that the £66 million bid of Sea Containers Ltd had been accepted. Control of Sealink UK Ltd was to pass on Friday, July 27, to the American company, which is based in Bermuda. A holding company, British Ferries Ltd, was established to own Sealink UK Ltd, and thus on July 27 1984 the railway links with the Channel Islands and north-west France were severed after a period of 142 years and the services were again in private hands. The new owner, Mr J. Sherwood, visited Jersey on August 14 and Guernsey the following day, to outline his proposals to the Islands authorities.

It will be interesting to see what changes the new owners will make, as another company wants to start a new passenger-freight service from Portsmouth to the islands, and if this occurs it will be the first competition on the islands' route since 1899. Who would have thought in the late 1950s of the changes which have occurred in the last decade? It is doubtful whether any operator other than BR could have weathered the problems that they produced. The Channel Islands have depended upon the services provided by the railway companies for nearly a century and a half, and I hope this book is a tribute to all those both afloat and ashore who have helped to maintain them.

Earl Granville *leaving Jersey on March 3 1984, without the British Rail emblem on her funnel (Author).*

Ship histories

These are set out in two different ways, whereby the regular ships have their entire history covered together with full particulars of the vessel, while the relief ships have only the details of the services they covered and brief details of the vessel during the time it was on service.

The name of the owner or operator is given at the time the ship first commenced service in the area and, in the case of railway ships from 1948 to 1978, the title British Railways is used, although the registered owner up to 1962 was actually the British Transport Commission.

Tonnage and dimensions have long caused problems to those interested in shipping and for this reason I include a few notes to explain the measurements used in this book. Alterations and their dates during the time the vessel was in railway service are also given.

It should be mentioned that some of the technical data and information on builders' yards, date of completion et cetera has not been recorded in the ensuing ship histories. This is due to a variety of factors — records have disappeared or been left incomplete and, certainly in the early days (c1824–1880), importance was not attached to the completion of detailed records. Where this is the case, the abbreviation 'n/a' for 'information not available' is used instead of a normal entry.

Tonnage

Up to 1835 the tonnage of a vessel was related to the weight of cargo it could carry and given by the formula,

$$\text{tonnage} = \frac{(L - \tfrac{3}{5}B) \times B \times \tfrac{1}{2}B}{94},$$

where L = length and B = beam. In steam ships the engine and boiler spaces were commercially unproductive and thus the length of these spaces was deducted from the registered length before the tonnage calculation was made. For example, the dimensions of the *Lord Beresford*, with a length of 100' 9" and beam of 18' 2", would give a tonnage of 158, but with a reduction of 43' 8" for the engine

and boiler spaces the ship's length becomes 57' 1" which gives the ship a tonnage of 81.

In 1836 the 'New Measurement' tonnage system was introduced, which was based on the internal volume of the ship below deck level, with steam ships having their engine-room space deducted to give net tonnage for the assessment of harbour dues. As ship construction developed and superstructures were added above deck level, the method of calculating the tonnage was again altered by the Merchant Shipping Act of 1854 (effective in 1857), whereby all enclosed areas of the ship were measured for the gross tonnage, while the crew's accommodation and navigation areas were added to the deduction to produce the net tonnage. This was known as the 'Moorsom' method of tonnage measurement. This method has remained to the present day, although changes in the deductions for net tonnage were made in 1884 and in 1914, the former reducing the net tonnage while the latter increased it. In this book the 'Old Measurement' tonnage system is given as 'Tons Burthen', while the 'New Tonnage' is given as 'Gross' and 'Net' tonnage, with the gross tonnage abbreviated to 'g' and the net to 'n'.

Dimensions

A ship has a given set of 'Registered Dimensions', to be found on the Registry Papers, namely length, breadth and depth. The length is from the fore-side of the stem to the aft-side of the stern post, while the breadth is the widest beam measurement to the outside of the hull and the depth is the distance from the floor of the hold to the underside of the main deck (or tonnage deck). In recent years, more use has been made of the ship's overall length from stem to stern (oa) and of the length between perpendiculars, as the distance from the bow at waterline to the sternpost (bp), is known. Since most vessels built before 1940 had straight stems the registered length equates closely with the (bp) length of modern raked bow vessels, and so for ships built after 1945 I have used the (bp) length as well as the overall length and

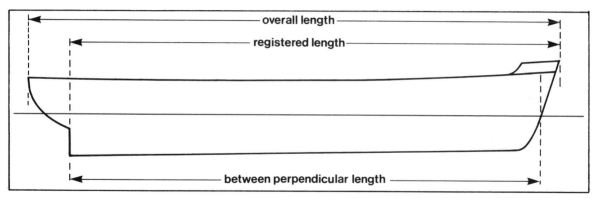

overall beam. The depth of a modern ship can vary greatly for the same type of vessel and therefore only the draft of the ship is included.

Propulsion

All the paddle ships were steam driven and therefore only the size of the cylinders is given, while for the screw vessels 'SR' denotes that steam-reciprocating machinery was used and this is given as well as the size of the cylinders. The steam turbine is self-explanatory and for modern oil engines the number of cylinders is given. For all types of engine I have given the horsepower where they can be detailed in the same units and, where known, the service speed of the vessel, rather than that obtained on trials.

Horsepower

This can be defined in a number of ways; in the early days a ship's papers would simply record HP while, since then, ihp (Indicated Horse Power), nhp (Nominal Horse Power), shp (Shaft Horse Power) and bhp (Brake Horse Power) have all been used as the units of measurement.

Indicated Horse Power is dependent on the size of the engine, the steam pressure in the unit and the speed at which the shaft is rotating. Nominal Horse Power is mainly used by the engine builders and the classification societies and is little used elsewhere. Shaft Horse Power and Brake Horse Power are measured while the engine is on the test-bed working into a load. It is difficult to relate these powers, but a very rough guide would be: the bhp and shp of a steam-reciprocating (SR) engine are about 90 per cent of the ihp; the bhp and shp of a diesel engine equal about 70 per cent of the ihp; and the nhp of a steam engine is about one seventh of the ihp, though this will vary, depending on the size of the engine.

The Ships

Ada

Owner London & South Western Railway. **Builder** Gourlay Bros & Co (Dundee) Ltd, Dundee **Completed** April 1905. **Yard no** 216. **Tonnage** 1905 529 g, 152 n; 1914 489 g, 198 n. **Dimensions** 175.3 (rl) 197.5 (oa) × 28.15 × 12.45 ft. **Propulsion**

Ada leaving St Peter Port (J.M. David).

Single screw, SR, 3 cyl 16" 26" 43"–33" 1,000 ihp. **Speed** 12 knots.

Completed in April 1905 at a cost of £13,200, *Ada* and her sister ship *Bertha* spent most of their service life on the Southampton–Honfleur route, but did run occasionally to the Channel Islands. To provide better protection for deck cargo, both ships had their bulwarks raised by two feet in early 1911. Withdrawn from service at the end of 1932, the ship was sold to the Darwen & Mostyn Iron Co, for £750 in March 1934 to be demolished.

Ailsa Princess

Owner Sealink UK Ltd. **Builder** Cantieri Navale Breda, Venice. **Completed** June 1971. **Yard no** 272. **Tonnage** 1971 3,715 g, 1,274 n; 1982 3,910 g, 1442 n. **Dimensions** 346' 6" (bp) 369' 5"(oa) × 57' 3" × 12' draft. **Propulsion** Twin screw. 16-cyl oil engines 14,560 bhp. **Speed** 19 knots.

This ship was built for the Stranraer–Larne route and entered service in July 7 1971. In December 1981 it was announced that she was to replace the *Maid of Kent* on the Weymouth–Cherbourg route and that alterations, including extra lounge accommodation on the promenade deck and a duty-free shop, were to be made and the engines converted to burn heavy grade fuel before she took up service on April 2 1982. The work was carried out by Smith's Dock Co at Middlesborough and cost £280,000. One other small change was the painting out of the long extensions to the Rail emblem on the funnel.

The ship was taken over by a crew from the Weymouth station at Middlesborough on February 17 1982 and, with the alterations completed, she arrived at Weymouth on March 27, making a trial trip to Cherbourg on March 31 before taking up the service on April 2. At the end of the season she helped out at Folkestone from October 2–19, and then went for relief work to Holyhead on 21–22 October and also on November 10. The ship had had an interesting period from November 16 1982,

when she sailed from Weymouth for Birkenhead where she commenced a ten-day charter on November 18 to the Ministry of Defence, which used her to test the feasibility of using ferries as minelayers.

Alberta

Owners London & South Western Railway. **Builder** John Brown & Co Ltd, Clydebank. **Completed** May 1900. **Yard no** 346. **Tonnage** 1900 1,242 g, 376 n; 1900 1,238 g, 329 n; 1904 1,236 g, 326 n; 1908 1,247 g, 319 n; 1914 1,125 g, 460 n; 1921 1,193 g, 481 n. **Dimensions** 270.0 (rl) 280.75 (oa) × 35.6 × 14.6 ft. **Propulsion** Twin screw, SR, 4 cyl 19½" 31½" 36½" 36½"–30" 5,000 ihp. **Speed** 19 knots.

Built to replace the *Stella*, the *Alberta* was ordered in August 1899, launched on April 3 1900, underwent trials on May 22 and arrived in the Channel Islands on her maiden voyage on June 2 1900. Improvements were made in 1908 which altered her appearance, the most noticeable being the addition of a poop with two lifeboats above and the plating in of the forward end of the promenade deck.

In late November 1913, two new lifeboats under Welin davits replaced the two forward cutters to meet new regulations and, at the same time, the bulwarks under the bridge were painted black, this following half a strake of brown being painted on the accommodation the previous year. During overhaul in October 1915, internal alterations to the smoke-room were made, the bridge moved aft of the foremast and the wheel-house removed.

The ship remained on the Channel Islands route during the Great War. She was requisitioned for a short period in March 1918, but the starboard crankshaft broke as she was leaving Southampton and she remained out of service until August of that year. During a three month refit early in 1920 a new funnel was fitted, and on July 21 of that year, the ship suffered the only major incident of her life, when she hit rocks off Guernsey when inward-

bound from Southampton. She was patched at St Peter Port and returned to service on August 15. On November 13 1920 the ship left Southampton bound for the Caledon Shipbuilding Co at Dundee to undergo a major refit. She was due back in service in time for the 1921 season, but a strike at the yard delayed her return and it was not until November 7 1921 that the ship resumed the Channel Islands service. During another refit early in 1925 the forward end of the promenade deck was enclosed, and the rails plated in to just under the second set of lifeboats. In 1927, trials with Radio Direction Finding (RDF) equipment were carried out on board and as a result all the passenger vessels had the equipment fitted.

In her last season of service she showed that she still had a good turn of speed, when on August 12 1929 the *St Julien* found that she was unable to overtake the old ship when on passage from Jersey to Guernsey. She arrived in the Channel Islands on her last voyage on December 12, sailing the next and was then laid up. She was sold to Greek owners and sailed from Southampton on June 11 1930. She retained her name until 1934 when she became the *Mykali,* but reverted to *Alberta* the following year. Her end .came on April 23 1941 when she was sunk by German aircraft at Punta (Salamis).

Alderney

Owner London & South Western Railway. **Builder** Wigham Richardson & Co, Newcastle. **Completed** May 1875. **Yard no** n/a. **Tonnage** 612 g, 395 n. **Dimensions** 175.0 (rl) × 25.2 × 19.5 ft. **Propulsion** Single screw, SR, 2 cyl 26½" 42"–27" 90 hp. **Speed** 11.36 knots.

This cargo vessel ran trials on May 1 1875, when she attained a speed of 11.36 knots, after which she spent most of her life on the services to Cherbourg, Le Havre and Honfleur. She had only a few incidents during her life with the L & SWR, the most serious being on September 24 1889 when she ran down the yacht *Ladybird* in the Needles Channel.

In October 1890 it was decided that her boilers were worn out and she was put up for sale, and in April 1891 passed to the Dundee & Newcastle SS Co, which retained her name. In late 1909 she was acquired by the Preston & Dublin Shipping Co without a change in name and in January 1913 appeared again in the Channel Islands when operating the service to the islands from Bristol. Late in the same year she passed to H. & C. Grayson and then to the Levant Transport Co (H. Tyrer & Co), which renamed the ship *Niggem*. A year later she was sold to Wilson & Reid of Belfast, but did not

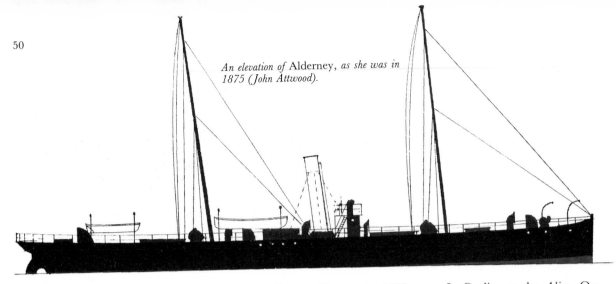

An elevation of Alderney, *as she was in 1875 (John Attwood).*

remain long with them, as she sank seventy miles from Malta on December 27 1914.

Aldershot

Owner London & South Western Railway. **Builder** Earl's Shipbuilding & Engineering Co Ltd, Hull. **Completed** August 1910. **Yard no** 572. **Tonnage** 1933 631 g, 256 n. **Dimensions** 192 (rl) × 29.2 × 14.17 ft. **Propulsion** Single screw, SR, 3 cyl 13½″ 25″ 40″–27″ 900 ihp. **Speed** 12.5 knots.

Formerly the *Brittany*, this ship was renamed *Aldershot* on March 31 1933 to free the original name for a new ship then building at Dumbarton. (See *Brittany* (II) entry for earlier history.)

From this date little took place in the life of the ship and when the *Minster* was moved from Dover to Southampton it allowed the *Aldershot* to be withdrawn in November 1936 and she was sold on December 16. Acquired by a D. Tripcovich of Trieste for £2,350, she was converted into a salvage vessel named *Hercules*. On November 24 1941 the ship was attacked by a submarine when off Candia and was reported sunk; the ship, however, was found in November 1945 as a wreck at Heraklion.

Alice

Owner London & South Western Railway. **Builder** Caird & Co, Greenock. **Completed** 1859 (The ship's register has no date for the year of construction but there is no doubt that she was built at the same time as *Fannie*). **Yard no** n/a. **Tonnage** 1869 635 g, 359 n; 1884 635 g, 294 n. **Dimensions** 231.6 (rl) × 26.2 × 13.4 ft. **Propulsion** Paddles, 2 cyl 60″ 60″–72″ 250 hp. **Speed** n/a.

Built as the *Sirius* in 1859 for a service between Lübeck and Kronstadt, she soon went to America, being involved in the civil war and registered at Nassau in 1863 to a J. Carlin as the *Alice*. On October 31 1865 her registry was passed to Messrs T. Salkeld & T. Hill of the Caledonian Railway Co. She remained with them until April 1869 when she was acquired by the L & SWR arriving at Southampton from Glasgow on May 3. After a short refit during which alterations were made to the decks, she underwent trials on June 22 and was then placed on the St Malo route, remaining on it until 1874, when she moved to the Le Havre service. She had short spells on the Channel Islands route between 1879 and 1882, and remained on the Le Havre route until late 1886. The following summer she took the Cherbourg service, acting as relief to Le Havre and St Malo as required.

Her last mention in the newspapers was on December 24 1887. She was then converted into a coal hulk, remaining with the company until November 10 1897, when she was sold with the hulk of the *Dispatch* for £450 to a Mr J.J. King, apparently ending her days at a breaker's yard in Holland.

Aldershot *in Southampton Water (B. Moody).*

Alliance

Owner London & South Western Railway. **Builder** Ditchburn & Mare, Blackwall, London. **Completed** July 1855. **Yard no** n/a. **Tonnage** 1855 361 g, 169 n; 1878 400 g, 230 n (189 n in 1884); 1889 387 g, 176 n; 1894 422 g, 195 n. **Dimensions** 175.5 (rl) × 23.7 × 14.7 ft. **Propulsion** Paddles, 1855 3 cyl 61″ 61″ 61″–54″ 225 hp; 1878 2 cyl 34″ 57″–54″ 146 hp. **Speed** n/a.

Built for the Southampton–Le Havre of the L & SWR, the *Alliance* was registered on July 13 1855. She first visited the Channel Islands on May 8 1860 but only rarely made the trip until late 1865, when the larger ships went on the Le Havre route. The *Alliance* then took relief duties, but these were still few and far between. Later, in February 1876 she commenced relief duties on the Jersey–France routes.

In the early part of 1878 the ship was re-engined and had a new boiler fitted, and in the space of the former aft stoke-hold a ladies' lounge was constructed. At the same time the aft funnel was removed and the sailing rig cut down.

There were two major incidents involving the *Alliance*. The first occurred on June 19 1878 when she collided with the French boat *Francois* on entering Le Havre, causing the loss of two lives, for which the master of the *Alliance* was held to blame. The second accident happened on September 6

1890, when she collided with the *Wolf* while on the Cherbourg route.

The ship came on the Jersey station permanently on May 20 1880 and remained there until July 31 1896, when she was replaced by the new vessel *Victoria*. Even so, it was normal for the *Alliance*, during her last years on this station, to be replaced during the summer months by a larger, screw steamer. In May 1897, the *Alliance* replaced the *Wolf* as a temporary hospital ship in Southampton Docks. Finally, she was sold for breaking up on February 28 1900 and left Southampton on March 9 bound for Holland.

Alma

Owner London & South Western Railway. **Builder** J. & G. Thomson Ltd, Clydebank. **Completed** December 1894. **Yard no** 275. **Tonnage** 1894 1145 g, 411 n; 1904 1150 g, 406 n. **Dimensions** 270.7 (rl) × 34.0 × 14.6 ft. **Propulsion** Twin screw, SR, 4 cyl 19″ 29″ 31½″ 31½″–30″ 3,740 ihp. **Speed** 19 knots.

Sister to the *Columbia*, this ship entered service on December 19 1894 on the Southampton–Le Havre route. Her first visit to the Channel Islands was on March 1 1899, when she was substituted for the *Frederica* for one trip, and then again in April, July and August of the same year when she helped cover the loss of the *Stella*; after August she was not seen in the Channel Islands again.

Above Alice *blowing off steam as she leaves Guernsey (J.M. David).*

Right Alliance *manoeuvring into position, prior to discharging her passengers, in St Malo (John Attwood).*

Early in 1907 the ship was reboilered and other extensive alterations were made, though these alterations were minor compared to the work carried out to her sister. Two years later, the forward end of the promenade deck was plated in. She had a number of collisions with sailing vessels, the worst being on April 1 1902 with the *Cambrian Princess,* which sank with the loss of 11 lives. The last incident under Railway ownership was when she grounded in fog on November 28 1911 off Octoville on her approach to Le Havre. Replaced in April 1912 by the *Hantonia* the ship was sold the following month to the Eastern Shipping Co Ltd, for use in the Penang Straits' settlement. In November 1916 she was sold to a Mr P. Heath of Shanghai and a year later passed to Japanese owners who renamed her *Shokiku Maru* No 2. She passed to a further owner before a Mr Hongo Ikichiro altered the name slightly to *Shogiku Maru* No 2 but she did not last long as such, as on June 17 1924 she stranded on West Saghalien and became a total loss.

Antelope

Owner Great Western Railway. **Builder** Laird Bros, Birkenhead. **Completed** July 1889. **Yard no** 569. **Tonnage** 1889 596 g, 141 n; 1890 668 g, 202 n; 1896 672 g, 206 n. **Dimensions** 235.5 (rl) × 27.6 × 13.1 ft. **Propulsion** Twin screw, SR, 3 cyl 16½" 26" 41"–30" 1,667 ihp. **Speed** 16 knots.

Built for the GWR when they decided to take over the operation of the Weymouth–Channel Islands service, the *Antelope* arrived in Jersey from Milford on Saturday August 3 1889, ready to make her maiden voyage to Weymouth on the 5th.

On June 10 1890 the ship hit the Cavale Rock off Guernsey and had to return to her builders for repairs. During a voyage from the Channel Islands on November 18 1893, in very bad weather, the ship ran out of coal and had to anchor in Swanage Bay, while a tug took out enough fuel for her to complete the journey.

The first-class ladies' sleeping cabins had been altered into one large cabin during a refit, early in 1890, and further changes took place in 1896, when the ladies' cabin replaced the captain's cabin on the quarter deck, the forward lifeboats were raised to give more deck space, the funnels lengthened and awnings erected over the decks to provide shelter; the ship returned to service on May 27 1896 being followed shortly afterwards by the *Gazelle.*

Even with the arrival of bigger ships in 1897, the *Antelope* kept her place on the service and covered for the *Ibex* when the latter was off service for the whole of 1900. From 1902 the ship had only a few short spells on the passenger service and in 1903 was moved to Plymouth to act as a tender for liners and operate local excursions, and for these operations her forward lifeboats were removed.

In the spring of 1907 the ship ferried men and equipment required for the salvage of the White Star liner *Suevic* which had grounded off the Lizard on March 17. The liner was cut into two sections by the use of explosives and the aft part was towed to Southampton where a new bow was fitted.

The *Antelope* returned infrequently to the Islands, the last period of such visits being during August to October 1911 when she helped cover the gap left after a mishap befell the *Roebuck.* The ship was also used on the French services of the GWR, but when these were withdrawn in 1912 it was decided to sell the ship. Thus in August 1913 she passed to Navigation à Vapeur 'Ionienne' (G. Yannoulato Frères), and renamed *Atromitos.* The owners changed their name in late 1929 to Hellenic Coast Lines, of Piraeus. The ship was broken up in late 1933.

Above right Aquila *berthed at the picturesque harbour front in Weymouth, 1865 (John Attwood).*
Below Antelope *moored in Jersey, showing the alterations made in 1896 (John Attwood).*

Aquila

Owner Weymouth & Channel Islands Steam Packet Co Ltd. **Builder** J. Henderson & Sons, Renfrew. **Completed** August 1854. **Yard no** n/a. **Tonnage** 1854 293 g 180 n; 1857 264 g, 138 n (altered to 123 n in 1879); 1881 270 g, 131 n (altered to 90 n in 1884). **Dimensions** 180.4 (rl) × 21.0 × 10.9 ft. **Propulsion** Paddle, 2 cyl 42″ 42″–42″ 110 hp. **Speed** 9 knots.

Built in 1854 for the Harwich–Antwerp service of the North of Europe SN Co, this ship was one of two, the other being the *Cygnus*. The service was not a success and the ships were laid up at Lowestoft. Both ships were chartered by the Weymouth & Channel Islands SP Co in 1857. *Aquila* arrived in Jersey from Lowestoft on April 14 and sailed on her first service to Weymouth on Friday April 17; soon afterwards, the ship was purchased by the Weymouth company, in November 1857. Major refits took place in 1860, when new boilers were fitted; 1868, when an enlarged bridge was installed; and 1873, when new boilers were again installed and a saloon was erected on the aft deck.

The ship helped out on the Weymouth & Channel Islands SP Co's service to Cherbourg and was also chartered to the GWR at times when they operated the route. When the GWR took the Weymouth–Channel Islands route over on July 1 1889, the Weymouth and Channel Islands SP Co sold the ships The *Aquila* made her last trip from the Channel Islands on June 28 1889 and was then sold, with her sister and a couple of other ships in Jersey to A. Tolhurst of London, who immediately re-sold her to the Plymouth & Channel Islands SS Co, which used her on a service from Plymouth to the Channel Islands and onwards to St Brieuc. On July 15 1892 she arrived in Jersey after a major refit, with her funnels now very close together and a long new foredeck. Despite the refit, she only remained in the Channel Islands until the end of the summer of 1894.

In 1895 she passed to J. Jones of Swansea and was renamed *Alexandra,* then in 1896 she passed to W.A. Paine of the Hastings & St Leonards SS Co, being renamed *Ruby,* and lastly in 1897 she was sold to W.T. Simonds of Boston, before being broken up in 1899.

Ardena

Owner London & South Western Railway. **Builder** A. McMillan & Son Ltd, Dumbarton. **Completed** (month n/a) 1915. **Yard no** 462. **Tonnage** 1,092 g, 433 n. **Dimensions** 250.1 (rl) 263.3 (oa) × 33.1 × 17.3 ft. **Propulsion** Single screw, SR, 3 cyl 21½″ 35″ 58″–27″ 2,000 ihp. **Speed** 16 knots.

This ship was built in 1915 as HMS *Peony,* a *Flower*-class sloop of the *Azalea* type. At the end of the war she was sold to a Mr. T.R. Sales, who in December 1919, in a deal arranged by James Transport Towage & Dredging Co Ltd, sold the ship to the L & SWR. The railway company sent the ship for conversion into a merchant ship to the Caledon yard at Dundee. The work took longer than expected, and it was not until December 6 1920 that the ship, now renamed *Ardena,* made her maiden voyage on the service to St Malo, before re-opening the Cherbourg service for the first time since the end of the First World War on July 6 1921. The summer service for 1925 was operated to Caen instead of Cherbourg, but this was not successful and was withdrawn after September 27 1931. She only visited the Channel Islands on three occasions, once on a football excursion and twice to take special parties to England.

It was intended that the *Ardena* should operate a summer service to Cherbourg again, in 1932, but she did not do so and remained laid up until July 1934, when she was sold. She was purchased through brokers, by a Mr Toyias of Greece who converted the ship, while retaining her name. During the War, following the fall of Greece, she was taken over and used by the Germans until she

Left SS Peony *in Southampton Water, seen just after her arrival from Malta on January 16 1920 (Southampton City Museums).*

Below Ardena, *at Cherbourg on July 6 1921, re-opening the route after the First World War (Southampton City Museums).*

Left Ariadne, *as depicted in a contemporary painting, arriving in Jersey (Société Jersiaise).*

Right *Another of the many excellent Ouless paintings of shipping in the Channel Islands, showing* Atalanta (I) *passing the Isle of Wight (John Vint).*

struck a mine on September 27 1943 off
Kephalonia, when she was lost, together with 700 of
the 1,000 Italians on board.

Ariadne

Owner Owned by many shareholders. **Builder**
William Evans, Rotherhithe. **Completed** May
1824. **Yard no** n/a. **Tonnage** 1824 133 tons
burthen; 1832 145 tons burthen; 1836 198 g 124 n;
1838 197 g, 117 n **Dimensions** 1824, 115.0 (rl) ×
19.2 × 8.'6; 1832 124.0 (rl) (lengthened); 1836
121.6 (rl) × 17.4 × 10.8 (remeasured) **Propulsion**
Paddle (further details n/a), 72 hp **Speed** n/a.

To this ship goes the honour of being the first
steamship on service between England and the
Channel Islands. She sailed from Southampton
early on June 8 1824 and, after being delayed by
fog, arrived at Guernsey at 7 pm, dropping anchor
in the Roads at St Helier at 10:30 pm and entering
harbour at high water the following morning, five
days ahead of her rival, the *Lord Beresford*. The ship
provided a once-weekly service during the summer
months.

During the winter of 1831–32 she was lengthened
and improved. She was acquired by the South of
England Co when it was formed late in 1835.

Replaced by the *Atalanta* in August 1836 on the
Channel Islands service the ship then opened a
summer service between Jersey and France until
replaced by the *Camilla* on July 31 1837. Little was
seen of the ship until June 14 1843, when she
opened a service from Torquay to the Channel
Islands which was maintained for three summers
until September 26 1846. With the formation of the
New South Western SN Co, which became her new
owner, in October 1846, the service was allowed to
lapse and the ship was not seen again. A press report
of November 27 1849 stated that the ship was one of
the company's fleet which was to be stripped and
broken up.

Atalanta (I)

Owner South of England Steam Navigation Co.
Builder Thomas White, West Cowes. **Completed**

August 1836. **Yard no** n/a. **Tonnage** 1836 309 g,
171 n; 1853 265 g, 129 n; 1857 313 g, 162.
Dimensions 1836 138.1 (rl) × 21.9 × 13.0 ft; 1853
160.4 (rl) × 22.1 × 12.7 ft. **Propulsion** Paddles
(further details n/a), 120 hp. **Speed** n/a.

One of the most famous vessels on the Channel
Islands service the *Atalanta* was the first ship built for
the South of England SN Co. Launched on June 2
1836 at Cowes, Isle of Wight, the ship went to
London for the installation of her machinery,
arriving in the Channel Islands on her maiden
voyage of August 24 1836 under the command of
Captain G. Babot. During the winter months, the
Channel Islands service was extended to St Malo
and the ship also helped cover the service to Le
Havre while the *Monarch* underwent overhaul.

With the merging of the rival companies in
October 1846, the ship became part of the New
South Western SN Co, and was withdrawn from
service for the winter. When she returned to service
on April 21 1847 she carried the Royal Mail for the
first time, remaining as relief vessel on this service
until October 1848, after which she was little seen in
the Channel Islands.

In October 1851 it was stated that the ship was to
be lengthened by 14 feet (in fact she was lengthened
by 22) to provide a larger cargo hold, but she was
not seen in the Islands until April 17 1856 when she
commenced a passenger and cargo service. She
received a major overhaul in 1862 and, two years
later, a spar deck was added. She remained on the
Channel Islands route until September 30 1865. She
then made the occasional trip to the islands, before
arriving in tow of the *Fannie* at Jersey on September
22 1869, where she was stripped and used as a coal
hulk for the railway steamers based in the island. In
January 1882 she was sold to a Mr Hunt and
broken up in Jersey.

Atalanta (II)

Owner London & South Western Railway. **Built**
Gourlay Bros & Co (Dundee) Ltd, Dundee **Completed** May 1907. **Yard no** 227. **Tonnage** 577 g, 57
n. **Dimensions** 170.3 (rl) × 32.2 × 15.3 ft

Propulsion Twin screw SR, 3 cyl 14⅓" 22" 36"–24" 1,800 ihp **Speed** 14 knots.

This purpose-built passenger tender entered service on May 28 1907 at Plymouth, replacing the smaller *Victoria*. On May 28 1910 the tender services at Plymouth passed solely into the hands of the GWR, and *Atalanta* sailed to Southampton. She did not remain there long, as she was sold to the GWR, leaving on June 10 1910 and being delivered at Fishguard three days later. She was used at Fishguard and Plymouth until 1924 when she was sold to the Royal Mail SP Co. Two years later she passed to P. Cottel & Cie at Cherbourg and then, in 1931, to G. Fougere & Cie, before passing to Cie de Remorquage & de Savage 'les Abellies' in 1933 and being renamed *La Bretonnière*.

The ship was scuttled at Le Havre on June 11 1940 and was dismantled by the Germans.

Autocarrier

Owner Southern Railway. **Built** D & W Henderson & Co Ltd, Glasgow **Completed** March 1931. **Yard no** 912M **Tonnage** 1946 985 g, 645 n. **Dimensions** 22.03 (rl) 230.0 (oa) × 35.6 × 14.1 ft, 11'6" draft. **Propulsion** Twin screw, SR 4 cyl 15" 25" 29" 29" 29"–21" 154 nhp **Speed** 15 knots.

Although this vessel can only be considered as a relief ship at the port of Southampton, she did much useful work after the Second World War to re-establish the SR's routes in the area. In 1930 the SR found that although greater numbers of passengers wanted to take their cars when they travelled to the Continent, there was not enough space in the company's passenger ships for this wish to be satisfied. To overcome this difficulty the SR invited tenders for the construction of a cargo passenger vessel and, on October 15 1930, accepted the price

of £49,150 from the above builders. The ship was to be called the *Camberley* but before she was launched on February 5 1931 this was changed to *Autocarrier* and the ship entered service on the Dover–Calais route on March 30 1931.

She was due to visit Jersey in the winter of 1932–33 to replace the *Vera*, but the latter stayed until a new ship was built, making it June 1940 before the ship visited the Channel Islands, to help with the evacuation before the German invasion.

Her first call to Jersey after World War 2 was on December 11 1945. Shortly afterwards on December 15, she took the first party of Alderney residents to return to their homes after their wartime exile. She re-opened the service between Jersey and France on January 15 1946 when she sailed to Granville as St Malo was not yet open. From April 16 the service was moved to the newly opened St Malo and maintained there until the *Brittany* returned to take over. It also fell to *Autocarrier* to re-open the passenger service between Southampton and Le Havre on January 13 1947, on which she was replaced, by the *Brittany* again, the following month. After this the ship came to Southampton every winter as a relief on the Jersey–St Malo route and, during the summer of 1949, she also provided a car-carrier service to Le Havre and St Malo.

With the advent of the *Normannia* in 1952, even the *Brittany* was not considered adequate as a relief ship and thus the *Autocarrier* was no longer required at Southampton, where her last spell of duty ended in February 1952. Replaced as the car carrier at Dover by the *Dinard,* the ship became a pure cargo carrier, remaining in the fleet until April 6 1954 when she left Dover in tow for ship-breakers at Ghent.

Above Autocarrier *in Jersey.*

Right Autocarrier *arriving in Alderney with returning islanders (Carl Toms).*

Bertha

Owner London & South Western Railway **Builder** Gourlay Bros & Co (Dundee) Ltd, Dundee **Completed** December 1905 **Yard no** 219 **Tonnage** 1905 528 g, 139 n; 1914 487 g, 195 n; **Dimensions** 175.3 (rl) 182.5 (oa) × 28 × 12.25 ft **Propulsion** Single screw, SR, 3 cyl 16″ 26″ 43″–33″ 1,000 ihp **Speed** 12 knots.

So pleased were the L & SWR with the *Ada* that they ordered a sister ship in May 1905. The *Bertha* joined the fleet in December of that year and the two ships then spent most of their time on the Honfleur cargo service.

The only recorded alteration occurred when, early in 1911 the bulwarks along the main deck were raised by two feet to give better protection for deck cargo.

From late October 1914 until mid-February 1915, the ship operated on the cargo services of the GWR out of Weymouth to the Channel Islands.

The ship had a predilection for hitting the quay walls in Southampton; on the fourth occasion on January 16 1923 such was the impact that the mainmast collapsed!

Following the closure of the Honfleur service the ship was put up for sale and sold, in November 1933, to Metal Industries Ltd, which used her at Scapa Flow in the raising of the sunken German fleet. Requisitioned in October 1939, the ship was sold to the Admiralty the following year and her registry closed on May 1 1940. Following war service, she was acquired by Risdon Beasley Ltd on November 27 1946 and renamed *Topmast No 6* in February the following year, being registered at

Southampton on April 19. She did not remain long with Risdon Beasley, as on August 23 1948 her registry was cancelled upon her sale to Belgian buyers for breaking up.

Brest

Owner French Railways (SNCF), Dieppe. **Built** 1950 **Tonnage** 1,059 g **Dimensions** 237′10″ (oa) × 34′6″

During the summers of 1957 and 1958, the *Brest* operated to the islands from Southampton and then, from March 1959 until February 1967 (with the exception of 1965), operated at various times,

mainly from Weymouth covering the overhauls of the *Roebuck* and *Sambur*. During 1965 the *Rennes* provided the service.

Bretonne

Owner Great Western Railway **Builder** Earl's Shipbuilding & Engineering Co Ltd, Hull. **Completed** (month n/a) 1893 **Yard no** 367. **Tonnage** 1,635 g 596 n. **Dimensions** 300.4 (rl) × 34.5 × 16.2 ft. **Propulsion** Twin screw SR 3 cyl 26″ 39½″ 61″–36″ 447 nhp. **Speed** n/a.

This ship was originally built for the Great Eastern Railway in 1893 for their services based on

Harwich and was named *Chelmsford*. Later re-christened as the *Bretonne*, she was to become holder of the record for the shortest time in service, being acquired by the GWR for their Plymouth–Brest service early in July 1910 and then being withdrawn at the end of September 1911 when French services were discontinued by the GWR.

After service with the GWR she was sold for service in the Mediterranean being renamed *Esperia* by her new owners, the National SN Co of Greece, which in 1920 renamed the ship *Syros*, she reverted however to *Esperia* three years later. The owners had ties with London and in 1924 the ship was registered with the Byron SS Co of London, where a year later

she reverted to the name *Syros*. She only remained with the London company for two years before returning to the Greek company and there were no further changes before she was broken up late in 1933.

Brighton

Owner Weymouth & Channel Islands Steam Packet Co Ltd **Builder** Palmer Bros & Co, Jarrow **Completed** (month n/a) 1857 **Yard no** n/a. **Tonnage** 1858 286 g, 180 n; 1878 316 g, 187 n (altered to 137 n in 1884). **Dimensions** 193.5 (rl) × 20.9 × 10.0 ft. **Propulsion** Paddles, 2 cyl 44″ 44″–48″ 140 hp. **Speed** n/a.

Above Brest *when she was in Jersey in 1957 (Author).*

Right Bretonne *lying off Brest (John Attwood).*

This ship first visited Jersey in 1857 when between May 24 and October 14 she operated the Newhaven–Jersey service of HP Maples. She was purchased by the Weymouth & Channel Islands SP Co in July 1858 and arrived in the islands on her first visit on the 31st of that month. Her main task was to operate the new service between Weymouth and Cherbourg which opened in September 1858, though she continued to call in at the Channel Islands. After the suspension of the Cherbourg service at the end of June 1859, she and other company ships took it in turns to maintain the Channel Islands service.

Brighton was not seen on the Channel Islands route from July 28 1874 until October 17 1878, the last seven months of that period having been spent in Jersey under repair. Eventually, she was lost on January 29 1887 when, approaching Guernsey from Weymouth in fog, she struck rocks off the north-east coast of the island and sank, without any loss of life.

Brighton photographed in Weymouth (John Attwood).

Brittany (I)

Owner London & South Western Railway. **Builder** John Ash & Co, London. **Completed** November 1864. **Yard no** n/a. **Tonnage** 1864 529 g, 351 n (altered in 1867 to 333.2 n); 1883 655 g, 313 n; 1890 625 g, 283 n; 1895 678 g, 327 n. **Dimensions** 1864 215.6 (rl) × 25.6 × 13.1 ft 1883 236.0 (rl) ft. **Propulsion** Paddles, 1864 2 cyl 60″ 60″–60″ 250 hp; 1883 2 cyl 40″ 68″–60″ 230 hp. **Speed** 14 knots.

Last paddle steamer to be built for the L & SWR, *Brittany* was launched in London on August 8 1864, underwent trials on November 11, and arrived in

An atmospheric illustration of Brittany *(I) entering Le Havre, showing her as she was after lengthening (John Attwood).*

the Channel Islands on her maiden voyage on November 17 1864. During a voyage to the Channel Islands on January 16 1866, the ship was forced to the east coast of Jersey, where the passengers were landed at St Catherines Bay — one of the few times that this can have occurred.

New boilers were fitted in 1871 and, at the same time, a forecastle was added to the ship. The ship saw little mail service from the time when the *Diana* was introduced in 1877 until October 12 1883, when she resumed her Channel Islands station, having just completed a major refit that included lengthening by 21 ft and the installation of new engines. She then remained in regular service until October 5 1889 after which, apart from a few calls in 1890, the ship was not seen in the Channel Islands again. She then moved to the Le Havre route where, after more refitting work in the summer of 1893, she helped to maintain an augmented service from November 1893 until the new ships arrived late in 1894. After that *Brittany* acted as a relief ship, appearing at the Spithead Review in August 1897 and taking an excursion to Yarmouth in July 1898. She was sold to the T.W. Ward Company for £2,500 on October 17 1900 and was broken up at Preston.

Brittany (II)

Owner London & South Western Railway **Built** Earl's Shipbuilding & Engineering Co Ltd, Hull **Completed** August 1910. **Yard no** 572 **Tonnage** 1910 618 g, 252 n; 1924 631 g, 256 n. **Dimensions** 192.0 (rl) × 29.2 × 14.17 ft. **Propulsion** Single screw, SR, 3 cyl 13½" 25" 40"–27" 900 ihp. **Speed** 12.5 knots.

Built for the Newhaven–Caen cargo service of the London, Brighton & South Coast Railway in 1910, the vessel was purchased with her sister *Normandy* in 1912 by the L & SWR and was delivered later that year to Southampton on June 3. When built, the ships had very tall funnels with little rake, so to improve their appearance the funnels were shortened and given a rake; the masts were raked, too. The vessel arrived after this work at Guernsey on December 5 1912.

The *Brittany* was reported to have been in a collision off the Isle of Wight on October 27 1916 and she was stated to have been lost on February 5 1918; the latter report was inaccurate.

In March 1933, the ship was renamed *Aldershot*,

to free her former name for a new ship then building, under which appellation she remained in service until December 1936. (See *Aldershot* entry for further information).

Brittany (III)

Owner Southern Railway. **Builder** Wm Denny & Bros Ltd, Dumbarton. **Completed** June 1933. **Yard no** 1261. **Tonnage** 1933 1,445 g, 554 n; 1946 1,522 g, 583 n. **Dimensions** 249.8 (rl) 260.0 (oa) × 39.1 × 14.0 ft. **Propulsion** Twin screw, geared turbines 2,500 ihp. **Speed** 16 knots.

Brittany made her maiden voyage on the Jersey–St Malo route on Sunday June 18 1933, replacing the *Vera* which had re-opened the route the year before. Apart from the regular St Malo service the ship also operated excursions to Guernsey, Sark,

Above right *The first arrival of* Brittany *(II) at St Helier, on June 22 1912 (Author).*
Right Brittany *(II) at the quayside (Author).*

Above Brittany *(III) seen at sea in 1958 (Author).*

Left Brittany *(III) anchored off Sark during an excursion from Jersey (Southampton City Museums).*

Far right Caesarea *(I) photographed in Jersey (J.M. David).*

Alderney, Granville and Cherbourg. For most of the winter periods before the Second World War the ship was laid up, and the service maintained in conjunction with the direct St Malo service, which was routed via Jersey in winter. In the summer of 1939, the ship helped out on the Southampton–St Malo route but, when war was declared, the *Brittany* was withdrawn, making her last trip on December 27 1939.

During this last trip the vessel had been painted grey during the time she was on 'stopover' in St Malo on the 26th. She then went to Folkestone from January 23 to April 19, but was back in Channel-Island waters to help with the evacuation of the islanders, making her last call to Jersey on June 21 1940.

Taken over by the Royal Navy for war service,

the ship went round Africa, called at Bombay, and passed through the Suez Canal. She then spent time in the Mediterranean before being released, after which she returned to Jersey on June 5 1946, proceeding to St Malo the next day. On March 10 1947 the ship took over the operation of the Le Havre service from the *Autocarrier*, operating this service until the *Hantonia* made her first crossing after the war on June 2. In the summer she was again stationed in Jersey and commenced an excursion programme. During one of these excursions, on August 28, 1947, she struck a rock off Gorey on the east coast of Jersey during a cruise round the island and was off service for six weeks.

The ship also operated direct services from Southampton to Jersey due to a shortage of ships in the SR fleet and, later, when a direct Southampton–

Guernsey service was commenced she operated a Guernsey–Jersey sailing to connect with it. It was usual, too, at this time for the ship to relieve the *Hantonia* during the latter's refits and, during one of these spells in November 1950, she lost her rudder in Le Havre and had to be towed back to Southampton; she did not return to service until the end of March 1951. Excursions from St Malo to Jersey were restarted in July 1956 and on one of these, September 24 1957, a baby was born while the ship was en route to the French port from Jersey.

It was maintained that the ship had never made a profit and, as her costs were mounting, it was announced on January 2 1963 that the service was to be discontinued and the *Brittany* sold. In the event, the service was maintained for a further few years, but the ship was still sold. The *Brittany* had made her last voyage from St Malo to Jersey on November 29 1962 and, upon her arrival at Southampton, was laid up for the winter. The ship did not remain at Southampton for long, being sold to Finnish buyers, and left Southampton on April 21 1963 as *Alandsfarjan*. She was converted into a roll-on/roll-off car ferry and remained in service till May 19 1972, when she grounded off Remmargrund in the Stockholm Archipelago. Although refloated she was declared a total loss and broken up at Salo, Finland.

Much of the interior fittings and panelling were saved by the owner and were later built into the Brittany Bar of the Park Hotel at Mariehamn.

One final note is that the ship was always considered to be underpowered and this might account for the frequency with which she hit quay walls. On one occasion, on June 10 1951, this caused the bow to be flattened, giving the ship a huge bow wave for the rest of the summer.

Caesarea (I)
Owner London & South Western Railway. **Builder** Aitken & Mansel, Whiteinch, Glasgow. **Completed** March 1867. **Yard no** n/a. **Tonnage** 1867 408 g, 210 n; 1874 463 g, 275 n; 1880 466 g, 279 n; 1884 468 g, 250 n. **Dimensions** 187.2 (rl) × 24.3 × 13.55 ft. **Propulsion** Single crew, SR, 1867 2 cyl 42" 42"–30" 130 hp; 1874 2 cyl 26" 52"–36" 120 hp. **Speed** 13 knots.

Built in 1867 for the service to St Malo, *Caesarea* was launched on January 7 and underwent trials on March 15 when she attained a speed of 13.43 knots. She entered service on March 22 1867 with Captain G. Clements in command.

Her first call in the Channel Islands was on April 16 1867, but her only regular spells of service to the islands were after she was re-engined in 1874. From January 1875 to February 1881 she operated on the

winter passenger and cargo service which was extended through to Granville. The ship also helped out on the Jersey–France services during the summers of 1876 and 1879 inclusive, but was seen rarely apart from these times.

The ship was lost while on a voyage from Southampton to St Malo on June 27 1884 when she was in a collision with the *Strathesk*, which was bound from Jersey to Littlehampton with a cargo of potatoes, and she sank 10 miles off Cap de la Hague.

Caesarea (II)
Owner London & South Western Railway. **Builder** Cammell Laird & Co Ltd, Birkenhead. **Completed** September 1910. **Yard no** 334. **Tonnage** 1910 1,499 g, 601 n; 1911 1,505 g, 603 n; 1912 1,500 g, 601 n; 1920 1,504 g, 598 n. **Dimensions** 284.65 (rl)

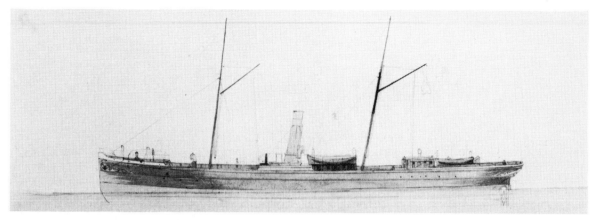

× 296.0 (oa) × 39.2 × 15.2 ft, **Propulsion** Triple
screw, direct drive turbines 6,350 ihp. **Speed** 20
knots.

Built with her sister to replace the *Frederica* and
Lydia, this ship was to be named the *Anglia*, but this
was not approved and she was launched as *Caesarea*
on May 26 1910. Delayed by strikes at her builders,
it was not until September 14 that the ship
underwent trials, when she attained a speed of 20.41
knots.

Her maiden voyage to the Channel Islands was
on September 24 1910, but after only five trips she
was withdrawn from service for alterations in the
engine-room. She was a triple-screw ship, with
direct-drive turbines, the centre shaft having a high-
pressure unit, while the outer shafts had low
pressure units. The centre and starboard propellers
were right-handed while the port one was left-
handed, which no doubt accounted for the difficulty
experienced in handling the ship. The ship had a
few spells on the Le Havre service, but the turbines,
being direct-drive, made the ship very uneconomic
to operate in the winter and she, and her sister ship
Sarnia, used to be laid up off Netley.

Above *An Ouless sketch of* Caesarea, *dated April 17 1867
(Société Jersiaise).*
Below Caesarea *(II) approaching land (Author).*

The ship was taken over for war service in
October 1914 and was converted into an Armed
Boarding Vessel, to be used off the north coast of
Scotland. In December 1915 she was converted into
a troop-ship and operated mainly out of Southampton; towards the end of this service she made a
number of trips to Bergen and is stated to have
called at Archangel when returning Russian
refugees. Handed back in October 1919, the ship
was sent to the Caledon yard at Dundee for reconditioning.

She arrived back in the Channel Islands on June
12 1920 and continued in summer service until July
7 1923, when outward-bound she struck a rock off
Noirmont Point off the south coast of Jersey.
Although badly damaged she was put ashore outside
the harbour at St Helier. After work by company
engineers, she was refloated at midnight on July 20

Caesarea *(III) approaching St Helier at speed on March 21 1973* *(Author).*

and left Jersey in tow of the tug *Canute* on August 4. When dry-docked at Southampton, however, it was decided not to repair her and she was sold to the Isle of Man SP Co, on December 5 1923.

Renamed *Manx Maid*, she ran trials from Barrow on June 12 1924, after which she remained with the Isle of Man SP Co until she was taken over for war service in 1940, when she sailed as HMS *Bruce*. Returning to her owners in 1945, she remained in their service till 1950 when she arrived at Barrow on November 12 to be broken up.

One point of interest is that in July 5 1923, two days before she struck off Jersey, the company meeting decided to call for tenders for (i) new boilers for the ship and (ii) the cost of a replacement vessel, as well as having considered, a month earlier, a possible change to oil fuel.

Caesarea (III)

Operator British Railways. **Builder:** J. Samuel White & Co Ltd, Cowes. **Completed** November 1960. **Yard no** 2008. **Tonnage** 1960 4,174 g, 2,271 n; 1969 3,992 g, 2,075 n. **Dimensions** 302′ (bp) 322′ (oa) × 53′ 8″ × 26′ 9″, draft 13′ 7″. **Propulsion** Twin screw, geared turbines 8,500 shp. **Speed** 19 knots.

This ship, together with her sister *Sarnia*, are the last of a long line of vessels built especially for the Channel Islands passenger service. Launched on January 29 1960, the ship made a VIP trip to the islands between November 18–22 1960, before arriving on her maiden voyage on December 3. During her first winter in service, the ship continued on to St Malo on a Saturday.

Apart from a few early teething troubles, the ship settled down well on the service and, with her sister, helped to regain traffic which had been lost to the aeroplane.

On December 14 1966 the ship arrived at Dover to relieve on the 'Golden Arrow' service, remaining until January 1967.

Early in 1971 internal alterations were carried out to provide better facilities. The cafeteria on 'D' deck was converted into a lounge and a new lounge area was created forward on 'A' deck, giving a total of 870 seats, numbered to allow the introduction of the new reservation system on May 1 1971.

With a multi-purpose service being introduced on the Channel Islands route in 1976, there was no requirement for these two classic ships and so *Caesarea* made her last sailing from the Channel Islands, on Monday October 6 1975, before moving to Dover in time for the 1976 season.

During her time at Weymouth there were only a couple of incidents of note, the first being on July 29 1964, when she hit a rock while leaving Guernsey, sustaining little damage, however. The second occurred on August 22 1968 when she was holed while entering Weymouth and had to go into dry-dock for repairs.

She sailed from Weymouth on February 3 1976 bound for Dover, but that was not the last that the islands saw of the ship, as, due to the *Earl Godwin* being held up in dry dock in 1978, the *Caesarea* resumed the Channel Islands' service from April 11 operating in tandem with the *Normannia* until Saturday May 6 1978, when both ships left the islands for the last time.

Caesarea returned to Dover and continued in service until October 3 1980, having operated special sailings for her last week there. On Saturday October 4, she made a public charter trip in aid of the RNLI from Folkestone to Boulogne. On October 7 she arrived at Newhaven to await sale and on December 20 1980 she sailed for Hong Kong, having been sold to Superluck Enterprises Inc of

Panama and renamed *Aesarea*. It was announced that the owner intended to convert her into a floating hotel, but no work was carried out on the ship.

Caledonia

Owner London & South Western Railway. **Builder** Cunliffe & Dunlop, Port Glasgow. **Completed** September 1876. **Yard no** n/a **Tonnage** 1878 539 g, 312 n; 1879 567 g, 355 n. **Dimensions** 195.1 (rl) × 26.25 × 14.0 ft. **Propulsion** Single screw, SR, 2 cyl 31″ 56″–33″ 150 hp. **Speed** n/a.

Built in 1876 as the *Hogarth* for the Aberdeen SN Co, the *Caledonia* was taken on charter by the L & SWR in June 1878 for use on the St Malo service. She made a call to the Channel Islands on October 9 of that year with mail, when it was stated that she had been acquired by the L & SWR, which renamed her *Caledonia* in the November. She remained on the St Malo service, though making the occasional mail call to the islands. On one of these calls, substituting for the *Fannie*, the ship came to her end. After a much delayed voyage to the islands, she arrived off Jersey early in the morning of February 19 1881, struck the Oyster Rock when approaching St Helier Harbour and sank. On April 2 she was sold to a Mr Gautier de Ste Croix for £140, who raised her engine on July 10, a few days after lifting the boiler. Part of her deck-house is still in use at St Brelade in Jersey today.

Caledonian Princess

Operator British Railways. **Builder** Wm Denny & Bros Ltd, Dumbarton. **Completed** November 1961, **Yard no** 1501. **Tonnage** 1961 3,630 g, 1,306 n; 1976 4,042 g, 1,769 n. **Dimensions** 331′ 6″ (bp) 353′ 0″ (oa) × 57′ 2″ × 12′ 0″ draft. **Propulsion** Twin screw, geared turbines 11,500 shp. **Speed** 19 knots.

This ship, built for the service between Stranraer and Larne, made her maiden voyage on December 16 1961. From July 1968, when a larger ship took over the route, the '*Cale P*' — as she was known to all — provided summer services on a number of routes, returning to Stranraer for the winters.

On July 1 1972 she moved to Fishguard and on August 14 1974 it was announced that she would move to the Weymouth–Channel Islands route in 1975 to replace the *Falaise*. When the *Falaise* had to be withdrawn in August 1974, her stop-gap replacement was the *Svea Drott*, until September 26 when the *Cale P* took over for a month before the *Normannia* was able to provide the service. When the *Svea Drott* was purchased it was stated that the *Cale P* would not now be required at Weymouth, but due to the length of time it took to refit the *Svea Drott*, the

Above Caledonia *pictured on February 19 1881 after she had run aground (John Attwood).*

Below Caledonian Princess *sailing out of St Peter Port on July 4 1977 (Author).*

Cale P again took up service, starting on July 15 1975. By this time it had been decided to make the Channel Islands service into a multi-purpose operation, which would require both the *Earl Godwin* (ex-*Svea Drott*) and the *Cale P*.

The ship remained on the service until January 31 1976 and then proceeded to Immingham where she was altered for the new multi-purpose role on the Channel Islands service that she took up on May 12 1976. She remained on the route until December 14, when she went back to Fishguard, from where she acted as relief until the end of February, January 18 1978 saw the ship take up service on the Newhaven–Dieppe route until early February, but this change of route had major repercussions as it delayed the overhaul of the *Earl Godwin*, which then became involved in a dispute at the yard necessitating the calling in of chartered tonnage.

The *Earl William* suffered generator troubles in May 1980 and the *Cale P* sailed from Weymouth to the Channel Islands on the evening of Sunday May 4, and took up the Portsmouth service from the Channel Islands the following day, while waiting for the chartered tonnage to arrive.

The introduction of the *Earl Granville* on the Portsmouth route in 1981 allowed the *Earl William* to replace the *Cale P* at Weymouth, and the ship made what was intended to be her last sailing from the Channel Islands on Saturday May 2 1981, to take up service after overhaul at Dover on May 31. A fire in the *Earl Granville* on June 22 1981 caused the *Cale P* to be sent back for Channel Islands service, operating from Portsmouth and also Weymouth, and it was not until Thursday July 16 that the ship made her actual last sailing from the islands. The ship's Dover season ended on September 26 and she sailed to be laid up at Newhaven on October 11, remaining there for over a year. She was sold in December 1982 to the Quadirini Group and, after being given an all-white hull and a red funnel, was towed to the River Tyne where she arrived on March 2 1983, where she was converted into a recreation centre named *Tuxedo Princess*, she is registered to Riverzest Ltd and is now berthed at Gatehead.

Calpe

Owner Commercial Steam Packet Co. **Builder** McGhie & Hawks, Rotherhithe. **Completed** February 1836. **Yard no** n/a **Tonnage** 259 g, 157 n. **Dimensions** 125.4 (rl) × 19.5 × 12.8 ft. **Propulsion** Paddles (further details n/a). **Speed** n/a.

Launched in December 1835 for the British & Foreign SN Co, the *Calpe* was placed on their service from London to Spain and the near end of the Mediterranean. Her first call in the Channel Islands was to Guernsey on May 1 1836, when she put in due to having run out of coal. A year later, on April 8 1837, she passed to the Commercial SP Co and continued operating on her route to Spain, with calls at Southampton being introduced in the September of that year to pick up the mail. In October 1838 the Peninsular Company took over the mail contract and the *Calpe* was placed on a London–Southampton–Weymouth service. September 1839 saw the ship on the Le Havre route for a time and then, a year later, she commenced on the Southampton–Plymouth route; she alternated between these services until taken over by the South-Western SP Co in May 1842. She had further spells of service on both these routes until the end of 1845 and then she undertook relief and cargo duties until made redundant by the amalgamation of October 1846, making few trips thereafter.

In November 1849 it was stated that the ship was to be stripped and broken up, but this was not the case, as on December 6 1850 the ship was registered to a Mr G. Finlay of London after being converted into a sailing ship. She continued in his service until 1852, when a report from Gibraltar dated April 18 stated that the ship had gone ashore near Tangiers and had broken up.

Camilla

Owner Owned by many shareholders. **Builder** William Evans, Rotherhithe. **Completed** June 1824. **Yard No** n/a. **Tonnage** 1824 102 tons burthen; 1833 122 tons burthen; 1837 173 g, 106 n. **Dimensions** 1824 107′ 10″ (rl) × 17′ 10″ × 10′ 0″; 1833 120′ 7″ (rl) (lengthened); 1837 117.6 (rl) × 16.2 × 10.7 ft (remeasured). **Propulsion** Paddle (further details n/a). **Speed** n/a.

Built in 1824 for the Le Havre route, the ship was owned by a partnership. But, due to late delivery, the advertised service was initially maintained by the *Medina*. The *Camilla* arrived at Southampton on June 22 1824, sailing the next day on her maiden voyage.

She remained on this service, being registered to the South of England SN Co in April 1837, when the *Monarch* was introduced on the route; the ship was then overhauled, after which she replaced the *Ariadne* on the Jersey–France service on July 31 1837. She maintained this service until October 31 1847, having also extended the service to Plymouth for the summer of 1844. She had passed to the New South Western SN Co in October 1846, and following her departure in October 1847 she was not seen again in the islands. In November 1849, she and other ships were stated to be in the process of being stripped and broken up. Her registry was officially terminated on January 27 1853.

Top *A sketch of* Camilla *passing a sailing ship (Author).*

Above Cherbourg *seen towards the end of her career at Berth 6 in Southampton (John Attwood).*

Left Colchester *in Jersey during 1969 (Dave Hocquard).*

Top right Columbia *steams into Le Havre, some time between 1906 and 1909 (A.M.S. Russell).*

Cherbourg

Owner London & South Western Railway. **Builder** P. & R. Swan, Dumbarton. **Completed** December 1873. **Yard no** n/a **Tonnage** 1873 386 g, 245 n (altered in 1884 to 227 n); 1889 373 g, 213 n; 1894 398 g, 224 n; 1904 397 g, 224 n; 1921 388 g, 191 n. **Dimensions** 165.6 (rl) 172.6 (oa) × 23.1 × 11.9 ft. **Propulsion** Single screw, SR, 1873 2 cyl 22″ 38″–27″ 65 hp; 1921 3 cyl 15″ 24″ 40″–26″ 650 ihp. **Speed** n/a.

This L & SWR ship was built in 1873 for the services to Cherbourg, Honfleur and Le Havre, and was seen little in the Channel Islands. In 1909 extensive repairs were made to the ship, including a new funnel and deck alterations.

It was decided in 1920 that the ship was to be disposed of at the end of the season but, due to the high replacement cost, the ship was given a boiler and engine bought from Mr R. James (founder of eponymous Towing and Dredging Co), for £5,000 and returned to service in November 1921.

On March 6 1930 the ship sailed from Southampton bound for Grangemouth where she was broken up by G. & W. Brunton who had bought the ship for £900. On her way down Southampton Water she passed the new *Isle of Guernsey* inward bound from her builders.

Colchester

Operator British Railways, Harwich. **Built** 1959. **Tonnage** 866 g. **Dimensions** 241′ 10″ (oa) × 37′ 10″.

Operated from both Weymouth and Southampton to the islands, first arrival in Jersey being on October 28 1968 and the last on May 7 1969.

Columbia

Owner London & South Western Railway. **Builder** J. & G. Thomson Ltd, Clydebank. **Completed** October 1894. **Yard no** 274. **Tonnage** 1894 1,178g, 469 n; 1894 1,145 g, 411 n (altered in 1903 to 408n);

1906 1,169 g, 455 n. **Dimensions** 270.75 (rl) × 34.0 × 14.6 ft. **Propulsion** Twin screw, SR, 4 cyl 19″ 29″ 31½″ 31½″–30 3,740 ihp. **Speed** 19 knots.

Built for the L & SWR service to Le Havre, this ship and her sister *Alma* were the first owned by the company to provide accommodation in mainly individual cabins for the first-class passengers. The ship entered service on November 1 1894 and was first seen in the Channel Islands in June the following year, when she was chartered by seventy members of the Article Club for a cruise from Southampton to Le Havre, Cherbourg and the Channel Islands.

Except for a few service calls to the islands (in 1898 and 1899) the ship remained on the Le Havre route, being reboilered in early 1906 when the forward stoke-hold was moved aft into the space previously occupied by the first-class cabins, which were rebuilt in the old stoke-hold. This resulted in the two funnels being very close together and thus a different alteration scheme was used for her sister ship when she was reboilered the following year.

In late 1909, the forward end of the promenade deck was plated in to provide more shelter, but the ship did not remain in service much longer, arriving at Southampton for the last time on April 2 1912. She did not remain long at Southampton, sailing on April 16 under the Spanish flag, having been sold to J.J. Sitges Frères of Algiers and registered at Alicante as the *Sitges*. She was sold to the French navy in 1915, being renamed *Corse*, and was torpedoed on January 24 1918 off La Ciotat.

Courier

Owner New South Western Steam Navigation Co. **Builder** Ditchburn & Mare, London. **Completed** October 1847. **Yard no** n/a **Tonnage** 1847 314 g, 196 n; 1857 265 g, 147 n. **Dimensions** 167.0 (rl) × 22.5 × 10.8 ft. **Propulsion** Paddles (further details n/a), 200 hp. **Speed** n/a.

First of two sisters ordered after the formation of

Left Courier *arriving at Jersey in 1853, depicted in her new colour scheme by Ouless* (Author).

Left Cygnus *in Jersey in 1887 (John Attwood).*

Above right Deal, *which first came to the islands in 1935, pictured in Jersey on May 28 1960 (Author).*

the New South Western SN Co in 1846, this vessel was registered as *Courier* but was always referred to as *Courier*. Built for the Channel Islands service, she made her maiden voyage on November 12 1847. On July 6 1852 the ship returned to service following a major refit, which included new boilers, funnels and davits, and the installation of a ventilation system. In 1859, a deck-house was added on the aft deck, and the ship remained on the route until 1861, after which she acted as relief ship. From 1864 she was mostly used on the newer services that the L & SWR were introducing, to St Malo, Cherbourg and Honfleur, but she did return to Jersey, when on December 11 1873 she arrived to replace the *Wonder* on the service to France. She performed these duties till January 2 1875 when she sailed for Southampton to be broken up.

Cygnus

Owner Weymouth & Channel Islands Steam Packet Co Ltd. **Builder** J. Henderson & Sons, Renfrew. **Completed** October 1854. **Yard no** n/a **Tonnage** 1854 286 g, 180 n; 1857 245 g, 133 n (altered to 118 n in 1879); 1881 250 g, 126 n (altered to 85 n in 1884). **Dimensions** 182.0 (rl) × 21.4 × 9.4 ft. **Propulsion** Paddle, 2 cyl 42⅜″ 42⅜″–42″ 120 hp. **Speed** 9 knots.

Cygnus was built with *Aquila* in 1854 for the Harwich station, but the service to Antwerp was not a success and the ships were laid up at Lowestoft. Both vessels were chartered by the Weymouth & Channel Islands SP Co in 1857, with *Cygnus* arriving at Weymouth on April 14 and entering service on April 17 1857. Apart from the Channel Islands service, the ship also acted as relief for the Wey-

mouth–Cherbourg route when it operated. The ship underwent improvement when, in January 1861, steam superheating equipment was fitted. She returned to service on October 8 1883, after a major overhaul during which her paddles were raised 15 inches and a forecastle was added. She remained on the service until the GWR took over the route, with her last trip arriving in the Channel Islands on June 27 1889. She sailed the next day in ballast for Southampton, having been bought with her sister by a Mr A. Tolhurst who resold her to a Mr T. Holden for a service in 1890 between Preston and Douglas. She soon passed to David MacBrayne being renamed *Brigadier* and was wrecked on December 7 1896 on Duncan's Rock off the Isle of Harris.

Deal

Owner Southern Railway, Dover. **Built** 1928 **Tonnage** 1928, 688 g; 1939 691 g; 1946 829 g. **Dimensions** 220.5 (rl) × 33.6 ft.

This ship first came to the Channel Islands in 1935 to provide extra cargo capacity at the height of the produce season. She returned in June 1940 to assist with the evacuation and she was one of the first SR vessels on the service after the liberation of the islands, arriving in Jersey on July 3 1945 and helping out until November. She reappeared in the islands in 1960 when she made a few trips at the end of May and beginning of June.

Diana

Owner London & South Western Railway. **Builder** Aitken & Mansel, Whiteinch, Glasgow. **Completed** February 1877. **Yard no** n/a. **Tonnage** 1877 738 g, 368 n; 1881 744 g, 379 n; 1881 745 g, 380 n (altered in 1883 to 334 n); 1888 724 g, 312 n; 1889 772 g, 356 n; 1892 779 g, 294 n. **Dimensions** 232.6 (rl) × 28.2 × 14.1 ft. **Propulsion** Single screw, SR, 1877 2 cyl 37″ 68″–39″ 210 hp; 1892 3 cyl 23½″ 37″ 57″–39″ 1,650 hp. **Speed** 14 knots.

This vessel has a very special place in the history of shipping to the Channel Islands, as she was the first screw-propelled ship to be built for the mail service. Owned by the L & SWR, she was launched on November 30 1876 and, on trials in Stokes Bay, on February 9 1877 the ship achieved a speed of 14.1 knots.

Her first voyage was to St Malo on February 14; on the 21st of the month, when bound for St Malo, she had to be towed into St Helier by the local tug due to a mechanical defect and it was not until March 3 that she left again for the French port. Her 'working-up' complete, she arrived in the Channel Islands on her first mail voyage on April 7 1877, staying on the route until July 25 1890. During this period, in October 1881, a boat deck was added. After moving from the Channel Islands service she took up the route to St Malo.

In 1892 the ship was re-engined with triple-expansion machinery, running trials on August 16, after which she returned to the St Malo service.

On June 21 1895, when on a voyage from the French port to Southampton, the ship grounded on rocks off Cap de la Hague in fog and, after the passengers and mail had been put safely ashore, the ship slid off the rocks two days later and sank.

Dinard

Owner Southern Railway. **Builders** Wm Denny & Bros Ltd, Dumbarton. **Completed** July 1924. **Yard**

no 1164. **Tonnage** 1924 2,291 g, 917 n; 1938 2,313 g, 939 n; 1947 1,765 g, 502 n; 1953 1,769 g, 584 n. **Dimensions** 316.0 (rl) 325.0 (oa) × 41.1 × 16.0 ft. **Propulsion** Twin screw, geared turbines 5,200 ihp. **Speed** 19 knots.

First vessel to be built for the newly formed Southern Railway, the *Dinard* and her sister ship were stated to be destined for cross-Channel services from Southampton. SR mentioned that they could run to the Channel Islands if the harbours were enlarged, but this could not be done before the ships entered service and the *Dinard* made her maiden voyage to St Malo on July 22 1924. She stayed mainly on the St Malo route, but also helped out on the Le Havre service. The only time she visited the Channel Islands was in July 1925, when she was acting as yacht for the SR Directors' tour of inspection. In late 1930, the third class accommodation was improved and the open rails of the poop were plated in.

At the start of the Second World War the ship was converted into a Hospital Carrier and used initially in northern waters, until June 25 1943 when the ship sailed from Glasgow for the Mediterranean. She was back in British waters in time for D-Day, but on the day after, June 7, she struck a mine and only just managed to remain afloat during the tow back to England. Converted into a troopship early in 1945 it was July 11 1946 before the ship arrived back at Southampton. It was then decided to convert the vessel into a car carrier, for service at Dover, to replace the smaller *Autocarrier* and so the *Dinard* sailed from her home port on August 8 bound for the River Tyne where she was converted. The work completed, she took up service from Dover on July 1 1947. In 1952, to improve her capabilities, stern doors were fitted to allow the cars to be driven on and off.

The move to Dover did not mean the end of her story at Southampton as, during the summer of 1952, the ship would steam back to her old home port to operate a weekend service on her earlier route to St Malo. She remained in service at Dover until the end of the 1958 summer season, when she was replaced by purpose-built ferries. There was still useful life in the ship and she was bought early the following year by Rederi A/B Vikinglinjen of Mariehamm, renamed *Viking*, and used for a service across the Baltic. She was altered several times, during her surviving period of service, which lasted until August 1970, when, after a period of being laid up she was broken up at Helsinki.

Dispatch
Owner New South Western Steam Navigation Co. **Builder** Ditchburn & Mare, London. **Completed** April 1848. **Yard no** n/a **Tonnage** 1848 320 g, 197; 1858 272 g, 149 n; 1878 288 g, 166 n. **Dimensions** 1848 166.7 (rl) × 22.1 × 11.6 ft; 1878 171.0 (rl) × 23.7 × 10.9 (remeasured). **Propulsion** Paddle, 2 cyl 61″ 61″–42″. **Speed** 13.2 knots.

Sister to the *Courier*, this ship was built for the New South-Western SN Co and made her maiden voyage to the Channel Islands on May 2 1848 from the Dorset port of Poole, but remained at Poole for only one week before taking the main mail service from Southampton to the islands.

In early 1853, she underwent a major refit which included new boilers, davits and being painted in new company colours. A further major refit took place in 1859 at which time an aft-deck saloon was added. Two years later, in 1861, major machinery alterations were carried out and this included the raising of the main paddle shaft by eight inches, new boilers again and the installation of superheating for the steam supply. On the measured mile in bad

Below left *Horses and wagons wait patiently for* Diana *to discharge her passengers and cargo (John Attwood).*

Above Dinard *being fitted out at Dumbarton, pictured on June 2 1924. Note her all-yellow funnels; being of a dark hue they appear almost black (Southampton City Museums).*

Right Dinard *as a car ferrry in dry dock at Southampton (John Attwood).*

Below *A painting by P. J. Ouless, showing the* Dispatch *passing La Moye, Jersey, in 1848 (The Selective Eye Gallery).*

Left Dispatch *seen leaving Granville in her single-funnelled configuration, as distinct from her previous two-funnelled design shown on the dust-jacket (John Attwood).*

Below Dora *leaving St Peter Port (John Attwood).*

Bottom right Duke of York *in Southampton on June 30 1950 (Southampton City Museums).*

weather the ship made a speed of 13.2 knots and returned to service on March 5 1861.

With the advent of larger ships on the Channel Islands route, the *Dispatch* came off the regular service in August 1864 and then spent time on other routes, including the opening of the regular service to Cherbourg on May 10 1869. Three years later she was put on the Jersey station, arriving on April 10 1872 and initially took up the Granville route. She remained based in Jersey till November 18 1881 when she sailed for Southampton, where she was converted into a coal hulk, with her registry being cancelled in April 1885, and remained as such until being sold on November 10 1897, together with the hulk of the *Alice*, for £450 to a Mr J.J. King.

One item which has not been determined is the exact date when her fore funnel was removed. The evidence would point to some time before 1872, as photographs of the ship at that time show only one funnel.

Dora

Owner London & South Western Railway. **Builder** R. Napier & Sons, Glasgow. **Completed** April 1889. **Yard no** 416. **Tonnage** 1889 741 g, 110 n; 1890 813 g, 185 n. **Dimensions** 240.0 (rl) × 30.0 × 14.3 ft. **Propulsion** Single screw, SR, 3 cyl 27" 40" 65"–36" 220 hp. **Speed** 16 knots.

This vessel must have been the most unsuccessful of all the L & SWR mail steamers built for the Channel Islands service. She was completed in 1889, as an improved version of the *Hilda*, and made her maiden voyage to the Islands on May 26. In August of that year the GWR placed their new twin-screw ships on the Weymouth–Channel Islands route, which, with their speed, outclassed the single-screw ships of the L & SWR. Modifications were made to the *Dora*, including the introduction of forced draught in the stoke-hold and the fitting of a new propeller, but to no real effect. The L & SWR were quick to build new ships, and when

these came into service in 1890, the single-screw ships were withdrawn. The *Dora* acted as a relief ship for a time. Once, when outward bound from Jersey on May 16 1893, the ship struck the Balleine Rock off Icart Point, Guernsey, and was towed by the *Lynx* to St Peter Port with the engine-room and stoke-hold full of water.

Replaced by the *Vera* in 1898, the ship was sold in July 1901 to the Isle of Man SP Co, which renamed her *Douglas*. This was not the last that the Channel Islands saw of the ship, however, as in 1915 the ship operated on the potato service from Jersey to Hull. The end of the ship came on August 16 1923, when she collided with the *Artemisia* in the Mersey and sank in twenty minutes.

Duke of York

Operator British Railways. **Built** 1935. **Tonnage** 3,759 g. **Dimensions** 339.2 (bp) × 52.2 ft.

This ship was based in Southampton for the summer of 1950, operating to Cherbourg twice a week and taking the Friday-night sailing to Guernsey. The ship arrived at Southampton on June 26 and, after a short refit, served from July 3 until the end of the season on September 29, after which she was converted for oil burning, losing one funnel in the process!

On May 6 1951 the ship was involved in a collision which cut off the forward section of the vessel from just beneath the bridge and she was then rebuilt with a raked stem.

Dumfries

Owner London & South Western Railway. **Builder** Scott & Co, Greenock **Completed** February 1857. **Yard no** n/a **Tonnage** 1863 125 g, 85 n. **Dimensions** 112.0 (rl) × 18.0 × 9.0 ft. **Propulsion** Single screw, SR (further details n/a), 30 hp. **Speed** n/a.

The smallest L & SWR ship in cross-Channel ser-

vice, this vessel was completed for the Dumfries, Glasgow & Liverpool Screw SN Co of Dumfries in February 1857. Two years later she was acquired by a Mr John Hutchison, but he sold her the same year to the Jersey SP Co and she arrived in Jersey on December 1 1859. She was used on the services to France until July 1863, when the L & SWR took over the route and the ship was laid up.

After acquisition by the L & SWR, the ship made one trip to St Malo on November 1 1863 before sailing for Southampton on the 5th of that month. She was then used on a cargo service to Le Havre, but within a couple of years she settled down on the Honfleur route, though she called in the Channel Islands and other ports at times.

The *Dumfries* was sold to a Mr P. McGuffie on October 3 1871, passing the following year to a Mr J.T. Hay, who immediately sold her to a Mr J. McArthur who had the ship lengthened. This expense was wasted, however, as the ship stranded in Killaloe Bay, Ireland on October 20 1873 and was lost.

Earl Godwin

Operator British Railways. **Builder** Oresundsvaret A/B, Landskrona. **Completed** June 1966. **Yard no** 202. **Tonnage** 1976 3,999 g, 1,869 n. **Dimensions** 298′ 10″ (bp) 325′ 5″ (oa) × 59′ 6″ × 14′ 6″. **Propulsion** Twin screw, 4 oil engines, 2 × 12 cyl 4,000 bhp, 2 × 6 cyl 2,000 bhp. **Speed** 18 knots.

This ship first visited the Channel Islands as the *Svea Drott* in 1974 when she took over the car-ferry service of the *Falaise*. Built in 1966 for the Helsingborg–Copenhagen–Travemunde service, she was owned by the Stockholm firm Rederi A/B Svea. Replaced in 1974 by a larger ship, she spent the summer on charter in the Baltic before taking over the Weymouth–Channel Islands car-ferry service on August 19. She remained on the route until Sept-

ember 26 and so impressed were British Rail that the ship was bought for their use in December 1974, by Lloyds Leasing Ltd, London.

The ship was delivered at Helsingborg on January 10 1975, being renamed *Earl Godwin* the same day. Major engine work then took place at Harwich before the ship moved to Holyhead in late April 1975. The refit took longer than expected, which meant that it was not until February 2 1976 that the ship entered service, when she sailed from the Channel Islands to Weymouth, the first time this had occurred since 1897. Due to the *Earl William* being delayed in coming into service, the *Earl Godwin* was used to inaugurate the new ro/ro (roll on/roll off) service from Portsmouth to the islands on November 8 1977 and remained on it until mid-January 1978. The ship then went to dry dock, where a labour dispute retained the vessel until early May.

1981 saw the ship operate the Heysham–Isle of Man route, while the *Manx Viking* was on refit, from March 25 to April 8.

Earl Granville

Operator Sealink (UK) Ltd. **Builder** Jos L. Meyer, Papenburg. **Completed** June 1973 **Yard no** 570. **Tonnage** 1981 4,658 g, 2,018 n. **Dimensions** 316′ 7″ (bp) 356′ 8″ (oa) × 56′ 7″ × 15′ 1″ draft. **Propulsion** Twin screw, 12 cyl oil engines 11,600 bhp. **Speed** 19 knots.

Built as *Viking 4* for Rederi A/B Sally, Mariehamm, Finland, the ship was acquired (by W & G Industrial Leasing Ltd) for use on the Portsmouth–Channel Islands service in 1980, being taken over at Bremerhaven on August 25 and renamed *Earl Granville*. The ship then went back to her builders, where she was re-engined and altered for her new duties, running sea trials on February 23 1981 and arriving at Portsmouth on March 20.

After being on view at Portsmouth and the Channel Islands the ship entered service on March 29 when she sailed from Portsmouth. On June 22 1981 the ship hit the headlines when a fire was discovered in the domestic boiler room only twelve miles south of the Isle of Wight and the ship had to return to Portsmouth, being off service until July 16. On Saturday July 2 1983 the ship made her first sailing on the Weymouth–Cherbourg route when the extended French service was introduced, which required both this ship and the *Earl William* to operate one sailing each over the weekend.

Earl Siward

Owner Sealink (UK) Ltd. **Built** 1965. **Tonnage** 3,641 g. **Dimensions** 369′ 0″ (oa) × 57′ 2″.

This ship was built as the *Dover* but renamed after alterations in 1977. She came on the Channel Islands service to help cover the period in 1981 when both the *Earl William* and *Earl Granville* were off service. She made three round voyages arriving in the islands on July 11, 12 and 13. These were in fact her last voyages under British Rail ownership, as the ship was afterwards laid up and sold in November.

Earl Siward made the record books as being the largest ship to have entered St Helier Harbour.

Earl William

Operator British Railways. **Builder** Kaldnes Mek Verksted A/S, Tronsberg. **Completed** July 1964. **Yard no** 160. **Tonnage** 1977 3,765 g, 1,836 n. **Dimensions** 295′ 3″ (bp) 326′5″ (oa) × 60′ 1″ × 14′ 6″ draft. **Propulsion** Twin screw, 12-cyl oil engines 10,200 bhp. **Speed** 18 knots.

Earl William was built as *Viking II* for Thoresen Car Ferries when they took over the Southampton–Le Havre route from British Railways and, at the same time, opened a route to Cherbourg.

Bottom left Earl Godwin *approaching St Helier on March 6 1976 (Author).*

Above Earl Granville *seen off Jersey on her VIP cruise of March 27 1981 (Author).*

Right Earl Siward *seen entering Weymouth on July 13 1981, on her last voyage in Sealink service before being sold (A.M.S. Russell).*

Below Earl William *inward bound to Jersey on April 18 1980 (Author).*

The ship often went on charter to other operators during the winter months and, when replaced at Southampton in 1974 by larger vessels, the ship was used to open a new service between Felixstowe and Zeebrugge on October 23 1974.

In December 1976 the ship was purchased by Lloyds Leasing Ltd for use by British Rail, being delivered on the 22nd of that month at Holyhead, where she was overhauled and converted for service on the Portsmouth–Channel Islands route. She was delayed during overhaul, thus it was not until January 16 1978 that the ship took up service. She worked the route until March 1981 when, upon being replaced by the larger *Earl Granville*, she was overhauled and then replaced the *Caledonian Princess* at Weymouth on May 3. On Sunday July 3 the ship made her first sailing on the extended Weymouth–Cherbourg service which required the ship also to operate on Saturdays from the Channel Islands to Portsmouth.

The ship has suffered a number of 'incidents' since being built, some before and some since being placed on the Channel Islands route, but she is a fine time-keeper and an easy ship on which to load freight.

Elk

Operator British Railways. **Builder** Brooke Marine Ltd, Lowestoft. **Completed** July 1959. **Yard no** 267. **Tonnage** 795 g, 308 n. **Dimensions** 210' 0" (bp) 228' 0" (oa) × 39' 6" × 13' 4¾" draft. **Propulsion** Twin screw, 6-cyl oil engines 1,800 bhp. **Speed** 14 knots.

Built in 1959 as part of a four-ship rebuilding programme, *Elk* was based at Southampton and made her first call at Jersey on August 6 of that year.

From the time she was built, she commenced calling at Weymouth, as well as operating on the Jersey–St Malo route during the winter when she was advertised to carry twelve male passengers during the crossings!

It was the *Elk* which made the last railway sailing from the port of Southampton, this being on September 29 1972, after which the cargo services moved to Portsmouth. *Elk*'s last railway service was from Guernsey to Weymouth, where she arrived on October 7 1972.

On October 19 1972 she was sold to the Valmas Shipping Co, sailing from Weymouth as the *Nikolas* on October 22. The following year she was renamed *Skiron* and, in 1975, she was sold to the Jupiter SS Co Inc of Panama who renamed the ship *Nasim*. The ship was lost under the cliffs of Gianautri Island in February 1976.

Ella

Owner London & South Western Railway. **Builders** Aitken & Mansel, Whiteinch, Glasgow. **Completed** July 1881. **Yard no** 109. **Tonnage** 1881 820 g, 495 n (altered in 1883 to 442 n); 1888 797 g, 355 n; 1890 851 g, 404 n; 1904 850 g, 397 n; 1914 813 g, 318 n. **Dimensions** 235.5 (rl) × 29.1 × 14.2 ft. **Propulsion** Single screw, SR, 2 cyl 37" 69"–39" 220 hp. **Speed** 14 knots.

Following the success of the *Diana*, the L & SWR had an improved version of the ship built in 1881 and named her *Ella*. Launched on May 28 1881, the ship ran trials on July 23, and arrived in the Chan-

Elk, with her original black hull and her old funnel colours, leaving Jersey on August 3 1961 (Author).

Right Ella *gleaming after her 1896 refit (Author).*

Below Empire Lifeguard *in St Helier in 1946 (J. Watts).*

nel Islands for the first time on July 31. She remained on the Channel Islands route till August 15 1890, being replaced by the new twin-screw steamers and then spent her time mostly on the Cherbourg route or acting as relief ship as required.

She had been given steam steering and a wheel-house in 1886, and ten years later had new boilers and a new deck installed, the work costing £8,435 which was carried out by the firm of Day Summers at Southampton.

During her life she had a number of interesting incidents. On December 7 1895, while on a voyage from Cherbourg to Southampton the funnel was carried away, all draught was lost, and the ship was ten hours late in arriving; later, on November 24 1906, she was in collision in the Race of Alderney with another of the company's ships, the *Princess Ena*. The last incident of note occurred on June 18 1912, when she hit and sank the hopper *Rosina* off Netley, with three of the latter's crew being drowned.

A year later on June 24 1913 the ship was sold to the Shipping Federation for £4,500 and was used to house out-of-work persons. She was pressed into service during the First World War, though remaining with the Federation till February 1929 when she was broken up by T.W. Ward at Gray's, Essex.

Empire Lifeguard
Empire Peacemaker
Empire Rest

Owner Ministry of Transport. **Built** 1944–45. **Tonnage** 1,333 g. **Dimensions** 252′ 0″ (oa) × 36′ 6″.

These ships were commenced as *Castle* class Corvettes but were converted into ocean-rescue vessels before completion. The three ships were placed under the management of the SR during the time that they were at Southampton, operating the military leave service to the Channel Islands. Each could carry about 130 servicemen and they sailed from Southampton at 9:00 pm each night, calling at Jersey, then Guernsey and arriving back in England between 8:00 pm and 9:00 pm the following day.

The *Empire Lifeguard* arrived in Jersey on January 1 1946 and remained until July 15 1946. The *Empire Peacemaker* arrived in Jersey on January 3, remaining until October 5, then going onto the Tobruk–Port Said route. The *Empire Rest* arrived in Jersey on January 2 and only served until April 14 before going to the Gravesend–Antwerp service.

Express

Owner New South Western Steam Navigation

Company. **Builder** Ditchburn & Mare, London.
Completed June 1847. **Yard no** n/a. **Tonnage**
1847 255 g, 152 n; 1858 215 g, 111 n. **Dimensions**
159.0 (rl) × 21.4 × 10.4 ft. **Propulsion** Paddle 2
cyl 55″ 55″–42″ 180 hp. **Speed** n/a.

First vessel to be built for the New South-Western
SN Co, this ship was of the same dimensions as the
Wonder but had two funnels. She joined the *Wonder*
on the Le Havre route in July 1847 and, the following year on March 2 1848, she made the headlines
when she arrived at Newhaven, having conveyed
the fleeing King Louis-Philippe of France from Le
Havre.

She arrived in the Channel Islands for the first
time on May 28 1848 as relief for one trip and then
covered for the regular vessels during their overhaul
period each winter. The ship was used to open the
L & SWR route from Weymouth to the Channel
Islands on April 13 1857, after which she divided
her time between that route and the Le Havre
service.

On September 20 1859 she was outward bound
from Jersey when, on taking the inner passage at
Corbière, she struck rocks and was put ashore in a
sinking condition in a bay on the south-west corner
of the Corbière headland. One person lost his life
and the ship broke up, but much of the gear and
fittings were saved.

Above Express *steaming at speed (Author).*
Below Falaise, *outward bound from Jersey, pictured on September
25 1948 (Author).*

Falaise

Owner Southern Railway **Builder** Wm Denny &
Bros Ltd, Dumbarton. **Completed** July 1947. **Yard
no** 1400. **Tonnage** 1947 3,710 g, 2,046 n; 1964
2,416 g, 853 n. **Dimensions** 299′ 9″ (bp) 310′ 6″
(oa) × 49′ 8″ × 12′ 6″ draft. **Propulsion** Twin
screw, geared turbines 8,500 shp. **Speed** 19 knots.

When launched on October 25 1946, it was stated
that 'the ship is intended primarily for the Channel
Islands traffic but that she could be used on the
Dover, Folkestone and Newhaven services and
short sea cruises'. In fact the ship was placed on the
Southampton–St Malo route, making her maiden
voyage on July 14 1947. On July 19 the ship arrived
in Jersey for the first time, operating a direct service
from Southampton once a week. On Saturday September 6, after a direct service to Jersey, she took the
8:00 am mail sailing from the Channel Islands and
therefore made her first call at St Peter Port. Her
first season finished on September 26 and, on October 19, she sailed for Dover where she relieved the
Invicta on the Golden Arrow service until November
7.

Falaise as a car ferry, leaving St Helier on July 2 1974 (Author).

The ship passed into the British Railways' fleet on January 1 1948 and, in that May of that year, commenced the first of her annual Short Sea Cruises, cruises which had been made very popular before the Second World War by the *St Briac*. In the autumn of that year she again covered the Golden Arrow service from October 17 to December 5, but this was the last time she undertook this task.

In 1949 the frequency of the St Malo service was increased to three trips each week and thus the ship only visited the Channel Islands during her cruises.

For the first four years of her service to St Malo the ship anchored on the river outside the port, as the big lock had been destroyed in World War 2, and it was not until May 16 1951 that the ship berthed alongside the Gare Maritime.

During the winter months the ship performed the occasional service as required but otherwise remained laid up in Southampton. With the introduction of the *Normannia* in 1952, however, the ship then relieved regularly on the Le Havre route and, after the reorganisation of the services from Southampton in the autumn of 1958, also operated to the Channel Islands.

In March 1960 the ship went to Barry where alterations were made to the hatches to allow more cars to be carried and the wheel-house was extended forward to take in the walkway. The ship operated two cruises from Folkestone from May 5 1961 and, at the end of the season, replaced the *Brittany* on the Jersey station for a trip to St Malo on October 3. She had to undertake the same task the following year and, also, on October 5 1962 left the Channel Islands on a cruise to Le Havre and Rouen for the weekend.

In April 1963 came the news that the ship was being considered for conversion into a car ferry for service on another route and, following her last trip from St Malo on September 29 1963, it was announced that the ship was to be converted and used to commence a new service from Newhaven. The ship left Southampton on January 4 1964 and proceeded to Vickers Armstrong (Shipbuilders) Ltd's Palmers Hebburn-on-Tyne yard, where the conversion took place, and she arrived at Newhaven on May 13 where, after trials, she entered service on June 1 1964. Outwardly the ship had not changed greatly with the exception of an extra deck of black paint (though in fact this was how the ship had appeared when she was first launched), a white line painted at the waterline and the cabs removed from the wings of the bridge. The first few years of her life at Newhaven were plagued with handling problems and she was rather overshadowed after the introduction of new French vessels on the route.

Early in 1965 the ship received new, blue, hull colours but, due to the joint-service working of the Newhaven–Dieppe service, kept her yellow funnel; the joint-service house flag was, however, added to the funnel in March 1967. The ship had saved the Newhaven–Dieppe route from being closed, which led in 1970 to a new larger ferry being ordered to replace her in 1973 and it began to be rumoured that the ship would be used to commence a car-ferry service to the Channel Islands.

The ship had a spell of duty at Dover from September 30 1971 to October 10, and on April 29 1972 sailed from Dieppe on a cruise to Guernsey, returning on May 1. She arrived at Newhaven on her last crossing from Dieppe on September 25 1972 and, after helping out at Dover from September 28 for three days, remained at Newhaven until January 8 1973, when she sailed for Holyhead to be converted for use on the new Weymouth–Jersey service.

She arrived at Weymouth on April 21 1973 and, after a trial trip and a VIP voyage, she entered service on June 1. Such was the success of the summer service that it was extended to become a year-round operation, with the ship making two voyages a week during the winter, calling in at Guernsey from October 30 1973. At Guernsey, cars disembarking had to be craned ashore from the ship's ramp. The ship was given an extended overhaul from December 15 to March 18 1974, but had to be withdrawn from service from April 29 to May 20 due to machinery problems. The ship used the new ramp at St Peter Port for the first time on June 26 1974 where she called twice a week, sailing on the remaining days direct to Jersey. The ship was then being worked harder than the mail boats and in August further machinery problems caused the ship to run late and on August 14 the ship was withdrawn, after a very late arrival at Weymouth.

Following some work at Weymouth the ship left on August 21 for Holyhead, where it was decided that the ship was not worth any further work and she was offered for sale. She was sold for breaking up in Spain and left Holyhead in tow of the tug *Fairplay XIII* on December 24 1974. A sad end for a ship which had set new standard when built, saved the Newhaven–Dieppe service from closure and then brought to the Channel Islands a method of transport which was to revitalise the railway shipping services.

Fannie

Owner London & South Western Railway. **Builder** Caird & Co, Greenock. **Completed** (month n/a) 1859. **Yard no** n/a. **Tonnage** 1869 640 g, 403 n; 1870 632 g, 354 n (altered to 372 n in 1887 and 294 n in 1883); 1888 616 g, 278 n; 1889 654 g, 314 n. **Dimensions** 231.5 (rl) × 26.2 × 13.3 ft. **Propulsion** Paddle, 2 cyl 60″ 60″–66″ 250 hp. **Speed** 13 knots.

Built as *Orion* in 1859 for a service between Lübeck and Kronstadt, *Fannie* was a sister to the *Sirius* (later named *Alice*). She became a blockade runner during the American civil war, being registered as *Fannie* at Nassau to a J. Carlin. She then returned to England and, in 1865, took up service between Stranraer and Belfast, before being acquired by the L & SWR in June 1869. She was used unaltered during the latter part of the year, before being overhauled and undergoing official trials on March 9 1870 during which she reached a speed of 13.64 knots. She took up service mainly on the French services but did call in at the Channel Islands, her first mail visit to them being on June 25 1870. In September 1871 she returned to service after a major overhaul that included the installation of a new deck and bridge.

During a voyage from Le Havre on November 1 1873, water accumulated in the boiler rooms, ultimately extinguishing the fires, and the ship drifted until the steamer *Eddystone* encountered her and towed her to Dover, arriving there on the 3rd. The 125 passengers were put ashore there and the ship later towed to Southampton by the *Wolf*. *Eddystone* was later awarded £1,500 salvage for her work. The ship was then reboiled at the L & SWR yard at Northam, after which she was placed on the Channel Islands route, where she arrived on May 24 1874. She remained as a regular Channel Islands vessel until October 12 1880 after which, following the introduction of screw steamers, she saw little service on this route, changing instead mainly to the

Fannie moving slowly past a large sailing barque (John Attwood).

Felixstowe *in Weymouth in September 1948 (John Attwood).*

Le Havre route. By the mid-1880s, the ship was spending her time on the Cherbourg route during the summer and filling in on other routes as required. On August 6 1890 it was decided that the ship was worn out and should be broken up, and her last mention in the papers was on August 30 1890.

Felixstowe

Operator British Railways. **Built** 1918. **Tonnage** 905 g. **Dimensions** 215.1 (rl) × 33.2 ft.

The ship operated during the summer of 1948 from Weymouth to the Channel Islands, but only made two calls at Jersey, on July 7 and August 29.

Fratton *heading out to sea (John Attwood).*

Fratton

Owner Southern Railway. **Builder** D. & W. Henderson & Co Ltd, Glasgow. **Completed** September 1925. **Yard no** 720 M. **Tonnage** 757 g, 305 n. **Dimensions** 220.3 (rl) 229.6 (oa) × 33.6 × 14.1 ft. **Propulsion** Twin screw, SR, 3 cyl 15″ 25″ 41″–24″ 1,850 ihp. **Speed** 15 knots.

Second of the class to be built for Southampton, this ship made the headlines on October 7 1927, when she struck the Vieux Bank off St Malo and had to be escorted back to Southampton by the *Haslemere*. She was taken over in 1940 and was used as a barrage-balloon vessel for three years, and was lost on August 18 1944 when at anchor off the Normandy beaches, while being used as a control-ship for the invasion.

Top Frederica *photographed after the alterations made to her in 1905 (John Attwood).*

Above Fredor *in Jersey before she was lengthened (Author).*

Left Free Enterprise II *arrives in Jersey on May 12 1980, on charter from Townsend Thoresen (Author).*

Frederica

Owner London & South Western Railway. **Builder** J. & G. Thomson Ltd, Clydebank. **Completed** July 1890. **Yard no** 250. **Tonnage** 1890 1,059 g, 193 n; 1903 1,066 g, 187 n; 1905 1,088 g, 209 n. **Dimensions** 253.0 (rl) 259.0 (oa) × 35.1 × 14.1 ft. **Propulsion** Twin screw, SR, 3 cyl 24″ 37″ 56″–33″ 5,700 ihp. **Speed** 19 knots.

Frederica was the first of three ships built by the L & SWR to answer the challenge from the GWR on services to the Channel Islands. This ship was launched on June 5 1890 and on trials in Stokes Bay on July 21 attained 19.5 knots under forced draught. She arrived in the islands on her maiden voyage in July 31 and, with Capt G. Allix in command, set the standard and speed for the service.

From September 6 1893 the ship helped out on the Le Havre route, making only one trip each week to the Channel Islands, and from December 1 the ship stayed on the Le Havre route to help operate the new extended service. It was January 30 1896 before the ship returned to the Channel Islands service permanently though, after the introduction of the *Alberta* in 1900, she saw little service until July 1903 when she arrived on the 17th with the funnel heightened by nine feet to allow lower-grade coal to be burnt. The ship also had two extra lifeboats positioned after of the mainmast and lifeboats had also replaced the cutters. The use of lower-grade coal was not a success and in 1905 new boilers were installed and a new funnel fitted, the height of which was mid-way between the former heights. A deck cabin was built and internal alterations carried out to bring her into line with the *Lydia*, and she returned to service on May 6 1905.

She was due to be replaced by a new ship in 1910, but its late delivery kept her in service until after the Spithead Review in June 1911. She sailed from the Channel Islands for the last time on Monday June 26 1911.

She was sold to Turkish buyers who renamed her *Nilufer*; her owner the following year were given as the Administration de Navigation à Vapeur Ottomane, which registered her at Constantinople. The ship was taken over for war service and was lost on November 22 1914 when, being used as a minelayer she struck a mine herself and sank off the eastern entrance to the Bosphorus.

Fredor

Owner A. E. F. Monsen. **Built** 1943. **Tonnage** 339 g; 1952 423 g. **Dimensions** 139.3 (rl) × 26.3 ft; 172.3 (rl) × 26.3 ft (lengthened).

Although not a railway-owned ship, the vessel spent much of her time on service from Weymouth. Her first call at Jersey was on September 2 1947 and, after lengthening was carried out in 1952, she remained on the Weymouth route until the end of September 1956.

The ship always caused attention when entering or leaving port due to the list she assumed when the helm was put hard over.

Free Enterprise II

Owner Stanhope SS Co Ltd (Townsend Thoresen Car Ferries). **Built** 1965. **Tonnage** 4,122 g. **Dimensions** 354′ 9″ (oa) × 60′ 4″.

This ship arrived in the Channel Islands on May 10 1980 to cover for the *Earl William*, but made only two trips on this service, as she did not have sufficient height in the car deck for the freight traffic. The *Viking III* took over the service and then the *Earl Godwin* was switched from Weymouth, and the *FE II* took up the Weymouth route from May 21 to June 11 1980.

Gael swinging in Weymouth, 1884 (J Lucking).

Gael

Owner Great Western Railway. **Builder** Robertson & Co, Greenock. **Completed** (month n/a) 1867. **Yard no** n/a. **Tonnage** 1884 403 g, 107 n; 1890 419 g, 158 n. **Dimensions** 211.0 (rl) × 23.2 × 10.6 ft. **Propulsion** Paddle, 2 cyl 45″ 45″–62″ 150 hp. **Speed** n/a.

Built for the services of the Campbeltown & Glasgow SP Joint Stock Co, the ship was acquired by the GWR in April 1884 to replace the lost *South of Ireland*. The ship did not have much time on the route as she suffered from machinery problems early the following year and, by the time these had been made good, the service had been closed, on June 30 1885.

This was not the end of the ship at Weymouth however, as she was held in reserve at Milford and, when the new vessels were not ready to open the GWR service on July 1 1889, she came to Weymouth to assist. In fact the ship sailed direct to Jersey where she arrived on June 30, ready to take the sailing from the Channel Islands on July 2. She operated the service until August 3 and was not seen again.

Sold to David MacBrayne in 1891 the ship retained her name and remained in the fleet until being broken up in 1924.

Galtee More

Owner London & North-Western Railway Co. **Built** 1898. **Tonnage** 1,112 g. **Dimensions** 276.1 (rl) × 35.1 ft.

The *Galtee More* had two periods of service to the Channel Islands, the first of which was in the Great War, when she maintained the GWR route from Weymouth between June 2 and 17 1915. The second time was in 1921 when, due to the *Alberta* being held up at Dundee, the ship was chartered by the L & SWR for two months from July 11; in the event this was extended to September 20, due to a mishap putting the *Hantonia* out of service.

Gazelle

Owner Great Western Railway. **Builder** Laird Bros, Birkenhead. **Completed** August 1889. **Yard no** 570. **Tonnage** 1889 596 g, 141 n; 1890 668 g, 202 n; 1896 672 g, 206 n (altered to 195 n in 1908 and to 169 n in 1913); 1914 613 g, 226 n. **Dimensions** 235.5 (rl) × 27.65 × 13.13 ft. **Propulsion** Twin screw, SR, 3 cyl 16½″ 26″ 41″–30″ 1,650 ihp. **Speed** 16 knots.

Third of the trio of vessels built for the GWR in 1889, this ship made her maiden voyage on September 8 of that year. The ship has a most uneventful life, one of the few things of note occurring on December 15 1895 as she was approaching Guernsey, when her port propeller-shaft broke.

The first class ladies' sleeping cabins were combined into one large cabin during refit early in 1890, with further changes taking place in 1896 in line with those on *Antelope*. The ship returned to service on June 30 1896.

She finished her regular service to the Channel Islands in February 1900, but acted as stand-by ship for the passenger service until late 1907, when she was sent for conversion into a cargo vessel, arriving back at Weymouth by May 8 1908. Her life was then spent mostly on the Guernsey fruit trade, and she was also used on the Weymouth/Plymouth services to Brest. Called up for war service in 1914, she then spent most of her time in the Mediterranean as a minesweeper.

She returned to Jersey for the first time after war service on May 1 1920 and remained on the cargo service to the islands until March 1925 when she was withdrawn and put up for sale, going thereafter to the breakers' yard.

Above right Gazelle *at her duties as a tender at Plymouth. Her forward lifeboats have been removed (D.B. Hoppins).*

Below Galtee More *was on the Weymouth–Channel Islands route during 1915 (A.M.S. Russell).*

Grand Turk

Owner Commercial Steam Packet Co. **Builder** Robert Duncan & Co, Greenock. **Completed** June 1837. **Yard no** n/a. **Tonnage** 369 g, 244 n. **Dimensions** 135.3 (rl) × 20.2 × 13.0 ft. **Propulsion** Paddle (further details n/a). **Speed** n/a.

One of the vessels taken over from the Commercial SP Co by the South Western SP Co in May 1842, this ship was built for Glasgow owners in June 1837 and before passing, in the same year, to the Commercial SP Co. In 1838 she appeared on the London–Southampton–Weymouth service while the following year she was on the Le Havre route and also made some calls to the Channel Islands. She remained on the Le Havre route until early 1846 when, with new ships entering service, she commenced a direct service from Portsmouth to Le Havre. The following year, however, she again changed service, by introducing a service from Southampton to Plymouth and Penzance, having been bought by the New South Western SN Co in 1846.

On January 9 1849 she sailed from Southampton for the Mediterranean on a two-year charter to Newbolt Hall & Bros, London, to operate a service between Alexandria, Jaffa and Beirut in connection with the P&O mail contract.

On May 12 1851 the ship opened a new service from Southampton to Morlaix calling at Guernsey, the service was not successful and lapsed after the end of the season. The ship then acted as relief vessel, and the last entry on the ship's papers was made on August 30 1854, after which her registry was closed on December 11 1856, the ship being broken up.

Granuaile

Owner R. E. V. James Ltd, Southampton. (See *Ulrica* entry for full technical details.)

The ship was acquired by Mr James in late February 1916 and in April was chartered to the L & SWR, which in July purchased the ship and renamed her *Ulrica* in early September 1916. (See *Ulrica* entry for further information.)

Granville

Owner London & South Western Railway. **Builder** (name n/a), Blackwall. **Completed** (month n/a) 1841. **Yard no** n/a. **Tonnage** 1868 131 g, 50 n. **Dimensions** 147.7 (rl) × 19.2 × 9.4 ft. **Propulsion** Paddle (further details n/a), 70 hp. **Speed** n/a.

This vessel was built in London in 1841, but was not registered until November 16 1853 when (named the *Comet*) her owners were given as the Gravesend New SP Co. On July 4 1856 she passed through Jersey as the *Comet*, bound for her new owner, M Durand in Granville, for a service to Jersey. She commenced service on July 20 as *Comète*, remaining with him until October 18 1859, when it was stated that the vessel was to be withdrawn and placed on the service between Cherbourg and Le Havre. This did not occur, however, and the ship came under the control of the La Société Granvillaise, recommencing service a month later. La Société Granvillaise went into liquidation in December 1863, but she remained on the route until acquired by the L & SWR in December 1867, sailing from Jersey to Southampton for overhaul on January 1 1868. She returned to the island on May 28 as the *Granville* and remained on

the service till October 9 1871, when she sailed from Jersey to Southampton. On November 13 1871 it was announced that the ship had been sold to owners in Cardiff and had left Southampton.

Early in 1872 the ship was owned by a Mr C. McConochie of Cardiff, but was never registered to him, and it was not until December 28 1872 that a Mr John Boyle had her registered at Cardiff. She did not remain long in his service, as her registry was closed on July 13 1875 upon being broken up.

Great Southern

Owner Great Western Railway. **Built** 1902. **Tonnage** 1,225 g. **Dimensions** 275.8 (rl) × 36.3 ft.

The ship was built for the Milford–Waterford service, and first came to the Channel Islands in 1916, when she arrived on July 30 to replace the *Ibex* for two weeks. She returned to Weymouth in 1920 to help out during the produce season, as she did in 1924 and, additionally, she provided relief passenger sailings in the latter year.

Great Western (I)

Owner Great Western Railway. **Builder** W. Simons & Co, Renfrew. **Completed** (month n/a) 1867. **Yard no** n/a. **Tonnage** 1867 447 g, 281 n (altered to 250 n in 1872); 1879 454 g, 255 n; 1881 466 g, 207 n. **Dimensions** 220.4 (rl) × 25.2 × 12.4 ft. **Propulsion** Paddle, 2 cyl 48″ 48″–45″ 190 hp. **Speed** n/a.

Built for Ford & Jackson when they operated steamer services for the GWR, she was acquired by the railway company after they had been granted powers to operate steamship services in February 1872. She came to Weymouth when the service to Cherbourg was commenced on August 1 1878 and remained on this service until it ended on June 30 1885. She then returned to Milford but, following the loss of the *Brighton*, the ship was chartered by Weymouth & Channel Islands SP Co to maintain the Channel Islands route during the summer. The ship arrived in the islands for the first time on June 6 1887 and for the following year she continued to be chartered. She again came on service in June 1889 and, as the new GWR vessels were not ready for the July 1 take-over, the ship remained on the route until August 4.

In 1890 the ship operated a service from Preston Quay to Douglas for the Preston & West Coast SS Co Ltd (owned by a Mr N. Miller) and in 1891 she was sold to the firm of David MacBrayne and re-

named *Lovedale*, with which she stayed, until being broken up in 1904.

Great Western (II)

Owner Great Western Railway. **Built** 1902. **Tonnage** 1,225 g. **Dimensions** 275.8 (rl) × 36.3 ft.

Sister to the *Great Southern*, this ship followed her twin to Weymouth in 1921 to operate in the produce season. Again, in 1922, she worked on this service, while in 1923 she also provided relief passenger sailings. The ship was back again in 1925 carrying out the same duties, but after this she only carried produce and was seen little in Jersey after 1929, though she came to Weymouth until 1932.

Griffin

Owner London & South Western Railway. **Builder** Laurence Hill & Co, Inch Green, Renfrew. **Completed** (month n/a) 1858. **Yard no** n/a. **Tonnage** 1865 216 g, 147 n; 1866 265 g, 195 n (altered in 1867 to 151 n); 1876 281 g, 163 n (altered in 1884 to 154 n); 1889 272 g, 145 n; 1894 292 g, 160 n. **Dimensions** 155.0 (rl) × 20.1 × 11.8 ft. **Propulsion** Single screw, SR, 1858 2 cyl 32½″ 32½″–26″; 1876 2 cyl 22″ 44″–26″ 70 hp. **Speed** n/a.

Right Great Western (II) first appeared at Weymouth in 1921 (John Attwood).

Built in 1858, the ship was owned by a Mr James Baird and registered at the Scottish port of Ayr. Acquired early in 1865 by the L & SWR, the ship was used to commence the Southampton to St Malo route, being replaced in late September by the new *Saint Malo*.

At the end of her first season with the railway company, improvements were made to the accommodation, with a large poop being erected, causing the ship to be known as the Chinese pagoda! The ship was then used during the winter months on the cheap-boat service to the Channel Islands, while in the summer she relieved on the Jersey–France service and also made some sailings on the Cherbourg route. In early 1876, the ship underwent a major refit that included a new engine and boiler, and she arrived in Jersey on relief duties on May 15.

The ship became a permanent Jersey-station vessel on November 17 1881, when she replaced the *Dispatch*, and maintained the Granville route till April 19 1890. She was then used mainly as a cargo ship until sold, on February 22 1895, to a J. Constant of London, who operated services in the Mediterranean. It is not known if the ship was used on these, but on May 12 1898 the register was

Below An Ouless sketch of Griffin, showing her after the addition of a poop deck (Société Jersiaise).

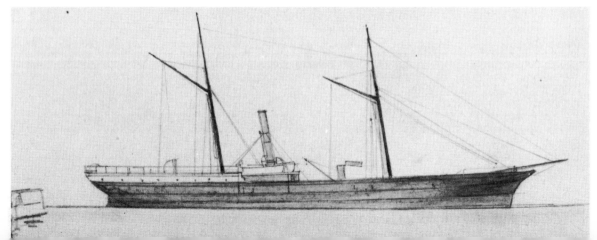

closed as the ship was sold to Cie de Nav et de Colon des Antilles and was renamed *Le George Croise*. She did not remain long with this company, as on March 29 1900 she sank outside San Domingo when bound for Cuba, going down with eighty passengers and some cattle.

Guernsey

Owner London & South Western Railway. **Builder** J. & W. Dudgeon, London. **Completed** May 1854. **Yard no** n/a **Tonnage** 1874 536 g, 306 n; 1878 545 g, 315 n (altered in 1884 to 280 n); 1888 521 g, 234 n; 1889 526 g, 149 n; 1890 572 g, 189 n; 1914 509 g, 200 n. **Dimensions** 195.5 (rl) × 26 × 13.4 ft. **Propulsion** Single screw, SR, 1874 2 cyl 35″ 61″–32″ 150 hp; 1889 3 cyl 21″ 34″ 59″–34″ 159 hp. **Speed** n/a.

Completed in 1874 the ship was placed on the St Malo service, though she did make three mail sailings to the Channel Islands in July 1874 and the same number in May 1875, and also called at Jersey during the potato season purely as a cargo vessel.

Replaced during summer months on the St Malo service by bigger ships from 1890, the *Guernsey* then helped out on other routes, and was on the Jersey–France services in the summers of 1890, 1893, 1897–99 and 1904–05.

In early 1908 the vessel was converted to a purely cargo configuration by company engineering staff at a cost of £1,000. She continued in service until April 9 1915, when she went ashore on Cap de la Hague and was lost with seven crew while sailing from Guernsey towards Southampton.

Guernsey Fisher

Operator British Railways. **Builder** NV Ijsselwerf, Rotterdam. Hull built by D & J Boots Scheeps De Industrie, Alphen. **Completed** December 1971. **Yard no** 1343. **Tonnage** 829 g, 390 n. **Dimensions** 249′ 4″ (bp) 269′ 7″ (oa) × 39′ 9″ × 12′ 0″ draft. **Propulsion** Single screw, 8-cyl oil engine 1712 bhp. **Speed** 13.5 knots.

Built in Holland for James Fisher & Sons Ltd of Barrow, the ship was 'bare-boat' chartered to

Guernsey Fisher *leaving Jersey at full speed on June 1 1973* (*Author*).

British Rail for their service to the Channel Islands. Initially based at Southampton, she made her maiden voyage to Guernsey on January 6 1972, moving to Portsmouth in the October of that year on the introduction of the 'Brit-Comm' agreement on October 2. The working of this agreement resulted in the two *Fisher* boats working mainly on the service to Jersey, but during the winter of 1975–76 the *Guernsey Fisher* moved to the Irish Sea and worked on the Heysham–Belfast service. She returned south, and arrived in the Channel Islands again on March 16 1976, but with British Rail changing the Portsmouth service over to a ro-ro operation from October 1977, the ship was no longer required by them. Her last call to the Channel Islands was to her namesake island on October 27 1977.

She then returned to her owners. She sailed from Manchester on July 26 1984 as the *Scafell*.

Hantonia

Owner London & South Western Railway. **Builder** Fairfield Shipbuilding & Engineering Co Ltd, Glasgow. **Completed** April 1912. **Yard no** 482. **Tonnage** 1912 1,560 g, 662 n; 1948 1,594 g, 594 n (altered in 1948 to 596). **Dimensions** 290.3 (rl) 300.0 (oa) × 36.1 × 16.1 ft. **Propulsion** Twin screw, geared turbines 4,750 ihp. **Speed** 19.5 knots.

Built in 1912 as a sister to the *Normannia* the L & SWR had difficulty in finding a name for the ship, as both *Aurania* and *Maya*, the company's first two choices, were not approved by the Board of Trade and she was launched without ceremony on December 23 1911 as the *Louvima*. The name *Hantonia* was agreed upon in January 1912 and the ship bore the name when she underwent trials in March, and made her maiden voyage to Le Havre on May 7 1912.

The ship remained with the company during the First World War, the Le Havre service being diverted to St Nazaire for a short period after September 1914 when the Germans were making rapid advances into France. In April 1915, the open area on the main deck under the second lifeboat was plated in and at the same time the rails at the forward end of the promenade deck were also replaced by solid bulwarks.

The ship made her first call to the Channel Islands on July 21 1923 when she replaced the damaged *Caesarea*. From the early 1930s it was usual for the larger ships from the St Malo service to take over much of the winter running on the Le Havre route, and the *Hantonia* and her sister found themselves taking over, in turn, the Southampton–Jersey–St Malo service from the smaller *Brittany*, which was withdrawn for the winter.

With the outbreak of the Second World War the ship found herself operating at Folkestone from September 11 1939, but she returned and for two weeks in February 1940 worked the Channel Islands route before taking the Le Havre service. She was back on the Channel Islands route in early May and maintained the St Malo service as an extension of this service. The last of these three services routed direct back to Southampton, and *Hantonia* made the last sailing to leave the French port during the war on June 16 1940 and her last trip from the islands on June 25.

The ship was then laid up until June 30 1941, when she went on charter to the GWR for the Fishguard–Rosslare service, remaining on it until January 14 1942. After a short period at Bideford she was chartered by the Ministry of Transport and sailed for the Clyde on May 5 1942. She remained there until December 1944 when, after a call at Portsmouth on the 15th, she left for the River Schelde where she acted as an accommodation vessel until February 1945.

She then returned to the Clyde for a short period, before going back to Southampton on June 18 1945.

Hantonia had a quick refit in London, before taking up the Channel Islands' service, sailing from Southampton at 9:00 pm on July 6 1945. She remained on the Channel Islands route until March 1947 and then, after overhaul and a couple of trips to the islands, returned to the Le Havre service, leaving Southampton at 11:15 pm on Monday June 2 1947. She stayed on this service until arriving at Southampton on Sunday March 2 1952 when she was replaced by the new *Normannia*. *Hantonia* remained at Southampton until Friday June 6 1952 when she was towed away by the tug *Englishman* to be broken up at Gray's, Essex. During her last night in Southampton some of the letters from her name on the port side were removed, and thus a small part of the old ship must be in her old home port somewhere!

Hantonia *leaving Guernsey, after the Second World War (John Attwood).*

Haslemere
Owner Southern Railway. **Builder** D. & W. Henderson & Co Ltd, Glasgow. **Completed** July 1925. **Yard no** 719M. **Tonnage** 1925 756 g, 305 n; 1950 832 g, 313 n. **Dimensions** 220.3 (rl) 229.6 (oa) × 33.6 × 14.1 ft. **Propulsion** Twin screw, SR, 3 cyl 15″ 25″ 41″–24″ 1,850 ihp. **Speed** 15 knots.

Haslemere *seen in St Helier towards the end of her career (Author).*

First of the new SR cargo vessels to be built for Southampton, this ship led a very quiet life. In 1940 she was taken over for use as a barrage-balloon vessel and was later used as a control vessel at the Normandy landings. The ship was the first SR vessel to arrive in Jersey after the Second World War which she did on June 23 1945, under the command of Captain Light. On November 23 1945 shortly after leaving St Peter Port the ship struck rocks and was off service until April the following year for repairs.

On December 2 1955, the ship was involved in a collision with another ship of the fleet, the *Winchester*, in the Solent and as her steering was damaged she had to be assisted into port. Her last call at Jersey was on July 7 1959 and after being sold

for breaking up, she arrived at Rotterdam on August 29 1959.

Havre

Owner London & South Western Railway. **Builder** Ditchburn & Mare, Blackwall. **Completed** June 1855. **Yard no** n/a. **Tonnage** 387 g, 200 n. **Dimensions** 184.7 (rl) × 24.0 × 14.5 ft. **Propulsion** Paddle, 3 cyl, 62″ 62″ 62″–54″ 220 hp. **Speed** n/a.

Built, as her name implies, for the Le Havre route, it was not until December 13 1859 that she made her first call to the Channel Islands and, even then, she made only one trip. It was not until 1870, with the introduction of the daily mail service to the Channel Islands, that the ship began to operate on the route, and then, on one such voyage on Febru-

Above Havre *reflected in a glassy sea at St Peter Port (John Attwood).*

Right Hilda *entering St Peter Port (John Attwood).*

ary 16 1875, she hit the Platte Boue rock north-east of Guernsey and was lost, fortunately without loss of life.

Hilda

Owner London & South Western Railway. **Builder** Aitken & Mansel, Whiteinch, Glasgow. **Completed** January 1883. **Yard no** n/a. **Tonnage** 1883 822 g, 393 n; 1888 796 g, 368 n; 1889 849 g, 413 n; 1904 848 g, 373 n. **Dimensions** 235.5 (rl) × 29.1 × 14.2 ft. **Propulsion** Single screw, SR, 2 cyl 37" 69"–39" 1,530 ihp. **Speed** 14 knots.

Built for the Channel Islands route at a cost of £33,000, this ship was launched in July 1882, but due to a strike at the yard it was not until January 19 1883 that she made her maiden voyage. She remained on the Channel Islands route until October 7 1890, when she was replaced by the *Stella*. She then helped out on the Le Havre route before taking up the St Malo station. In February 1892 she was specially chartered to convey General Booth of the Salvation Army from Cherbourg to Southampton at the end of his world trip. In 1894 the ship had a major refit, which included new boilers and the fitting of electric light.

Eleven years after this she met a frightful end. On November 18 1905, after a voyage from Southampton which had been bedevilled by fog, the ship arrived off the entrance to St Malo where, after waiting some time, the master decided to make this approach. In so doing, the ship struck the Grand Jardin reef and was lost with 128 lives, with only six managing to survive the night to be picked up the next morning.

Hogarth

Owner Aberdeen Steam Navigation Co. (See *Caledonia* entry for full technical details.)

The *Hogarth* was chartered by the L & SWR in June 1878 and later acquired by them, being re-named *Caledonia* in November 1878. (See *Caledonia* entry for further information.)

Holyhead Ferry I

Operator British Railways. **Built** 1965. **Tonnage** 3,879 g. **Dimensions** 369′ 0″ (oa) × 57′ 2″.

On March 9 1973, this ship was on passage from Dover to Holyhead when she was diverted to Weymouth to cover for the *Caesarea*. She took the 12:30 am sailing from Weymouth on March 10, but as she was considered too long to enter St Helier Harbour the service terminated at Guernsey, with the Jersey passengers being taken to their destination by Condor hydrofoils. The ship remained in St Peter Port over the weekend and took the return sailing on the Monday to Weymouth. *Holyhead Ferry I* was later altered and renamed *Earl Léofric*.

Honfleur

Owner London & South Western Railway. **Builder** Aitken & Mansel, Kelvinhaugh. **Completed** February 1874. **Yard no** 68. **Tonnage** 1874 410 g, 228 n; 1884 413 g, 208 n (altered to 123 n in 1888); 1889 398 g, 107 n; 1889 429 g, 133 n; 1907 440 g, 122 n. **Dimensions** 176.4 (rl) × 24.1 × 12.35 ft. **Propulsion** Single screw, SR, 1874 2 cyl 26" 52"–30" 100 hp; 1888 3 cyl 19½" 31" 51′–33" 125 hp. **Speed** n/a.

This small passenger and cargo vessel was completed in February 1874 for the secondary services of the L & SWR. From October 2 of that year and in subsequent winters until late spring 1880, the ship operated to the Channel Islands by providing an extra mail service and then taking the service onwards to Granville. The ship also spent two or three months every year based on Jersey to cover during the overhaul periods of the regular ships.

The ship was re-engined and boilered in 1888, and on April 20 1890 replaced the *Griffin* on the Jersey station for the Granville service, remaining until 1896 when she was replaced by the *Victoria*. She returned to the island when the *Victoria* went to Plymouth in 1904. In early 1907 she was re-boilered with a boiler from the *Alma* and other alterations were carried out at the same time. With the permanent return of the *Victoria* to the Jersey station in April 1909, the *Honfleur* became the number two vessel and was withdrawn from the island in June 1910.

In February 1911 she was sold to Mr S. Galbraith of Glasgow who resold her in May 1911 to Nav à Vap 'Ionienne' G. Yannoulato Frères. She was then registered at the Greek port of Argostoli under the name *Chryssalis* — this name, however, was spelt as *Chrysalis* in the 1916–17 edition of Lloyds Register. The ship was acquired by the French Government in 1917, which renamed her *Fauvette* and remained with them until 1924, when she passed to Ihsan Bey and was registered at Constantinople as the *Ihsanie*. Later the same year or early in 1925 she passed to other members of the Bey family and renamed *Aidin*, which was changed in 1928 by the Beyler brothers, Hadji Ali and Mahmud, to *Aydin*. She returned to the Beys in 1933 and was renamed *Cihat* and remained with them until 1938 when Mehmet Kasim Basak renamed her *Demirhisar*, and the ship has remained with him ever since — for longer than her railway days and 110 years after her maiden voyage from Southampton to Le Havre on February 16 1874.

Hythe (II)

Owner Southern Railway, Dover. **Builder** D. & W. Henderson & Co Ltd, Glasgow. **Completed**

Above Holyhead Ferry I *arrives at St Peter Port on March 10 1974 (Guernsey Press).*

Right *In a contemporary postcard we see* Honfleur *entering St Malo, some time between 1907 and 1910 (John Attwood).*

Below Hythe *working at Weymouth on March 11 1954 (John Attwood).*

June 1925 **Yard no** 706M. **Tonnage** 1925 685 g, 269 n; 1939 688 g, 267 n; 1948 844 g, 306 n. **Dimensions** 220.6 (rl) 229.6 (oa) × 33.6 × 14.1 ft. **Propulsion** Twin screw, SR, 3 cyl 15″ 25″ 41″–24″ 1,850 ihp. **Speed** 15 knots.

The *Hythe* (II) came to Southampton to supplement the cargo service to the Channel Islands during the produce seasons of 1933 and 1934, and assisted with the evacuation of the islands in June 1940. The ship reappeared at Southampton in June 1948 for the summer and became a permanent member of the SR fleet in May 1949, though she went off on relief duties to other ports including Weymouth. By 1955 she was looking extremely decrepit, and she made her last visit to Jersey on August 23. Then, after a spell of relief duty, she was delivered at Dover on January 31 1956 to be broken up by Dover Industries Ltd.

Ibex

Owner Great Western Railway. **Builder** Laird Bros, Birkenhead. **Completed** August 1891. **Yard no** 581. **Tonnage** 1891 1,161 g, 373 n; 1893 1,150 g, 309 n; 1902 1,062 g, 232 n; 1914 951 g, 388 n. **Dimensions** 265.0 (rl) × 32.8 × 14.2 ft. **Propulsion** Twin screw, SR, 3 cyl 22″ 34″ 51″–33″ 4,250 ihp. **Speed** 18 knots.

One of the most noted ships ever to have been built for service to the Channel Islands, the *Ibex* was intended to operate the GWR's new daylight service to the islands, but this was put back. She sailed from Milford on September 4 1891, arrived in Jersey on the 5th and sailed the same day for Guernsey before arriving at Weymouth on the 7th. Her maiden

voyage to the islands was on September 9.

The first major incident in her life occurred on April 16 1897 (Good Friday) as she was approaching Jersey in close company with the L & SWR's *Frederica*. Both ships wanted to make harbour first, and in attempting this the *Ibex* struck the Normontaise Rock off the Corbière Lighthouse causing serious bottom damage and losing most of her propeller blades. With her decks almost awash she was put ashore in Portelet Bay and her passengers taken to land in her boats. Refloated, she was sent to Barrow for repairs, and arrived back in the islands on July 2 1897.

With the advent of two large new ships in 1897 and after agreement between the GWR and the L & SWR in 1899, the *Ibex* then acted solely as a relief ship during the summer, while taking over the whole of the winter running. On January 5 1900 the ship was on a voyage from Weymouth to the Channel Islands when, just north of Guernsey, she struck rocks and sank outside St Peter Port. Due to the winter weather it was decided to wait before salvaging her, and so it was not until July 21 that she was finally raised. After a great deal of repair work, she was sent to Birkenhead to be reconditioned, making her virtually a new ship when she arrived back in the Channel Islands on April 23 1901. During her reconditioning alterations were made to the vessel, the most noticeable being the extension of the bridge deck by twelve feet.

On June 24 1913 the ship arrived in the islands with two extra lifeboats slung above the poop deck

Ibex arriving at Jersey, probably in 1909 (Author).

and, a year later, radio equipment was fitted, to house which a radio room was erected just aft of the wheel-house; the ship arrived for the first time this configuration on June 15 1914.

She was the only vessel of the Weymouth fleet to remain on service to the islands during the Great War, during which period she both missed being torpedoed and sank a German submarine. On September 19 1917 she collided with and sank the cargo ship *Aletta* which was on charter to the GWR. In the spring of the following year, she had a short spell on the Dover–Calais route and in early 1919 she was used on the Weymouth–Le Havre trooping service, operating on both these services under Government orders.

In June 1922 the ship returned to service after a major refit, during which a shelter deck was added. The following month on July 9 she was hit by a huge wave which broke over the ship, entering much of the passenger accommodation and causing panic amongst the passengers. In early 1925, with two new passenger ships being built to take over the service, the *Ibex* made her last trip to the Channel Islands, arriving on Good Friday, April 10, and staying in Jersey until Tuesday the 14th when she sailed at 08:30 direct for Weymouth. On her departure she was given one of the most memorable send-offs ever. She was then sent to Plymouth to be laid up and was sold at the end of the year for breaking up at Sharpness.

Isle of Ely moving out of Southampton Docks in 1972 (Dave Hocquard).

Isle of Ely

Operator British Railways, Harwich. **Built** 1958. **Tonnage** 866 g. **Dimensions** 241' 10" (oa) × 37' 6".

This ship made three voyages to the Channel Islands from Southampton, the first of which arrived at Jersey on July 6 1972.

Isle of Guernsey

Owner Southern Railways. **Built** Wm Denny & Bros Ltd, Dumbarton. **Completed** March 1930. **Yard no** 1234. **Tonnage** 1930 2,143 g, 862 n; 1947 2,152 g, 834 n; 1956 2,188 g, 845 n; 1956 2,189 g, 846 n. **Dimensions** 296.4 (rl) 304.4 (oa) × 42.1 × 14.2 ft. **Propulsion** Twin screw, geared turbines 5,400 ihp. **Speed** 19 knots.

Second of the *Isle* class, the *Guernsey* was launched on December 17 1929 and arrived in the Channel Islands on her maiden voyage on April 5 1930. When she entered service all her ventilators and tanks were painted brown, but in early 1934 these were repainted white and the superstructure given an extra strake of white. Improvements, including extra seating and deck awnings were made in 1937, and at the outbreak of war the ship made some journeys to France for the army, in addition to her roster to the islands. Her last trip from the Channel Islands was on September 22 1939, after which she was taken over as a Hospital Carrier and used as such at Dunkirk. At the end of the year, she was converted into a target ship and used mainly in northern waters. In late 1943 she was converted into a landing ship and as such took part in the Normandy landings in June 1944.

The invasion over, the ship was used as a troop transport, until January 15 1945 when, still in camouflage livery, she re-opened the Newhaven–Dieppe service for the SR — the first cross-Channel service since 1940. It also fell to the ship to re-open the service to the Channel Islands where she arrived on June 26 1945 proudly flying both the SR and GWR house flags. At this time she had an all-grey hull but the funnels had been repainted yellow and black.

She made only five trips on the service before returning to Newhaven, remaining there until July 26 when she arrived back at Southampton. She then underwent a major refit, which meant that it was not until April 23 1947 that the ship ran trials; she returned to the Channel Islands on April 26. On July 30 1953 the ship sailed from the islands covering for the *St Julien*. Early in 1956 improvements were made to the third-class accommodation and the buffet area, with more seats being installed.

Isle of Guernsey as she was built and as she was up to 1934; up to this date a smaller proportion of the superstructure was painted white—compare Isle of Jersey on the facing page, pictured at a later date. Her brown vents may also be noted (John Attwood).

Apart from an occasional trip on the Le Havre service, the ship remained on the Channel Islands route until May 13 1961 when she ended the passenger service from Southampton.

The ship then went to Weymouth to take the duties of the third (relief) ship pending the arrival of the *Sarnia*. Apart from the weekend sailings, the ship made two excursions to Guernsey, one from Weymouth on June 5 and the other from Torquay on June 7. Her last sailing was the direct sailing from Jersey to Weymouth on Saturday June 10 1961, after which she was laid up in Southampton. Sold for breaking up later in the year, the ship arrived at Ghent on November 20 1961.

Below left Isle of Jersey *as she looked after 1935 (Author).*

Above Isle of Jersey *arriving at the island after which she was named, between 1937 and 1939 (John Attwood).*

Isle of Jersey

Owner Southern Railway. **Builder** Wm Denny & Bros Ltd, Dumbarton. **Completed** January 1930. **Yard no** 1233. **Tonnage** 1930 2,143 g, 864 n; 1948 2,144 g, 830 n; 1956 2,180 g, 842 n. **Dimensions** 296.5 (rl) 304.4 (oa) × 42.1 × 14.2 ft. **Propulsion** Twin screw, geared turbines 5,400 ihp. **Speed** 19 knots.

First of the *Isle* class vessels, this ship was launched on October 22 1929, arriving in the Channel Islands on her maiden voyage on March 13 1930. She remained on the Channel Islands service until August 24 1939 when she made her last departure from the islands until after the war.

She was converted into a hospital ship and sailed for Scapa Flow where she arrived in early September 1939. She remained at the base until the Normandy landings when from June 8 to July 16 1944 she made eleven voyages to the beaches. She then returned again to Scapa Flow where she remained for the rest of the war, being reconditioned in London before being handed back to the SR on October 3 1945. She returned to the islands on October 10 1945 and spent a year on the route before moving to the Newhaven–Dieppe service. On March 14 1947 the ship arrived back at Southampton and four days later was back in the islands, fitted with radar. The ship then carried on with her normal routine until 1956 when, from January 1 she was at Weymouth, covering for the *St Julien*. She also underwent improvement during that year.

Her first major accident occurred on September 7 1957 when, approaching St Helier Harbour, the ship continued to swing after rounding Elizabeth Castle and struck the SE rock, causing damage which required dry docking. She was the first of the Channel Islands' fleet to be withdrawn, arriving in the islands for the last time on October 31 1959, sailing 'light' back to Southampton the same day.

She was sold to Mohamed Senussi Giaber of Tripoli, Libya, and left Southampton under tow on March 31 1960 bound for the Tyne, where she underwent conversion before sailing on April 28 for Tripoli as the *Libda*. A Jersey resident saw the ship in late 1960 and stated that she seemed in a poor state and little used on the Tripoli–Benghazi route. She lasted until early 1963 when she was scrapped at La Spezia.

Isle of Sark

Owner Southern Railway. **Builder** Wm Denny & Bros Ltd, Dumbarton. **Completed** January 1932. **Yard no** 1257. **Tonnage** 1932 2,211 g, 876 n; 1946 2,188 g, 831 n; 1956 2,233 g, 855 n. **Dimensions** 296.7 (rl) 304.1 (oa) × 42.1 × 13.9 ft. **Propulsion** Twin screw, geared turbines 5,400 ihp. **Speed** 19 knots.

The success of the two 1930 *Isle*-class vessels and the increase in the tourist traffic to the islands, prompted the building of a third ship in the class. Built with an experimental Maierform bow, she also had enclosed bulwarks for most of the foredeck and, at the time of her launch on November 12 1931, these were painted black but, before her trials, the ship had an extra strake of white paint added to the superstructure and was the first ship into the fleet to have white paint down to her main-deck level.

She arrived in the Channel Islands on her maiden voyage on March 19 1932. Four years later she was selected as the first vessel to have a set of stabilisers installed. She ran trials with the new stabilisers on March 31 1936 and, during a demonstration for potential customers on September 17 in Southampton Water, the ship was made to roll 20° on a flat, calm sea, which caused alarm to those looking on!

Like her sisters she was improved in 1937, and she remained on the Channel Islands' route until June 28 1940 when she made her last sailing from the islands.

The ship went on charter to the GWR early in 1941, when she covered the Fishguard–Rosslare route for a month from early February. She was then laid up at Bideford until December of that year when she was requisitioned for war service and converted into a radar training vessel, the equipment for which required the ventilators in front of the forward funnel to be raised in height and they remained like this even after her reconversion.

Her war duties over, she arrived at Southampton on December 29 1945 and, after being refitted by Thornycroft's, she re-entered service to the Channel Islands on June 24 1946 and had the distinction of being the first mailboat to arrive fitted with radar. For the first two weeks of January 1950 she operated the Weymouth–Channel Islands service, a task she again undertook in September 1956, but this time on the daylight service. Like her sisters, her accommodation was improved in early 1956.

In her last year in service she hit the Albert Pier in Jersey, flattening her bows and thereafter pushed a huge bow wave. She arrived in the islands at the end of her last voyage on Saturday October 29 1960 and sailed 'light' back to Southampton the same day. Sold for breaking up, she arrived at Ghent on April 7 1961.

Isle of Thanet

Owner Southern Railway. **Built** 1925. **Tonnage** 2,789 g. **Dimensions** 339' 9" (oa) × 45' 1".

This ship was originally built for services across the Dover Strait and first operated from Southampton in 1939 when, during the summer, she ran on the route to St Malo.

During the summer of 1949 and from 1952 to 1958, in addition to her duties at the eastern end of the Channel, she would come round to Southampton and operate a Friday night sailing to Guernsey with a daytime return, before returning up the Channel for the rest of the week. Her last sailing from Guernsey was on September 6 1958. She remained in service until September 1963 and left Dover in tow on June 10 1964 to be broken up at Blyth, in north-east England.

Jersey Fisher

Operator British Railways. **Builder** NV Ijsselwerf, Rotterdam. **Completed** February 1972. **Yard no** 146. **Tonnage** 829 g, 390 n. **Dimensions** 249' 4" (bp) 269' 7" (oa) × 39' 8" × 12' 0" draft. **Propulsion** Single screw, 8-cyl oil engine 1,712 bhp. **Speed** 13.5 knots.

Second of the ships 'bare-boat' chartered by British Rail from James Fisher & Sons Ltd of Barrow, this ship made her maiden voyage to Jersey on February 21 1972. She remained on the route until September 29 1977, when she sailed for the last time from Jersey as a British Rail ship. With the end of the Brit–Comm agreement, and the Commodore Shipping Co Ltd taking over all the unit traffic to

A unique picture of Isle of Sark *taking the Jailer Passage off Corbière (Author).*

Right Isle of Thanet *leaving Southampton for St Malo in August 1939 (Southampton City Museums).*

Below Jersey Fisher *loading cars at Weymouth in August 1974 (Dorset Transport Circle).*

the Channel Islands, the ship was chartered to the Commodore Company being renamed *Commodore Challenger*, arriving as such in Guernsey for the first time on October 13 1977. She remained in the service of the company until October 3 1983. She arrived in Glasgow as *Loch Awe* on April 4 1984 for overhaul before further trading.

Lady de Saumarez

Owner British & Foreign Steam Navigation Co. **Builder** Henry Wimshurst, Millwall. **Completed** December 1835. **Yard no** n/a. **Tonnage** 1835 172 tons burthen; 1836 265 g, 148 n; 1846 273 g, 157 n. **Dimensions** 1835 131′ 5″ (rl) × 21′ 4″ × 12′ 10″; 1836 127.2 (rl) × 20.0 × 12.85 ft (remeasured). **Propulsion** Paddle (further details n/a). **Speed** n/a.

The British & Foreign SN Co was formed late in 1835 and, after the purchase of a second-hand ship fell through, the company purchased this nearly completed vessel from her builders. Registered as the *Lady de Saumarez* at Southampton on December 31 1835, she arrived at her home port on January 4 1836 and sailed on her maiden voyage to the Channel Islands the following day. In August 1837 the Channel Islands service of the British & Foreign SN Co was taken over by the Commercial SP Co, with which she remained until she became part of the fleet which was taken over by the South-Western SP Co in May 1842. Apart from being one of the foremost vessels on the Channel Islands route, she also helped out on the service to Le Havre. The joining of the two companies in October 1846 and the building of new vessels meant the end of the ship's role as a mailboat, her last scheduled voyage as such being on June 5 1847. After this she was rarely seen, her last call to Jersey being on May 2 1849. On February 1 1853 her registry was closed upon her being broken up.

Laura

Owner London & South Western Railway. **Builder** Aitken & Mansel, Glasgow. **Completed** May 1885. **Yard no** 132. **Tonnage** 1885 617 g, 247 n; 1888 595 g, 226 n; 1890 641 g, 265 n; 1922 592 g, 223 n. **Dimensions** 207.0 (rl) 215.6 (oa) × 26.8 × 13.25 ft, 12′ 11″ draft. **Propulsion** Single screw, SR, 2 cyl 33″ 64″–36″ 1,050 ihp. **Speed** 14 knots.

Built in 1885, at a cost of £23,500, as a replacement for the *Caesarea* on the St Malo route, this ship was launched on March 20 and made her maiden voyage on May 18 1885. With larger ships taking the route from the summer of 1891, the *Laura* then operated to Cherbourg with winter relief to St Malo and for the peak summer months from 1891 until 1914, with four exceptions, worked on the Jersey–France service. During the Great War the ship relieved the *Victoria* as required and, in 1916, was even pressed into service on the mail run to the Channel Islands when the regular vessels were damaged. On September 20 1918 the ship entirely took over the Jersey–France route from the *Victoria* and stayed on the route until closing it on March 27 1919.

A pen-and-wash rendering of Lady de Saumarez *(Société Jersiaise).*

During the winter of 1921–22 the ship was converted into a pure cargo ship and a year later passed to the SR. On November 7 1925, while on a voyage from St Malo to Southampton, the ship lost her rudder when in mid-Channel and was towed into Cowes Roads by the *Magic Star*. With the introduction of new cargo steamers in 1925–26, the *Laura* was no longer required and was sold to the Bahamas Shipping Co on October 26 1927.

The ship sailed from Southampton on November 22 to the Clyde and from Glasgow to Miami on December 9 1927. During the crossing the ship ran low on coal and the wooden interior of the ship had to be used to keep the boilers alight. She eventually arrived at her destination on January 19 1928. In October 1928 the Bahamas Shipping Co went into liquidation and the ship passed into the ownership of the Florida Inter-Island SS Co Ltd, which renamed the ship *City of Nassau*. She remained with them until 1937, when she was broken up late in the year.

Laura *departing from Jersey (John Attwood).*

Liverpool

Operator Taylor & Farina & Co. **Built** 1830. **Tonnage** 206 tons burthen. **Dimensions** 137' 5" (rl) × 22' 0". (Further details n/a.)

The *Liverpool* was owned by the Glasgow & Liverpool SS Co. She was chartered by her London-based operators after they had set up a distilling firm in Guernsey. The ship first arrived in Guernsey from Liverpool on June 6 1835, leaving the same evening for Southampton and London. She maintained this Islands–Southampton–London service until July 2, after which the London calls were dropped and the ship entered into direct competition with the regular vessels. As she was much larger she drew a greater following and consequently a price war broke out. The ship did not stay long on the service and after her trip from the Channel Islands on August 20 1835 she was not seen again, perhaps understandably as her charters left a trail of debts in Guernsey! The ship went on to the Iberian service and in February 1842 passed to P & O and was registered in London.

Lord Beresford

Owner Owned by many shareholders. **Builder** William Scott & Sons, Bristol. **Completed** May 1824. **Yard no** n/a. **Tonnage** 1824 81 tons burthen; 1832 118 tons burthen. **Dimensions** 1824 100' 9" (rl) × 18' 2" × 11' 9"; 1832 117' 11" (rl) × 18' 2" × 8' 9". **Propulsion** Paddle. (Further details n/a.)

Although she did not have any direct ties with the railway shipping services this ship is included as she was the second steamer on service to the Channel Islands and, notably, the first to use Portsmouth as her English terminal.

The ship was expected to be the first steamer in service but delays at Swansea caused her not to arrive in Jersey until late on Firday June 11 1824 and she entered harbour the next morning. On Monday, June 14 she took a party to Guernsey for the day and on Wesnesday, June 16, she sailed on her maiden voyage to Portsmouth via Guernsey, arriving late the same day. She operated during the summer only and, for summer 1825, the English terminal was moved to Southampton, which meant that she was in direct competition with the *Ariadne*. During the winter of 1831–32, the ship was lengthened by 17 ft and, during the winter of 1835–36, new boilers were installed and new paddle wheels fitted, while the whole of the interior was refitted and the vessel converted into a passenger-only ship. While this work was taking place the South of England SN Co and the British & Foreign SN Co had both been formed, and when the *Lord Beresford* re-entered service on August 23 1836 there were on the service two new large passenger vessels,

not leaving any traffic for the smaller ship. After only one trip she was switched to the Le Havre service, but only for a short time before she was withdrawn. On June 17 1837 she was advertised for sale by private tender, but little could have come of this, as on August 31 1839 she was advertised for sale by public auction to be held on September 2. The next mention of the vessel is on September 11 1841 when she was advertised as commencing a service from Falmouth to Southampton and was registered on October 29 1841 to the Falmouth & Southampton SP Co.

The service could not have been a great success, as the last date that the *Lord Beresford* can be proved to have been on the route was March 26 1842. She then moved to Swansea, being registered to a Mr T. Price on November 28 1843 and then, on March 26 1855, she was registered to Messrs H.H. and E. Price. The last item recorded in her register was for October 19 1863 when she was broken up.

Lord Warden

Operator British Railways **Built** 1952. **Tonnage** 3,333 g. **Dimensions** 362' 1" (oa) × 60' 8".

Due to the *Maid of Kent* taking longer than expected on overhaul, the *Lord Warden* opened the Weymouth–Cherbourg service on March 20 1978 and operated it for three weeks. She left Weymouth for Dover on April 9.

Lorina

Owner London & South Western Railway. **Builder** Wm Denny & Bros Ltd, Dumbarton. **Completed** December 1918. **Yard no** 1021. **Tonnage** 1918 1,457 g, 577 n; 1920 1,504 g, 605 n; 1928 1,578 g, 629 n. **Dimensions** 291.3 (rl) 300.0 (oa) × 36.1 × 14.7 ft, 12' 9½" draft. **Propulsion** Twin screw, geared turbines 4,748 ihp. **Speed** 19 knots.

In October 1913, the L & SWR were looking for a replacement for the *Lydia* and, after talks with Wm Denny & Bros Ltd, accepted on June 25 1914 a tender of £83,850 for a ship to be delivered by June 1915. The war effort delayed the building of the ship and work was suspended altogether in August 1915. By 1917 the Government was short of this type of tonnage and, on December 20 1917, the L & SWR agreed to have the ship completed as a troop ship. The ship was launched on August 12 1918 as the *Lorina*, arriving at Southampton on December 30, and entered military service on January 8 1919. She had finished in this role by October 9 1919 and, as her builders were unable to refit her, she was sent to the Caledon Shipbuilding and Engineering Co at Dundee, for the work to be carried out.

She arrived back at Southampton, on completion of the work, on March 28 1920, with the total cost of the ship now being £135,971. Her maiden voyage

Top Lord Warden *pictured at Weymouth in April 1978, while working on the Cherbourg service (Dorset Transport Circle).*

Above Lorina *in St Malo, shortly after entering service (John Attwood).*

Left *In this photograph of* Lorina *entering St Helier Harbour in 1936, the plating in of the promenade deck, carried out in 1928, can be clearly seen (John Attwood).*

Right Lune Fisher *sailing out of St Helier on October 1 1971 (Author).*

was to the Channel Islands where she arrived on April 1. For a short period she went onto the Le Havre route, before taking up regular service to St Malo for the summer months and acting as relief vessel during the winter.

With the advent of new ships on the St Malo route in 1924, the *Lorina* moved to the Channel Islands station to replace the *Caesarea*, which had been sold after her accident. In 1927 and again in 1928 the ship was off service due to turbine troubles and, during the second period of repair, the dining saloon was extended and the cabins on the same deck enlarged, this being made evident by the plating in of the promenade deck. She remained a front-line ship until the end of October 1931, when she was replaced by the *Isle of Sark* (early in 1932), after which she provided extra sailings to the islands at the weekends. In the autumn of 1935 it was decided to withdraw the *Brittany* from the Jersey station and to operate the Jersey–St Malo service as a service from Southampton. On the second such sailing, October 23, the *Lorina*, when leaving Jersey on return to Southampton, grounded on some rocks shortly after leaving and had to put back for repairs.

In 1937, she provided extra excursions on the St Malo–Jersey route and the following year she had two long spells back on the Channel Islands mail service. The ship was withdrawn from the Channel Islands area early in September 1939 and was lost at Dunkirk on May 29 1940.

Lune Fisher

Owner Seaway Coasters Ltd (James Fisher & Sons Ltd). **Built** 1962. **Tonnage** 1,012 g. **Dimensions** 217' 6" (oa) × 33' 9".

This ship first arrived in Jersey on charter to British Railways on April 6 1963, but operated for only a short period that year. The following year, however, she spent seven months operating to the Channel Islands. The ship was back in Jersey on

June 17 1965 and then remained on permanent service until January 31 1972, by which time the second of the two new container ships chartered from James Fisher was nearing completion.

Lydia

Owner London & South Western Railway. **Builder** J. & G. Thomson Ltd, Clydebank. **Completed** September 1890 **Yard no** 251. **Tonnage** 1890 1,059 g, 193 n; 1904 1,175 g, 271 n; 1914 1,133 g, 480 n. **Dimensions** 253.0 (rl) 259.0 (oa) × 35.1 × 14.8 ft. **Propulsion** Twin screw, SR, 3 cyl 24" 37" 56"–33" 5,700 ihp. **Speed** 19 knots.

Second of the *Frederica* class, this ship was launched on July 16 1890, made 19.55 knots during trials held on September 29 in Stokes Bay and arrived in the Channel Islands on her maiden voyage on October 7. The following year, on May 6 1891, the ship hit the La Rond Rock off Guernsey; refloating herself, she steamed for St Peter Port and ran aground in the harbour with her foredeck awash.

On December 16 1901 when raising steam in St Helier Harbour down-draught caused a blow-back in the furnace that set the furnace casing alight and the outbreak took an hour to extinguish. In early 1904 the ship was given an internal rebuild, with a new ladies' first class suite being built on the aft promenade deck; this allowed the dining saloon to be moved up a deck and the resulting space was used to provide extra cabin accommodation. One of the outward changes was the removal of the main-mast, but this had to be refitted from November 11 1905 to meet new regulations that called for a light on each mast, to help indicate in which direction the ship was proceeding.

Although major boiler repairs were carried out in 1899, further work was required by 1908, and it was decided to install new boilers at a cost of £4,400. These were fitted early in 1909 and at the same time

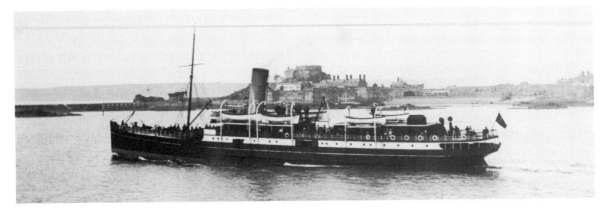

Above Lydia *as she was from June 1904 to November 1905, with only one mast (Author).*

Left Lydia *in drab wartime colours leaves St Peter Port and the islands for the last time on September 21 1919, having brought back troops of the Guernsey contingent from Le Havre (John Attwood).*

Below Lynx *showing how the three sister ships looked when they were first built (John Attwood).*

a new, taller funnel was added, and she returned to service on June 2.

The ship gained a new lease of life on July 22 1910 when, instead of becoming a relief ship, she opened a new daylight service at the weekends from Southampton to Le Havre. This should have been an easy year for the ship, but due to the non-arrival of new ships for the Channel Islands' route, the *Lydia* also operated to the islands and to St Malo at times. At the end of 1913 the L & SWR sought to replace the ship and, in June 1914, an order was placed with Wm Denny & Bros for a ship to be delivered by the summer of 1915. World events overtook these plans, and *Lydia* remained in service until March 12 1915 when she sailed from the Channel Islands for the last time as a mailboat, being then taken over for military service as Admiralty Transport No 280. One of her first voyages was to Jersey where she arrived on March 20 with prisoners-of-war for internment. She spent most of the war on the military service between Southampton and Le Havre which was operated on behalf of the Government by the L & SWR. Her last call in the islands was to Guernsey on September 21 1919 when she conveyed the Guernsey contingent back home. Her military service ceased at the end of October 1919 and the ship was returned to the L & SWR which, on December 18, sold her through the offices of R.E. James to a Mr Thomas Sales for £20,000, this being linked with the purchase from him of the *Peony*, then at Malta. The sale was completed by February 19 1920, but the ship remained at Southampton and in June was registered to the James Dredging Towage & Transport Co, and was moved on June 16 from the Docks into Southampton Water. She remained with this company until March 26 1921 when she passed to a Captain Montague Yates, who sailed from Southampton on March 28 for the Mediterranean to operate a service between Malta and Syracuse. The ship hit the headlines in the September of that year when Captain Yates resisted arrest at Syracuse after a two-day siege by Italian police. James recovered the ship and, in September 1922, sold her to Coast Lines Ltd, for a service between Preston and Dublin. She was short-lived in their employ, being sold in May 1923 to SA Ionienne de Nav à Vap 'Yannoulatos' which renamed the ship *Ierac*. She remained in their service until 1937 when she was broken up.

Lynx

Owner Great Western Railway. **Builder** Laird Bros, Birkenhead. **Completed** July 1889. **Yard no** 568. **Tonnage** 1889 596 g, 141 n; 1890 668 g, 202 n; 1896 672 g, 206 n; 1904 671 g, 206 n; 1906 672 g, 206 n; 1912 670 g, 166 n; 1914 609 g, 230 n. **Dimensions** 235.5 (rl) × 27.65 × 13.15 ft. **Propulsion** Twin screw, SR 3 cyl 16½" 26" 41"–30" 1,650 ihp. **Speed** 16 knots.

First of three ships built for the GWR in 1889, the *Lynx* made 16.5 knots during trials held on July 4 and arrived in the Channel Islands on her maiden voyage on August 4 1889.

On September 5 1890 she was in collision with the *Oevelgonne* when 15 miles south of Portland and, on March 20 1897, she grazed a rock while on passage from Weymouth to Guernsey, and had to proceed to Barrow for repairs.

Alterations for the first class ladies accommodation had taken place in 1890 and further improvements were made in 1896 to keep her in line with her sisters. The forward lifeboats were raised to provide more deck space and awnings erected; the ship returned to service on April 2 1896. With the exception of a two-month spell in early 1902, the ship saw

Lynx working cargo in Guernsey, shortly after the First World War (John Attwood).

little passenger service after June 1900, going in early 1903 to Plymouth for tender duties. She did appear, however, on the Guernsey produce service and on July 16 1906 arrived in Jersey for a two-month charter, making excursions to the other islands and France.

Converted into a cargo vessel in early 1912, she worked the Jersey potato season that year, but was rarely seen in the island again until 1920, working instead on either the Guernsey fruit trade or the services to France. Taken over for war service in 1914 she, like her sister, spent most of her time in the Mediterranean, being renamed HMS *Lynn* for the duration. She arrived in Jersey for the first time after the war on March 12 1920. One of the first people on board was Captain H. Bond, the commander of the ship during the war who was able to dismiss as untrue, the rumour that the *Lynx* had arrested her old sister *Antelope* (then the *Atromitos*).

On December 31 1924 when on passage from Jersey to Guernsey the ship was hit by a huge wave, which carried away the wheel-house. She was withdrawn from service in early 1925, being replaced by two new cargo ships and was sold to W.M. Constamb & Co for breaking up.

Maid of Kent
Operator British Railways. **Builder** Wm Denny & Bros Ltd, Dumbarton. **Completed** May 1959.

Maid of Kent *leaving Cherbourg on September 26 1980 (A.M.S. Russell).*

Yard no 1492. **Tonnage** 3,920 g, 1,335 n. **Dimensions** 348' 0" (bp) 373' 0" (oa) × 60'3" × 13' 0" draft. **Propulsion** Twin screw, geared turbines 11,500 shp. **Speed** 19 knots.

Built for the Dover–Boulogne car-ferry service, the *Maid of Kent* has as a result limited height in the car deck, which made her of little use when high-sided commercial lorries started to be carried on the route in October 1965. The ship remained to cater for cars and coaches until moving to commence a new motorists' route to the Continent between Weymouth and Cherbourg in 1974.

The ship made a trial run to Cherbourg on March 27, returning the next day, and opened the summer-only route on Saturday April 6 1974. On only the third day in operation the ship suffered turbine trouble and had to return to Weymouth, and did not sail again until April 30.

The ship visited Guernsey on April 6 1977, to take a backlog of trade cars which had built up at Weymouth, and also helped out at Stranraer in April 1975 and at Holyhead in October 1979. Sealink gave good notice that 1981 was to be the ship's last season on the route and the ship was given a grand send-off when she closed the summer route on Friday October 2. That should have been her end but, due to the *Earl William* being withdrawn from service, the *Maid* was called in to operate both service and excursions to Guernsey until October 30.

The ship was sold for breaking up and left Newhaven in tow for Spain on April 6 1982.

Right Maid of Orleans *swinging round in St Helier Harbour on her second Channel Islands service in 1974 (Dave Hocquard).*

Below Maria, *as purchased in 1872 (John Attwood).*

Maid of Orleans

Operator British Railways, Dover. **Built** 1949. **Tonnage** 3,777 g. **Dimensions** 341' 6" (oa) × 52' 3".

This ship had two short spells on the Weymouth–Channel Islands service, the first being in 1972 when she covered for the *Caesarea*. She arrived 'light' at Jersey from Folkestone on July 20 and operated a service to Weymouth. The next day she took the 1:30 pm sailing to the Channel Islands, with the 9:45 pm return sailing routed to Newhaven so that the ship could be back at Folkestone quickly, but fog held her up off Guernsey and it was not until 6:35 am on July 22 that she cleared St Peter Port.

Her second period of service was in 1974 when she replaced the *Sarnia* from July 1–8.

Maria

Owner London & South Western Railway. **Builder** H. Murray & Co, Port Glasgow. **Completed** October 1871. **Yard no** n/a. **Tonnage** 1872 271 g, 170 n; 1888 261 g, 146 n; 1895 278 g, 155 n. **Dimensions** 155.7 (rl) × 21.1 × 11.0 ft. **Propulsion** Single screw, SR, 2 cyl 19" 33"–24" 50 hp. **Speed** n/a.

Built as a pure cargo ship, *Maria* was completed in October 1871 for the Liverpool owners M.R. Nolan & W. Johnston who, in April 1872, sold the ship to the L & SWR. She spent most of her life on the service to Honfleur, but did serve the other Normandy ports and also visited the Channel Islands at the height of the produce seasons. In March 1876, her propeller shaft broke near Guernsey and on September 8 1904 she was in collision with the *Avonmore* off the Owers and, with her forward hold full of water, she was towed stern-first to Spithead by the *Columbia.*

She was sold on April 12 1907, on which date she had four owners — the L & SWR sold her to a W. Summers, who sold her to a M. Schultz, who sold her to a Mr R.J. Campbell of Galata, Constantinople, who a month later registered the ship to the Anatolian SS Co. She sailed from Southampton on April 18 1907 and arrived at Constantinople on May 4, and then traded in the Black Sea area.

In November 1908 she was sold to Joseph Constant who, the following month, registered her in the name of the Little Eastern SS Co Ltd. In March 1910 the Little Eastern changed its name to the Patriotic SS Co Ltd and the ship was registered in London, but for some unknown reason her register was closed by the Customs and Excise in May 1910 and the ship then appeared in Lloyds Register without a port of registry. In late 1913 she was bought by a Mr H. Himminghoffen, renamed *Myra* and registered at Altona, where remained with the same owner until late 1926, when it is assumed she was broken up.

Mellifont

Owner Lancashire & Yorkshire Railway Company. **Built** 1903. **Tonnage** 1,207 g. **Dimensions** 260 (rl) × 35.6.

This ship had only one short period on the Weymouth–Channel Islands route when, with the *Ibex* off service, the ship took over the route from the *Galtee More* on June 18 1915, remaining until July 6, when she sailed from the islands for the last time.

Melmore

Builder David J. Dunlop & Co, Port Glasgow. **Completed** (month n/a) 1892. **Yard no** n/a. **Tonnage** 412 g, 168 n. **Dimensions** 156.2 (rl) × 25.8 × 11.3 ft. **Propulsion** Single screw, SR, 3 cyl 15″ 23″ 28″–27″. **Speed** 10 knots.

Acquired by the GWR from the Earl of Leitrim

early in 1905, *Melmore* was intended for service as required on the Waterford and Channel Islands routes. Her first call at Jersey was on May 14 1905 and she operated the potato service each season up to 1909. She was then moved to operate the GWR service to Nantes and, when this was discontinued in September 1911, the ship was put up for sale. She made three trips to Jersey in May 1912 but on June 26 she was sold through the shipping agents, C. W. Forbes, to a Mr J. Constant, who on August 19 resold her to a Mr H. Whitworth.

In the newspapers of June 11 1912 it was reported that the ship had been sold for about £4,500 to a Canadian buyer and was being prepared at Plymouth for a trip to Cocos Island in an attempt to recover gold and jewels worth £20,000. The ship sailed from Barry on September 25 and, after calling at Cocos Island, arrived at Panama on February 23 1913, but it is not known if the valuables were recoverd. The ship left Panama on April 11 and, afterwards, called at Punta Arenas on April 17, finally arriving at Vancouver on June 13. It would appear that the ship was then repossessed by J. Constant who sold her to J.E. Darby (E. Beazley, Manager) (sic) and in 1914 she passed to the Melmore SS Co (Union SS Co of British Columbia). Two years later, in 1916, she was owned by Milne & Co and, a year later than that, she was sold to a Mr G.E. Leith, renamed *Santa Elena* and registered at Callao in Peru.

In 1936 she was sold to the Peruvian Government (Minister of Marine [sic]) and was renamed *Condestable Celendon* and her last entry in Lloyds Register was in the 1946–47 edition, contact thereafter being lost.

Minster

Owner Southern Railway. **Builder** D. & W. Henderson & Co Ltd, Glasgow. **Completed** August 1924. **Yard no** 634M. **Tonnage** 1924 682 g, 267 n; 1937 707 g, 278 n. **Dimensions** 220.4 (rl) 229.6 (oa) × 33.6 × 14.1 ft. **Propulsion** Twin screw, SR, 3 cyl 15″ 25″ 41″–24″ 1,850 ihp. **Speed** 15 knots.

Built for the cargo services at Dover, this ship was

the second of the class, being delivered on August 18 1924. The introduction of the Train Ferry Service in 1936 caused a marked reduction in the general cargo traffic and thus *Minster* was transferred to Southampton in October to replace the elderly *Aldershot*. Her first call at Jersey was on October 24 and, in February 1937, the decision was taken to build accommodation for passengers, so as to bring her into line with other ships of the class based at Southampton which had had the facility from new.

The ship helped with the evacuation of the Channel Islands and in August 1940 was taken over by the Admiralty and fitted out as a Net Layer. She was lost in the Seine estuary when she struck a mine on June 8 1944.

Monarch

Owner South of England Steam Navigation Co. **Builder** Rubie & Blaker, Northam, Southampton. (The original register certificate of the builder was signed by what appears to be a 'J. Blatier'.) **Completed** March 1837 **Yard no** n/a. **Tonnage** 1837 312 g, 172 n; 1840 314 g, 174 n. **Dimensions** 137.7 (rl) × 21.0 × 13.1 ft. **Propulsion** Paddle (further details n/a), 120 hp. **Speed** n/a.

Ordered when the South of England SN Co was formed in late 1835, this ship was launched on May 1 1836, though it was not until April 4 1837 that she made her maiden voyage from Southampton to Le Havre, replacing the *Camilla*. During the winter of 1837, she also worked to the Channel Islands to cover for the refit of the *Atalanta*.

Passing to the New South-Western SN Co in October 1846, she was laid up until June 8 1847 when she was placed on the Channel Islands mail service, where she ran opposite the *Wonder* for the summer, her last regular call being on November 18. She made only a few calls in 1848, but on one she towed from Jersey the Chinese junk *Keying* to London. In September the following year she was sold to C.B. Robinson and H. Smith of London, who converted her into a square-rigger sailing ship, and then set out for New Zealand and Australia. In June 1852 she was registered in Sydney to E.M. Sayers, then sold in 1861 to J. & C. Burke of Melbourne. The ship was finally lost by stranding at Hobson's Bay, Victoria, on July 17 1867.

Moose

Operator British Railways. **Builder** Brooke Marine Ltd, Lowestoft. **Completed** October 1959. **Yard no** 268. **Tonnage** 795 g, 308 n. **Dimensions** 210′ 0″ (bp) 228′ 0″ (oa) × 39′ 6″ × 13′ 4¾″ draft. **Propulsion** Twin screw, 6-cyl oil engines 1,800 bhp. **Speed** 14 knots.

Sister to the *Elk*, this vessel was launched on May 25 1959, arriving at Southampton on October 12. She sailed on her maiden voyage to Guernsey in the evening of October 16 and maintained the new style of cargo services then being introduced. Her one claim to fame occurred on December 19 1964, when it fell to her to be the ship to close the railway's service between St Malo and Jersey.

The ship became closely associated with the build-up of the special car shipments to the Channel Islands during the holiday season and her last year in service saw her spend the whole of the summer on this service. Her last sailing from the islands was from Jersey on October 7 1972, after which she was laid up until sold on the 19th of the same month to the Valmas Maritime SA, leaving Weymouth as the *Rena* on November 11 1972. The company renamed her *Syros* in 1973 and *Zefiros* in 1975, and in late 1976 sold her to the Mykonos Shipping SA, also of Greece, which renamed her *Mykonos*.

Normandy (I)

Owner London & South Western Railway. **Builder** John Ash & Co, London. **Completed** September 1863. **Yard no** n/a. **Tonnage** 425 g, 252 n (altered to 204 n in 1867). **Dimensions** 209.9 (rl) × 24.1 × 12.7 ft. **Propulsion** Paddles (further details n/a), 225 hp. **Speed** n/a.

This ship was launched on June 17 1863 by a Miss Dutton and made a trial trip to the Nore on August 5. She arrived at Southampton on September 7, underwent trials on the 12th and arrived in the Channel Islands on her maiden voyage on September 19. Except for June 1868 and June 1869, the ship remained on the islands route.

Shortly after leaving Southampton on April 21 1864 she was in collision with the liner *Bavaria* and suffered serious damage. The end of the ship came on March 17 1870 when, 25 miles south of the Needles, she collided with the steamer *Mary*. The speed of the *Normandy* caused the bow of the other

Below Moose *with the monastral blue hull of British Rail, pictured on September 4 1972 (Author).*

Bottom *Another Ouless painting, this time of* Normandy (I) *off Corbière, dated 1869 (Author).*

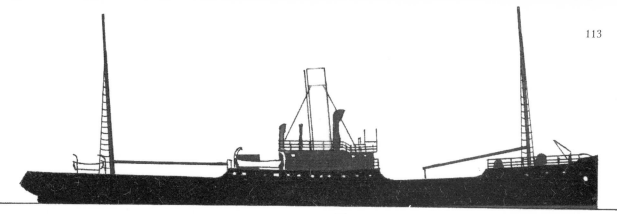

Above Normandy *(II) seen in an elevation drawn by the author.*
Below Normannia *(II) moored at the harbour front in Le Havre*
(John Attwood).

ship to cut deep into the hull just aft of the starboard
paddle box, with the result that she sank with some
loss of life. The court of inquiry held the *Normandy*
to blame for the collision.

The ship also made history as she was the first in
the fleet to use a small auxiliary steam engine to
provide the vacuum for the engine, giving much
easier and quicker control of the engine. Previously
the pump had been driven by the main engine
through an intermediate shaft, meaning that there
was no vacuum when the main shaft was stationary.

Normandy (II)

Owner London & South Western Railway. **Builder**
Earl's Shipbuilding & Engineering Co Ltd, Hull.
Completed (month n/a) 1910. **Tonnage** 1912 618
g, 251 n. **Dimensions** 192.0 (rl) × 29.2 × 14.7 ft.
Propulsion Single screw, SR , 3 cyl 15½″ 25″ 40″
-27″ 900 ihp. **Speed** 12.5 knots.

Acquired with her sister ship *Brittany* by the L &
SWR in May 1912 from the London, Brighton &
South Coast Railway Co, this ship and her sister
was altered at the end of the year.

The *Normandy* had a short life with the L & SWR
as she was torpedoed on January 25 1918 while on
the Cherbourg service, with only 13 of the 45 people
on board being saved.

Normannia (I)

Owner London & South Western Railway. **Builder**
Fairfield Shipbuilding & Engineering Co Ltd,
Glasgow. **Completed** March 1912. **Yard no** 481.
Tonnage 1,567 g, 676 n **Dimensions** 290.3 (rl)
300.0 (oa) × 36.1 × 15.3 ft. **Propulsion** Twin
screw, geared turbines 4,750 ihp. **Speed** 19.5 knots.

First ship in the world to be fitted with geared
turbines, the *Normannia* thus has a special place in
shipping history. Launched on November 9 1911,
she ran trials in the Clyde on February 22–23 1912
and arrived at her home port, Southampton, on
February 26. Her maiden voyage to Le Havre was
to have been on March 16, but due to a coal strike,
this was delayed until April 2.

Her first call to the Channel Islands was on May
9 1926 when, due to the General Strike, the regular
vessels had no coal, and the *Normannia* took over as
she had already coaled in Le Havre. Her next
service to the islands was from July 7 1928 to
September 28, when she replaced the *Lorina*, which
had suffered turbine damage. She was back again
on the run from March 8 to April 13 1929 to cover
for the *Alberta*.

In early 1931 the ship was fitted with a new type of rudder, an Oertz, to help improve handling.

In the mid-1930s it was usual for the *Brittany* to be withdrawn for most of the winter and the Jersey–St Malo service was covered by either the *Lorina* or *Normannia*, or the latter's sister.

With a number of the regular Channel Islands vessels taken over for war service in late 1939, the *Normannia* went on the Channel Islands route on September 11, remaining till May 3 1940. Soon after going off service she was lost at Dunkirk, on May 30.

Normannia (II)

Operator British Railways. **Builder** Wm Denny & Bros Ltd, Dumbarton. **Completed** January 1952. **Yard no** 1454. **Tonnage** 1952 3,543 g, 1,912 n; 1964 2,219 g, 717 n. **Dimensions** 299′ 1″ (bp) 309′ 2″ (oa) × 49′ 8″ × 12′ 6½″ draft. **Propulsion** Twin screw, geared turbines 8,000 shp. **Speed** 19.5 knots

Built to replace the *Hantonia* on the Le Havre route, this ship was launched on July 19 1951 and arrived at Southampton on January 18 1952. Of similar design to the *Falaise* she was a neater-looking vessel due to being a deck lower at the bow and stern, a modification introduced after the difficulty experienced by dock cranes of working cargo in the *Falaise* in some ports at high water.

An official cruise in Southampton Water took place on February 27 and her maiden voyage commenced on March 3 1952. On December 26 that year, just after her first overhaul, the ship, leaving Southampton in fog, hit the liner *Arundel Castle* which was moored at the quay. From September 14 1953 the ship had a short spell on the Harwich–Hook of Holland route.

Five years later she made her first visit to the Channel Islands, where she arrived on November 13 1958. That winter, she and the *Falaise* covered the Le Havre and Channel Islands routes and the *Normannia* also took the Jersey–St Malo service. Reductions the following winter meant that only one ship was required at Southampton and the *Normannia* was able to replace the *St Patrick* on the Weymouth–Channel Islands route from January 2 to February 24 1960. Two months later it was the turn of the *St Patrick* to stand in at Southampton, from May 6, as with the usual cruise ship *Falaise* not ready for service, the *Normannia* undertook the short-cruise programme from Dover.

The ship returned to Weymouth in 1963, replacing the *Caesarea* on March 12–20, when the latter had to be withdrawn due to compass trouble. By this time it had been decided that the ship was to be converted into a car ferry for use at Dover. She arrived on her last trip from Le Havre on December 4 1963 and sailed the next day for Hawthorne Leslie's yard on the Tyne where the work was carried out. The car ferry *Normannia* arrived at Dover on April 5 1964 and entered service on the 20th to Boulogne but had a number of calls to Newhaven during the next few years to replace the *Falaise* which had a habit of hitting quays! The ship went further afield in 1965, when on July 9 she opened the new car-ferry service from Holyhead as the new *Holyhead Ferry I* was not ready for service, and during October 25–26 1968 when the ship made one round trip from Harwich to the Hook of Holland due to problems with the *St George*.

Great changes took place on the short sea routes in 1972, with two new large ferries entering service and Folkestone having a ramp installed. To adjust the number of ships within the Sealink group, the *Normannia* was transferred to the SNCF (French state railway company) and the French flag for the 1973 season; this caused something of a surprise when she arrived in Jersey from St Malo with a charter party on April 28. She made a day trip to Guernsey the next day before returning to St Malo on May 1, but that was not the last the islands saw of the ship that year as, after being handed back to the British, she was overhauled and then replaced *Falaise* on the Weymouth–Channel Islands route from December 18 1973 to March 15 1974. The ship was hardly back at Dover before the *Maid of Kent* had engine failure on the new Weymouth–Cherbourg route so the ship returned to Weymouth to take up service on April 11. Before these duties were finished, however, the *Falaise* started to have generator trouble so, after the repair and return of the *Maid*, the *Normannia* took up the Channel Islands service from April 29 to May 20.

The ship had been back at Dover for only a month when, on moving berth, she struck the footings of an old pier, which caused bottom damage and the flooding of the engine room. After being patched, the ship was towed to Middlesbrough for repairs and, upon their completion in October, she went straight back to Weymouth to take over the Channel Islands service, as by this time the *Falaise* had been withdrawn from service. For the winter of 1974–75, the car ferry was the sole vessel on the route and so extra seating was added to cater for the increased number of travellers at weekends.

The ship remained on the service until July 15 1975 — the longest spell of duty ever recorded — and then returned to Dover. Problems with other ships on the Channel Islands service, however, ensured that the ship kept returning. Trouble with the *Earl Godwin* brought the ship back between

Top Normannia *(II) leaving St Helier on January 9 1960* (Author).
Above Normannia *(II) as a car ferry, pictured on April 5 1976* (Author).

March 26 and April 5 1976 and she made one round trip on May 10–11 to cover for the *Caledonian Princess*. After returning to Dover it then fell to the *Normannia* to open the car-ferry service to the new port of Dunkerque Ouest on July 5 1976.

Her season finished on October 25, when she went to be laid up at Newhaven, and in mid-December she was put up for sale. In January 1977, however, she was called back to work at Dover from the 13th to the 20th and even then her work was not done. A strike took place at the repair yard where the *Earl Godwin* was undergoing refit, so the *Normannia* found herself again on course for Weymouth, where from March 20–31 1978 she maintained the service to the islands. Chartered

tonnage then took over, but the overhaul programme was well behind and thus, from April 11, the ship went back into service with the *Caesarea*, helping with the passenger traffic until Saturday May 6 when both ships sailed from the Channel Islands for the last time.

The *Normannia* then returned to Newhaven and it looked as though a buyer had been found, when on June 11 the port of registry was altered to Panama and a thin white line was painted on the funnel, while the ship was made ready for towage to Rotterdam. The ship was to be altered for a service in the Red Sea, but the deal fell through and eventually on November 29, 1978, the ship left Newhaven under its own power with a Sealink crew, bound for Spain where she was broken up.

Pembroke
Owner Great Western Railway. **Builder** Laird Bros, Birkenhead. **Completed** (month n/a) 1880.

Yard no 485. **Tonnage** 1896 971 g, 199 n; 1898 977 g, 196 n; 1913 965 g, 411n; 1916 918 g, 311 n. **Dimensions** 254.0 (rl) × 30.9 × 15.0 ft. **Propulsion** Twin screw, SR, 3 cyl 19" 30" 46"–30" 3,300 ihp **Speed** 16 knots.

Built in 1880 as a paddle steamer for the GWR's Irish Sea services, this ship suffered a major breakdown in 1895 and as a result was converted into a twin-screw steamer. She was then mainly used as a cargo ship and in June 1897 helped out on the Guernsey fruit traffic. On July 13 that year she was pressed into passenger service to the Channel Islands when the new *Roebuck* developed a fault and had to be withdrawn. The ship took the service to the islands until August 2, when she was replaced by the new *Reindeer* and sailed direct from Jersey to Milford on the August 3.

In 1906 the port of Fishguard was developed to provide a fast link with the Irish port of Rosslare and, at the same time, efforts were made to rival Plymouth as a port of call for Atlantic liners. To this end the ship was converted into a tender with a certificate for 665 passengers within the three-mile limit. The tender service was not a great success and the ship was used when required as a cargo ship.

In 1916 it was difficult for the GWR at Weymouth to find a ship to relieve the *Ibex* and in desperation they brought the *Pembroke* round from the Irish Sea. She arrived in the Channel Islands for the first time on March 30 1916 but was only permitted to carry up to twelve passengers, except when granted a special licence sometimes during *Ibex*'s off-service periods. She continued a heavy schedule

to the islands until August 1920 after which she operated mainly during the islands' produce seasons.

The ship continued in service until July 4 1925 when she arrived at Weymouth from Guernsey for the last time. On August 4 1925 she left Weymouth in tow for Charlestown on the Firth of Forth to be broken up.

Princess Ena

Owner London & South Western Railway. **Builder** Gourlay Bros & Co (Dundee) Ltd. **Completed** July 1906. **Yard no** 224. **Tonnage** 1906 1,203 g, 521 n; 1907 1,198 g, 501 n. **Dimensions** 250.6 (rl) 260.0 (oa) × 33.3 × 15.15 ft, 14' 1" draft. **Propulsion** Twin screw, SR, 3 cyl 16" 26" 36"–24" 2,700 ihp. **Speed** 16 knots.

Built to replace the *Hilda* on the route to St Malo, this ship can only be described as an odd member of the fleet, in that her builders styled her with a long forecastle and with the funnel set well aft, making her outside the trend which the L & SWR were following at the time. She was built in a very short space of time, being launched on May 25 1906, running trials a month later on June 22 and making her maiden voyage to St Malo on July 16. She led a rather charmed life, going ashore in dangerous positions on no less than three occasions, the first being on May 20 1908 when she hit the Paternoster reef off the north-west coast of Jersey in fog, after which she was refloated and safely made St Helier Harbour. The following year on September 10 1909 she grounded off the south coast of the Isle of Wight, near the Needles, and again refloated and made port; but the most serious incident occured on August 14 1923 when, in dense fog, she went ashore

Pembroke at the jetty-side in Guernsey in 1917, awaiting cargo (John Attwood).

A fine shot of Princess Ena *at speed (John Attwood).*

on the Minquiers. The passengers were put into the lifeboats for safety, but two boats were lost in the fog and, when the ship refloated, the master proceeded to St Malo, and it was not until sixteen hours later that the *Bertha* found the two boats tied to one of the navigational buoys off the reef.

In March 1911 the company agreed to alter the name of the ship to *Ena* and the publicity material for that year gave the name as such, but the renaming did not take place; no reason was ever given for this.

In early 1914 two new larger lifeboats were fitted to the ship, and on April 27 1915 the ship was taken over for service as a 'Q' ship, working out of Falmouth with HMS *Baralong*, her master at the time being Commander F.M. Simon RN, a Jerseyman. In October of that year she was converted into a troopship, sailing on the 18th from Southampton for the Dardanelles where she spent much of her time on the Salonica–Mudros route. At the end of the war she was reconditioned by the Admiralty at Devonport, arriving back at Southampton on July 7 1920. With the advent of new larger ships on the St Malo service in 1924, the *Princess Ena* spent her summers helping out on other routes, mostly Cherbourg and Caen (Ouistreham), while she returned to the St Malo route for the winter. With the withdrawal of the Cherbourg service in 1931 there was even less for the ship to do, but she helped out on excursion work between France and the Channel Islands and at weekends carried groups of Scouts and their equipment across the Channel.

In the evening of Saturday August 6 1932 the ship towed the damaged *St Patrick* from St Aubin's Bay into the Harbour at St. Helier, a quite unique feat as she towed her line-astern right through the narrow pierheads and to her berth, with only the local tug astern to stop her. The end of the ship came on August 3 1935 when, after discharging a group of Scouts in Jersey, the ship sailed 'light' for St Malo. When twelve miles south of the island, a fire was discovered and although all efforts were made to extinguish it, the ship was gutted and sank twenty-four hours later.

Princess Maud

Operator British Railways. **Built** 1934. **Tonnage** 2,883 g. **Dimensions** 330′ 0″ (oa) × 51′3″.

This ship first visited Jersey on September 3 1945 when she arrived in the island with a party of servicemen from Dover. She came to the Southampton station in 1951 when, between July 3 and September 18 she made two sailings a week to St Malo and also took the Friday night-sailing to Guernsey.

Rathmore

Owner London & North-Western Railway. **Built** 1908. **Tonnage** 1,569 g. **Dimensions** 299.5 (rl) × 40.2 ft.

This ship operated the Southampton–Channel Islands route from July 28 to August 14 1920, when she replaced the damaged *Alberta*.

Reindeer

Owner Great Western Railway. **Builder** Naval Construction & Armaments Co Ltd, Barrow. **Com-**

Top Princess Maud *backing out of St Peter Port in 1951 (Author).*

Above Rathmore *in Jersey while on the Southampton service as a replacement for the* Alberta *on August 1 1920 (John Attwood).*

Left *Just about to leave Jersey on her first Mail service,* Reindeer *presents a fine side view to the photographer, on August 3 1897 (John Attwood).*

Right Rennes *on Channel Islands service in 1965 (Dave Hocquard).*

pleted July 1897. **Yard no** 257. **Tonnage** 1897 1,281 g, 415 n (altered to 238 n in 1898); 1901 1,193 g, 309 n (altered to 312 n in 1912); 1914 1,193 g, 497 n; 1914 1,101 g, 455 n. **Dimensions** 280.0 (rl) × 34.5 × 16.8 ft. **Propulsion** Twin screw, SR, 3 cyl 23" 36" 56"–33" 5,300 ihp. **Speed** 19 knots.

Second of the GWR ships built for their 'daylight' service in 1897, this ship's first service was to carry returning day-excursioners from Guernsey to Jersey on August Bank Holiday Monday August 2 1897. The ship then took the Tuesday morning sailing from the Channel Islands to Weymouth and, apart from a month later on September 3 when she hit the paddle steamer *Brodick Castle* when entering Weymouth, the ship led a very quiet, uneventful life.

Like the *Roebuck*, she had a coaling gantry fitted in 1909 and, at the start of the Great War, was used as a troopship before taking up the Fishguard station in August 1914. She did not remain there long, as in October she was requisitioned for war service and was sent to the Mediterranean where she was used as a minesweeper and tender in the Dardanelles.

When she returned from the Mediterranean, she spent some time as a troopship between Weymouth and Cherbourg, before being refitted and arriving back in the islands on 8th February 1920. During a refit at Birkenhead in 1923 the ship was fitted with a shelter deck which extended from the bridge to the funnels and a bar was installed in the smoke-room; she returned to duty on March 13.

With the arrival of new ships in 1925, the ship became the relief vessel, and when required to replace the *St Helier* which had rammed the pierheads in Jersey on March 12 1926, the *Reindeer* steamed into Jersey and hit exactly the same spot, and had to be withdrawn from service.

It was found that the two new ships, *St Helier* and *St Julien*, could cope well on their own with the services to the islands and, on February 23 1928, the old ship left the Channel Islands for the last time. After spending the summer laid up, she arrived at Briton Ferry on November 30 1928 to be broken up by T. W. Ward Ltd.

Rennes

Owner French Railways (SNCF). **Built** 1947. **Tonnage** 1,053 g. **Dimensions** 237' 10" (oa) × 34' 5".

Rennes operated between June and September 1965 on the cargo services to the Channel Islands.

Rina

Owner London & South Western Railway. **Builder** Ardrossan Dry Dock & Shipbuilding Co Ltd, Ardrossan. **Completed** March 1902. **Yard no** 186. **Tonnage** 548 g, 227 n. **Dimensions** 170.0 (rl) × 27.1 × 11.4 ft. **Propulsion** Single screw, SR, 3 cyl 14" 22½" 37"–27" 500 ihp. **Speed** 9.5 knots.

Built in 1902 for R.H. Penny & Sons, Shoreham, as the *Algethi*, this ship was purchased in June 1922 by the L & SWR, arriving at Southampton on July 16. The name *Martha* was not approved by the authorities and thus the ship was renamed *Rina*. At

the end of the year, electric light was fitted in the ship, but she did not remain in the fleet long, being sold to York Line for £1,250 in February 1926. On March 1 she was resold to a Mr L.S. Richards who the same day sold her to a London firm; finally, on March 12, she was sold to a G. Dormio of Bari, Italy and was renamed *Costanza*. She remained with him until late 1940 when she was acquired by the A. Alfino e Figli Company and registered at Catania where she spent the rest of her time, becoming a war loss in August 1941.

Ringwood

Owner Southern Railway. **Builder** D. & W. Henderson & Co Ltd, Glasgow. **Completed** June 1926. **Yard no** 730M. **Tonnage** 755 g, 304 n. **Dimensions** 220.7 (rl) 229.6 (oa) × 33.6 × 14.2 ft. **Propulsion** Twin screw, SR, 3 cyl 15″ 25″ 41″–24″ 1,850 ihp. **Speed** 15 knots.

Last of the standard cargo vessels to be built for the SR, this ship was launched on April 13 1926 and made her maiden voyage to Guernsey on June 18 1926. On October 8 1927, the ship hit rocks off the Grand Jardin lighthouse at the entrance to St Malo but refloated and made port. Later the same year

Above Rina *as the* Algethi, *in the colours of R.H. Penny. When in L & SWR service she had no mizzen mast (John Attwood).*

Bottom Ringwood *at No 1 Berth in Jersey, pictured in 1950 without her mainmast (Author).*

the ship was altered for the transport of export cattle from the Channel Islands, which meant the ship also called at Plymouth and London.

In 1940 the ship was taken over for use as an Auxiliary Net Layer and served most of the War as such.

One of the last SR ships to return to normal service after Second World War, the ship made her first call at Jersey on June 11 1946 and, apart from time taken off during the replacement of her mainmast in 1954, the ship went about her duties until October 9 1959, when she sailed from Jersey on her last voyage to Southampton.

Robert Burns

Owner Commercial Steam Packet Company. **Builder** R. Duncan & Co, Greenock. **Completed** May 1838. **Yard no** n/a. **Tonnage** 1841 309 g,

125 n. **Dimensions** 132.1 (rl) × 19.4 × 10.5 ft. **Propulsion** Paddles (further details n/a). **Speed** n/a.

First registered to an owner at Glasgow in May 1838, the *Robert Burns* was placed on the London register in August 1841 and, in November of the same year, she was registered to Messrs C. Bleaden, J. Harman and J. Whilson (trustees of the Commercial SP Co). In the December of 1841, the ship was first seen at Southampton when she was advertised to be operating a service from that port to Plymouth. She remained on this route until early 1842, when she became part of the South-Western SP fleet and took up service to Le Havre. She also made seven trips to the Channel Islands during the summer, the only time she was seen in the islands. She was not advertised as being in service for the 1843 season and it was not until April 4 1846 that she again appeared on advertisements. She became part of the New South Western SN Co in late 1846, but she was replaced by new tonnage and her registry was closed in February 1852, upon being broken up.

Roebuck (I)

Owner Great Western Railway. **Builder** Naval Construction & Armaments Co Ltd, Barrow. **Completed** June 1897. **Yard no** 256. **Tonnage** 1897 1,281 g, 415 n (altered to 398 n in 1898); 1901 1,186 g, 303 n (altered to 493 n in 1914); 1914 1,094 g, 453 n. **Dimensions** 280.0 (rl) × 34.5 × 16.8 ft. **Propulsion** Twin screw, SR, 3 cyl 23″ 36″ 56″–33″ 5,300 ihp. **Speed** 19 knots.

Launched on March 6 1897, *Roebuck* ran trials on June 1 when she achieved a mean speed of 20.25 knots. Her first duty was to convey the GWR directors to the Naval Review at Spithead on June 25.

Her maiden voyage to the Channel Islands was on July 1, the day the improved 'daylight' service was commenced, but on July 12 the vessel had to proceed to Milford for repairs to her machinery, returning to service on August 23.

With her sister *Reindeer*, she only operated to the islands during the summer months, spending the winters laid up at Milford. During one such period of laying up, on January 26 1905, the ship caught fire and the weight of water used to extinguish the flames caused the ship to sink. She was refloated on February 4 and was back in service on June 1.

In September 1906 the ship sailed from Jersey bound for Fishguard to go on the service to Rosslare, and the next noticeable event that occurred in the ship's life was her spectacular grounding on the Kaines Reef close under the cliffs on Jersey's southwest coast, shortly after leaving St Helier on Wednesday July 19 1911. She remained with her bow high out of the water at low tide until refloated on July 28 and put ashore in St Brelades Bay. On August 14 she was towed to St Helier, having to be beached at Belcroute Bay on the way, and finally left Jersey on August 29 for repairs by Harland & Wolff at Southampton. She returned to service on January 10 1912.

On September 30 1914 the ship made her last service call to the islands before being taken over for government service. She was converted into an armed cruiser and renamed HMS *Roedene*, and as such was at Portland on November 25 1914. The end of the ship came on January 13 1915 when she dragged her anchor when in Scapa Flow and fell across the bows of the old battleship HMS *Imperieuse*, and sank in five fathoms of water. It was stated that the ship was blown up, but her remains were seen during the Second World War.

Roebuck (II)

Owner Great Western Railway. **Builder:** Swan, Hunter & Wigham Richardson Ltd, Newcastle.

A rare shot of Roebuck *(I) at Brest while on the service from Plymouth (A.M.S. Russell).*

Completed April 1925. **Yard no** 1204. **Tonnage** 1925 769 g, 304 n; 1927 776 g, 307 n; 1947 804 g, 310 n; 1950 863 g, 315 n; 1952 866 g, 315 n. **Dimensions** 201.2 (rl) 211.2 (oa) × 33.7 × 15.3 ft. **Propulsion** Twin screw, SR, 3 cyl 14½″ 23″ 38″-27″ 1,350 ihp. **Speed** 13 knots.

Initial design of this ship and of her sister *Sambur*, called for an extra hold aft of the accommodation but, due to the restricted length of the berth in

Jersey, the design was amended and for all their lives the ships appeared to 'sit up' and 'beg'.

The maiden voyage of the ship was from Weymouth to Jersey where she arrived on May 19 1925. She arrived in Guernsey on April 2 1928 after overhaul at Cardiff, where two cabins were made for twelve passengers in the space of the officers' mess, which was moved to the lower deck.

The ship helped at Dunkirk and were taken over by the Admiralty. She was fitted out at Penarth as a barrage-balloon vessel and during 1940–41 accompanied convoys between Sheerness and Southampton. In 1942 the ship was renamed *Roebuck* (II), and was laid up when the barrage balloon unit was disbanded in 1943. In 1944 she was taken over for use by the army, working in connection with restoring the recaptured ports for normal working, as well as working on the Mulberry Harbours.

The ship returned to Jersey for the first time after the war on October 17 1945 and became part of the British Railways fleet on January 1 1948. From 1960, she started calling at Southampton, but ceased to do this at the end of 1963.

The ship remained in service until February 27 1965, when she arrived at Weymouth from Guernsey, staying there until July 29. She then sailed for Sheerness, having been sold to Lacmots for breaking up but, on September 17 1965, she was moved to the Washer Wharf and resold to breakers at Brussels where work commenced in December.

St Andrew (I)

Owner Murray Bros. **Completed** 1881. **Tonnage** 558 g **Dimensions** 190.5 (rl) × 28.9 ft.

This ship took up the GWR service from Weymouth to Cherbourg on March 10 1885, replacing the *Gael* which had boiler trouble. She remained on the route until it closed at the end of June the same year, but the ship had a short life, foundering on July 11 1886 in a position 21° 03′ north 74° 17′ west.

Above left Roebuck *(II) slicing through the water at speed, pictured towards the end of her career on June 14 1962 (Author).*
Left St Andrew *(II), in a unique shot taken in 1928, berthed in Southampton (John Attwood).*
Above St Briac, *gaily bedecked as the Southern Railway cruise ship (A.M.S. Russell).*

St Andrew (II)

Owner Fishguard & Rosslare Railways & Harbour Co. **Built** 1908. **Tonnage** 2,495 g. **Dimensions** 351.1 (rl) × 41.1 ft.

This ship came to the English Channel in July 1923 when she took a party of GWR directors on a fact-finding tour, which commenced at Weymouth then went to the Channel Islands and then to the rest of the company ports, the result of the tour being the harbour improvements and new ships of 1925. The ship was chartered by SR in 1928 to operate the Southampton–Le Havre roster of the *Normannia* from August 11 until September 22, while the latter ship replaced the *Lorina* on the Channel Islands route.

St Briac

Owner Southern Railway. **Builder** Wm Denny & Bros Ltd, Dumbarton. **Completed** September 1924. **Yard no** 1165. **Tonnage** 1924 2,292 g, 918 n; 1938 2,312 g, 938 n. **Dimensions** 316.0 (rl) × 325.0 (oa) × 41.1 × 13.9 ft. **Propulsion** Twin screw, geared turbines 5,200 ihp. **Speed** 19 knots.

Second of two ships ordered by the SR, it was rumoured that she was to be named *Parame*, after the tourist resort next to St Malo, but she was launched as *St Briac* on June 2 1924. She arrived at Southampton on September 10 and made her maiden voyage on the Le Havre route on October 3. She was the running mate of the *Dinard* on the St Malo service, but spent much of her time in the winter on the Le Havre route.

During the winter of 1930–31 the second class accommodation was improved and, at the same time, the open rails round the poop deck were plated in. In 1932, the ship began to operate cruises during the summer months, taking in the French ports of Le Havre, Rouen, Cherbourg and St Malo, and also calling at Jersey and Guernsey. The ship remained with the SR when war broke out in 1939 and worked the Le Havre route. Once, when outward bound on March 13 1940, she was in collision in Southampton Water with the *Somersetshire* and sustained bow damage which took nearly two months to repair. She had just returned to service when the route was closed with the last round voyage being on May 18–19 and then operated the service from St Malo until May 27.

The ship was taken over for war service in June 1941 and, by the end of the year, was working off the east coast of Scotland as a target ship; while on these duties she struck a mine and sank on March 12 1942.

St David (II)

Owner Fishguard & Rosslare Railways & Harbour Co. **Built** 1947. **Tonnage** 3,352 g. **Dimensions** 321' 4" (oa) × 50' 5".

This ship only had one short period on the Weymouth–Channel Islands route from September 4 to October 4 1947, to see if there would be any problems with the introduction of the *St Patrick* on the route the following year.

Top St David *passing La Moye, Jersey, on September 5 1947 (Author).*

Above St Helier *in St Peter Port, as she was built and as she looked until 1927 (Author).*

Left St Helier *entering Weymouth between 1928 and 1936, now a single-funnelled ship (John Attwood).*

St Helier

Owner Great Western Railway. **Builder** John Brown & Co Ltd, Clydebank. **Completed** June 1925. **Yard no** 510. **Tonnage** 1925 1,885 g, 780 n; 1937 1,952 g, 810 n; 1947 1,949 g, 789 n. **Dimensions** 282.2 (rl) 291.5 (oa) × 40.0 × 16.3 ft. **Propulsion** Twin screw, geared turbines 819 nhp. **Speed** 18 knots.

Second of the two passenger ships built for the GWR in 1925, the *St Helier* arrived in the Channel Islands on her maiden voyage on June 17 1925. On April 10 1926, the ship rammed the pierheads at Jersey and was off service for repairs until early May. Two years later, on April 11 1928, the ship arrived in the islands having had one funnel removed and internal alterations made. Further work to the accommodation was made in 1937, with the first-class saloon being extended to the full width of the ship and the large windows in this area being replaced by fewer smaller ones. At the same time, the remaining funnel was shortened by four and a half feet and a bonnet fitted.

Withdrawn from the Channel Islands route after September 9 1939, she was used on Government work to many places along the French coast and helped with the evacuation at Dunkirk. Taken over by the Admiralty in November 1940, she was converted into a landing ship in 1942 and took the Canadians to the Normandy landing beaches in 1944. On May 12 1945 she arrived off St Peter Port with the command personnel for the liberation of Guernsey and, on July 16 1945 was in collision off the Nore with the collier *Lightfoot*. This caused the ship to be put into dry dock on August 8 and, on August 14 the ship was handed back to the GWR. Converted into a troopship, she commenced service on November 15 from Harwich to the Hook, remaining there until March 17 1946 when she sailed for Newport for conversion back to a mailboat.

She received a great welcome on June 13 1946, when she arrived back at Weymouth, and on Sunday June 16 she was once again back in the Channel Islands with a red funnel which had a thin black top-band, while the hull as in pre-war days was all black. A thick black top-band was added later to the funnel and, at the same time, the forecastle had half a strake painted white.

The ship became part of the British Railways fleet on January 1 1948, under the control of the Western Region. Thus when the ship returned to service on May 31 her funnel was yellow and the white paint of the superstructure had been taken down to main deck level. On November 1 1948, control of the ship passed to the Southern Region and twelve years later she was called upon to undertake the service

from Jersey to St Malo on December 20 1958, when the *Normannia* had been unable to made the trip.

In 1959 the ship lost half a strake of her white paint. With new ships building for the route, the *St Helier* sailed on her last mail service from the islands on September 12 1960, while her last duty was an excursion from Torquay to Guernsey on the 14th. Sold to Belgian ship-breakers, the ship arrived at Antwerp on December 19 1960 in the tow of the tug *Schouwenbank*.

St Julien

Owner Great Western Railway. **Builder** John Brown & Co Ltd, Clydebank. **Completed** May 1925. **Yard no** 509. **Tonnage** 1925 1,885 g, 780 n; 1937 1,952 g, 811 n; 1947 1,943 g, 785 n. **Dimensions** 282.2 (rl) 291.5 (oa) × 40.0 × 16.3 ft. **Propulsion** Twin screw, geared turbines 819 nhp. **Speed** 18 knots.

Part of the GWR 1923 modernisation programme, this ship was launched on February 24 1925 and arrived in the Channel Islands on her maiden voyage on Sunday, May 24 1925. As built, the ship had two funnels and the masters suggested, in an effort to improve the handling, the removal of the aft one. To show how the ship would look one of them would always complete the company's jigsaw of the ship minus the aft stack! The hint was taken and, on June 3 1928, the ship arrived back in the Channel Islands with only one funnel, without the high aft docking bridge and with improvements in the saloons. As such the ships were fine-looking vessels, but on February 26 1937, after further improvements to the accommodation, the ship returned to service with four and a half foot cut from the top of the funnel and with an added cowl, which gave a most unbalanced aspect to the ship.

Her last sailing before the Second World War was on September 9 1939; in October she was converted at Southampton into a Hospital Carrier. The work completed, she went to Newhaven and took part in the evacuation at Dunkirk before going north to work at Scapa Flow. On June 25 1942 the ship sailed from Glasgow for the Mediterranean, not returning to Britain until April 20 1944, when she arrived at Penarth. In late 1945 the ship was operating out of Southampton, still on Government work, and only in January the following year was the ship released, going to Penarth to be refitted.

She arrived in the islands on her first post-war voyage on December 1 1946, sporting a red funnel with a thick black top-band and a forecastle smartened up with a strake of white, and on January 1 1948 became part of the British Railways Western Region fleet. When she returned to service on June 1 her funnel was yellow and the hull had an

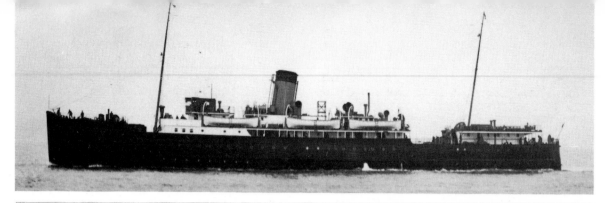

extra strake of white. On November 1 1948 she was transferred to the Southern Region of British Railways.

On September 8 1957, the ship replaced the *Brittany* on a day excursion from Jersey to St Malo.

Three years later the ship came to the end of her career. Her last trip from the Channel Islands was on September 27 1960. She sailed bedecked with bunting and, at St Peter Port, her name pennant was presented to the Maritime Museum. The ship remained laid up until April 1961 when she was sold to Belgian ship-breakers and arrived at Ghent on April 14.

Saint Malo

Owner London & South Western Railway. **Builder** Aitken & Mansel, Whiteinch, Glasgow. **Completed** October 1865. **Yard no** n/a. **Tonnage** 1865 301 g, 210 n (altered to 171n in 1867); 1884 309 g, 154 n (altered to 145 n in 1885); 1889 304 g, 141 n; 1895 325 g, 151 n; 1899 318 g, 137 n. **Dimensions** 161.0 (rl) × 22.25 × 12.15 ft. **Propulsion** Single screw, SR, 1865 2 cyl; 1873 2 cyl 25″ 50″–30″ 90 hp. **Speed** 12 knots.

The first screw-propelled vessel to be built for the

Top St Julien *as she appeared between the years 1937 and 1939 (John Attwood).*
Above St Julien *off Jersey on July 12 1948. She had a yellow funnel at this time (Author).*
Top right Saint Malo *sitting high out of the water at low tide in Honfleur (John Attwood).*
Above right St Patrick (I) *worked on the Southampton–Le Havre route in 1923 (John Attwood).*

L & SWR, she was launched on August 8 1865 and ran trials on September 27 when she made 12.25 knots on the measured mile. She took up service on the route to St Malo and, from November 1 1865, she operated to St Malo via Jersey, maintaining this service until May the following year, the only period for which she did this. Replaced by the larger *Caesarea* in 1867, the *Saint Malo* then spent most of her time on the shorter routes to Normandy but helped out on the St Malo and Channel Islands routes as required.

In 1882, 1883 and from 1887, the ship came to Jersey nearly every year to provide relief cover for the ships based there. In 1899, however the ship was converted into a pure cargo vessel. On November 15 1905, she was sold to James Power & Co for £300

but the ship remained in Southampton and was not registered to the new owner. Through a bill of sale dated May 31 1906, the ship passed to Mr J. Constant. In fact, the ship had already been towed from Southampton on May 21 bound for Holland where she was broken up.

St Patrick (I)

Owner Fishguard & Rosslare Railway & Harbour Co. **Built** 1906. **Tonnage** 2,531 g. **Dimensions** 350.8 (rl) × 41.1 ft.

This ship was chartered for service at Southampton from July 15 1923 at a cost of £450 per week to replace the *Hantonia* on the Le Havre service. The *Hantonia* replaced the *Caesarea* on the Channel Islands route, as the latter had struck a rock and been withdrawn from service. The charter lasted for two months.

St Patrick (II)

Owner Fishguard & Rosslare Railways & Harbour Co. **Builder** Alexander Stephen & Sons Ltd, Glasgow. **Completed** March 1930. **Yard no** 525. **Tonnage** 1,922 g, 792 n. **Dimensions** 281.3 (rl) × 41.1 × 16.3 ft. **Propulsion** Twin screw, geared turbines, 887 nhp. **Speed** 18 knots.

Built as a relief vessel for both the Irish and Channel Islands service, this ship was launched by a Mrs Milne on January 15 1930. Her maiden voyage to the islands was on April 18 and she remained on the route until early September, after which she only came to Weymouth for July and August each year, though her stay was sometimes extended by a week or so.

On Friday August 5 1932, the ship sailed from Weymouth at 1:39 pm on a direct Jersey sailing and, during a foggy approach to the island, hit rocks off Corbière and was disabled. The local tug, *Duke of Normandy*, and the *Isle of Sark* came out from St Helier and took off the passengers, and the *St Julien* which was anchored off Guernsey at the time also went to the scene. The *St Julien* later towed the *St Patrick* to St Aubin's Bay, from where she was taken into port by the *Princess Ena*. After inspection, the tug *Seaman* towed the ship to England where repairs were effected.

In 1937, the ship had an extended period on the route as, due to the *St Helier* being at Penarth for improvements, the ship commenced service early on May 16. The ship left the Channel Islands for the last time on September 2 1939, and was bombed and sunk near Fishguard on June 13 1941.

Above *A fine picture of* St Patrick *(II) showing her at speed off Corbière (Author).*

Left St Patrick *(III) operating the winter service, pictured on October 9 1959; her funnel was red at this time (Author).*

Above right Sambur *seen departing from Jersey (Photo by Dave Hocquard).*

St Patrick (III)

Owner Fishguard & Rosslare Railways & Harbours Co. **Builder** Cammell Laird & Co Ltd, Birkenhead. **Completed** January 1948. **Yard no** 1183. **Tonnage** 1948 3,482 g, 1,402 n; 1961 3,460 g, 1,318 n. **Dimensions** 300′ 0″ (bp) 321′ 4″ (oa) × 50′ 5″ × 13′ 3″ draft. **Propulsion** Twin screw, geared turbines 8,500 shp. **Speed** 19 knots

Built to replace her namesake, this ship was launched on May 20 1947. Her maiden voyage from Weymouth to the Channel Islands was on February 4 1948. Being owned by the Fishguard & Rosslare Railways & Harbours Co the ship was not part of British Railways and thus continued to wear her red funnel, while the GWR house flag was replaced by the former company's own flag. She remained on the route until October 26 and then went to Fishguard. On January 1 1950, the management of the ship passed from the Western Region of British Railways to the London Midland Region, but this did not stop the vessel moving round to Weymouth each summer. At the end of the 1953 summer the ship had a two-week spell on the Southampton–Le Havre route from September 14, covering for the *Normannia*.

The ship also had a spell on the Holyhead–Dun Laoghaire service in 1950 and 1951, but the major change took place at the end on the 1959 summer season, when the ship remained on the Weymouth station to become part of the reorganisation of the

Channel Islands services. The ship was officially transferred to BR on December 17 1959 and, following her refit early in 1960, she returned to service on February 27 in full BR livery with a yellow funnel. In the May of 1960 she again helped out on the Le Havre route. Following the introduction of the new *Caesarea* in December 1960, the ship proceeded to Cardiff where she was converted into a single-class vessel to bring her into line with the new service to the Channel Islands which was to commence on May 13 1961. At the same time the black paintwork was carried up an extra half strake, and gone was the graceful, red-funnelled ship, which for so many years had been the pride of the Channel Islands.

The new single-class service based at Weymouth required the third ship only at weekends and thus the *St Patrick* spent the rest of the week operating day excursions from Weymouth and Torquay to Guernsey. Following the sale of the *Brittany* early in 1963, the *St Patrick* was used to operate a service between Jersey and St Malo. With the cut-back in services from Southampton, *Normannia* was required for conversion into a car ferry, with the result that *St Patrick* moved from Weymouth to Southampton in October 1963 and took over the Le Havre service on December 5. The Le Havre route was closed on May 10 1954 and the ship then operated the service to St Malo in place of the *Falaise*, as well as making trips from Jersey to St Malo and Weymouth to St Malo, and also working some day trips from Weymouth to Guernsey — a very complicated timetable! At the end of the season she closed the St Malo route on September 27 1964 and, the next day, sailed from Southampton for Newhaven,

where she was overhauled. During overhaul, she was the first Southern Region vessel to be painted in the new livery, and was then dry docked and altered before arriving at Dover in December where she replaced the *Canterbury*.

It was not the last that the Channel Islands saw of the ship, however, as she replaced the damaged *Caesarea* in August 1968 and, in April 1969, she carried a charter from St Malo to Jersey. Additionally, in May 1970 she operated a couple of excursions from Guernsey to Jersey and from the latter to St Malo in May. The last time she visited Jersey was in May 1971 when she operated for a week from St Malo carrying parties of French schoolchildren. Her last departure from Jersey was on May 8 1971; she then went back to Dover where her last season ended on September 26 and she arrived at Newhaven on September 29 to await sale.

On March 9 1972, she was renamed *Thermopilae*, having been sold to Gerasimos S. Fetouris, a Greek shipowner, and left Newhaven the same day for Piraeus where she arrived on March 28. She operated a service from Greece to Italy but, early in 1973, she was sold to Agapitos Bros, who renamed her *Agapitos I* and used her in the Greek Islands.

She was only slightly altered for her Mediterranean service, the upper deck being extended to the stern, but she did not remain long in service being withdrawn and laid up in 1976, and she passed into the hands of the shipbreakers at Piraeus early in 1980.

Sambur

Owner Great Western Railway. **Builder** Swan, Hunter & Wigham Richardson Ltd, Newcastle.

Completed May 1925. **Yard no** 1206. **Tonnage** 1925 769 g, 304 n; 1927 776 g, 311 n; 1947 801 g, 305 n; 1949 861 g, 320 n. **Dimensions** 201.2 (rl) 210.0 (oa) × 33.7 × 15.3 ft. **Propulsion** Twin screw, SR, 3 cyl 14½" 23" 38"–27" 1,350 ihp, **Speed** 13 knots.

Like her sister *Roebuck*, the *Sambur* was initially conceived as being longer than she was when she arrived in Guernsey on her maiden voyage on May 25 1925. Both ships had alterations made to their accommodation in 1928, both helped in the evacuation of France in 1940, and both became barrage-balloon ships in 1940. She was renamed *Toreador* in 1942 and laid up when the barrage-balloon unit was disbanded in 1943. She was used by the Army's Royal Engineers for Mulberry-Harbour work and also for the recommissioning of the French ports.

The ship was the first GWR vessel to visit Jersey after the war when she arrived on September 19 1945. In September 1947, the ship sustained damage when entering Weymouth and had to be towed to Penarth by the tug *Empire Sanoy* for repairs; she returned to service in mid-December.

She passed to British Railways in January 1948 and from 1960 to 1963 also made calls at Southampton. Her last voyage was from Guernsey to Weymouth on March 29 1964. The ship was then laid up at Southampton, which she left on June 10 1964, under the tow of the tug *Pool Zee*, to be broken up in Holland.

Sarnia (I)

Owner London & South Western Railway. **Builder** Cammell Laird & Co Ltd, Birkenhead. **Completed** April 1911. **Yard no** 335. **Tonnage** 1911 1,498 g, 598 n; 1911 1,503 g, 600 n; 1912 1,498 g, 598 n. **Dimensions** 284.65 (rl) 296.0 (oa) × 39.15 × 15.8 ft. **Propulsion** Triple screw, direct-drive turbines 6,350 ihp. **Speed** 19 knots.

Sister to the *Caesarea*, this ship was due for delivery by March 30 1910 but, due to strikes at the yard, her entry into service was delayed by a full year. It was intended to name the ship *Gallia*, but this was not approved, and she was launched as *Sarnia* by a Mrs H. Pollitt on July 9 1910. Initial trials were run on December 23 1910, but the troubles experienced by the *Caesarea* led to modifications being carried out, and final trials were held in the Mersey on April 3 1911.

The ship arrived in the Channel Islands on her maiden voyage on April 13, but spent very little time on the route as, due to their heavy fuel consumption, she and her sister usually spent the winter laid up off Netley in Southampton Water. The *Sarnia* would be overhauled in time to operate to the Channel Islands in April and May each year, before taking up station on the St Malo route for the summer, at the end of which she was again laid up. In May 1912 extra life-saving equipment was added to the ship, and this included two lifeboats on the bridge deck but these caused the ship to roll even more than before.

With the outbreak of war, the ship made her last trip from the islands on November 20 1914, and was then taken over by the Admiralty and converted into an Armed Boarding Vessel by Harland & Wolff at Southampton. These duties ceased in late 1915, and the ship was converted into a transport and sent to the Mediterranean, where on October 29 1915 she collided with and sank the Dover-based railway cargo steamer *Hythe* off Cape Helles. In May 1916 the ship was mentioned in despatches for her work as a ferry steamer plying between Mudros and the Peninsular carrying troops and military stores. Her

Sarnia (I) entering St Peter Port. Note the lifeboats on the bridge deck (A.M.S. Russell).

master at this time was Commander H.G. Muir.

Her end came in the evening of September 12 1918 when, shortly after leaving Alexandria, she was torpedoed. The ship was in railway service for only three and a half years, one of the shortest periods on record.

Sarnia (II)

Operator British Railways. **Builder** J. Samuel White & Co Ltd, Cowes. **Completed** June 1961. **Yard no** 2009. **Tonnage** 1961 4,174 g, 2,271 n; 1969 3,989 g, 2,072 n. **Dimensions** 302′ 0″ (bp) 322′ 0″ (oa) × 52″7″ × 13′ 7½″ draft. **Propulsion** Twin screw, geared turbines 8,500 shp. **Speed** 18 knots.

The last ship to have been specifically built for the Channel Islands passenger services, *Sarnia* was launched on September 6 1960 and, after a VIP call at Guernsey on June 14 1961, arrived in the islands on her maiden voyage on June 17. The one major incident during her life occurred soon afterwards when, on December 9 1961, while she was entering St Peter Port she hit the quay, cutting a large hole in the hull on the starboard side.

From April 12 to 17 1962, the ship was at Folkestone covering for the *Canterbury* and she was at Dover from November 19 1962 to January 30 1963, operating the Golden Arrow service. She had one other short period operating at Folkestone over Easter 1967.

Early in 1971, the ship had internal improvements made including extra seating, some of which was put forward on the boat deck, protected by newly fitted draught doors, as can be seen from photographs, just forward of the bridge.

When the multi-purpose service was introduced in 1976, the ship was kept to help out at peak times and operate some excursions, but in her last few years in service she suffered from turbine trouble several times.

Her last regular service voyage to the Channel Islands was on Sunday September 4 1977 and her last call at Guernsey was on Saturday September 10, when she operated an excursion.

She was sold the following year to Supasave Supermarkets (Midland) Ltd of Guernsey and sailed from Weymouth on May 24 1978 for Hull, where she was converted into a floating supermarket and renamed *Aquamart*. She was operated by Channel Cruises Ltd of Guernsey and entered service on July 24 1978 based in Ostend, but the venture failed and she was laid up in London on August 4. Sold at the end of the year, she left London in tow on January 20 1979 under the name *Golden Star*, given by her new owners, Grecian Fertility Inc, of Greece. Late in 1981 she was sold to Hitta Establishment of Saudi Arabia and renamed *Saudi Golden Star*, and as such operates from Port Said to Aqaba and Jeddah. She was seen at Suez by a Jersey resident, early in 1982, in a very poor condition.

Selby

Operator British Railways. **Builder** James Lamont & Co Ltd, Port Glasgow. **Completed** June 1959. **Yard no** 395. **Tonnage** 1970 963 g, 375 n. **Dimensions** 215' 0" (bp) 232' 1" (oa) × 39' 5" × 13' 2¾" draft. **Propulsion** Single screw, 7-cyl oil engine 1,880 bhp. **Speed** 12.5 knots.

Built in 1959 for the Associated Humber Lines Ltd, for their services to the Continent from Goole, the *Selby* remained with them until March 1965 when, due to a reduction in services, she was transferred to British Rail, London Midland Region, and converted at Holyhead into a container vessel. She returned to service after this work and was placed on the Heysham–Belfast route.

Having been replaced by a larger vessel, she came south to Southampton where she replaced the *Winchester* on the service to the Channel Islands, her first visit being to Jersey on December 31 1970. She spent the next two years mainly working out of Southampton but, with the introduction of the new *Fisher*-class boats early in 1972, she switched to Weymouth where she was used to transport tomatoes from Guernsey. Being a single-screw ship she proved to be something of a handful in the Channel Islands harbours, proving the point on January 23 1971 when, while she was leaving the harbour in Jersey in gale force winds, she was blown ashore; this caused damage to her rudder and she

had to be towed to England for repair.

It was decided that from 1973 a chartered vessel would be used to cater for the BR tomato traffic to Weymouth and so, after spending the first week of October 1972 standing in for the *Jersey Fisher* on the new service to Portsmouth, the ship worked the last few weeks of tomato traffic, leaving Guernsey for the last time on October 20 at 8:35 pm with 25,836 trays of fruit.

She was sold ten days later to a Mr H.G. Pounds of Portsmouth and left Weymouth the same day to lay up there. She was sold early the following year to a Mr W.J. Sutton and registered in Panama, and arrived at London from Portsmouth on April 1. She was renamed *Raven* in January 1974, and in 1975 was sold to Ocean Services International Inc also of Panama, who resold her in 1977 to Trevelen Nav Inc which renamed her *Jean R*. Late in 1980 she passed to United Shipping Co SA, which renamed her *Victory*, but she soon passed to the Alkinoos Shipping Co, which resold her late in 1982 to the Phoenix Shipping Co of Greece and she is now named *Agios Nikolaos*.

Snaefell

Owner Isle of Man Steam Packet Co. **Built** 1876. **Tonnage** 786 g. **Dimensions** 251.3 (rl) × 29.3 ft.

This ship arrived in the Channel Islands on September 10 1890 to replace the *Lynx* for ten days.

South of Ireland

Owner Great Western Railway. **Builder** W. Simons & Co, Renfrew. **Completed** July 1867. **Yard no** n/a. **Tonnage** 1873 475 g, 299 n; 1879 483 g, 279 n; 1881 498 g, 239 n; 1883 502 g, 214 n. **Dimensions** 220.2 (rl) × 25.8 × 12.4 ft. **Propulsion** Paddle, 2 cyl 50" 50"–48" 200 hp. **Speed** n/a.

This vessel was built for Ford & Jackson, when they operated steamer services for the GWR, and was acquired by the railway company in February 1872, when they had been granted powers to operate steamship services. The ship came to Weymouth when the service to Cherbourg was commenced on August 1 1878, but was lost at Warbarrow near Lulworth on December 25 1883 when inward bound to Weymouth.

Southampton

Owner London & South Western Railway. **Builder** Palmer Bros & Co, Jarrow. **Completed** September 1860. **Yard no** n/a. **Tonnage** 1860 475 g, 299 n; 1880 611 g, 356 n; 1888 585 g, 341 n; 1894 614 g, 358 n. **Dimensions** 1860 215.5 (rl) × 25.4 × 12.7 ft; 1880 236.1 (rl) × 25.4 × 12.9 ft. **Propulsion** Paddle, 1860 2 cyl 60" 60"–60" (hp n/a); 1880 2 cyl 40" 68"–60" (hp n/a). **Speed** 13.5 knots.

Above Snaefell, *which ran from Weymouth in 1890 (John Attwood).*

Below South of Ireland, *one of the ships that helped open the Weymouth–Cherbourg route of the GWR in 1878 (John Attwood).*

Above *Seen in her original form, with two funnels and no forecastle,* Southampton *lies alongside in St Helier, 1871 (John Attwood).*

Below Southampton *arrives at Le Havre in her final form (John Attwood).*

Last of the traditional clipper-bowed paddle steamers to be built for railway service, this ship was launched on April 5 1860 and underwent trials on September 24, but these were not a great success as the ship made only 13.06 knots. Further trials were held two weeks later, when a speed of 13.75 knots was achieved, and the ship made her maiden voyage to the Channel Islands on October 13. In November 1864 the *Normandy* entered service and this allowed the *Southampton* to be switched to the Le Havre route, though she acted as relief ship to the islands as required. She returned to the Channel Islands route in June 1870 and, five years later, underwent a major refit during which a forecastle was added and her funnels altered after work on her boilers.

She was withdrawn from service in December 1879 for major work to be carried out; the hull was lengthened by twenty feet and a new engine and boilers were installed. The latter alterations resulted in the removal of the fore funnel, which made her easily distinguishable from the other twin-funnelled units of the fleet when she re-entered service to the Channel Islands on June 26 1880. She remained on this station till August 7 1883, when she again moved to the Le Havre route, where she remained until June 1894. She then took up the Cherbourg service and she last appeared in the Southampton

papers on August 21 1897, and was then sold to Mr J. Constant, who in turn resold her to a Mr A.F. Yarrow for use as an accommodation ship in February 1898. Later in the same year she was sold to F. Rijadijk (ship-breakers) and was broken up in Holland.

South-Western (I)
Owner South Western Steam Packet Company. **Builder** Ditchburn & Mare, Blackwall. **Completed** June 1843. **Yard no** n/a. **Tonnage** 1843 204 g, 132 n; 1857 167 g, 105 n. **Dimensions** 143.0 (rl) × 18.0 × 10.8 ft. **Propulsion** Paddle (further details n/a), 90 hp. **Speed** n/a.

This ship has a special place in the history of the L & SWR shipping fleet, as she was the first vessel built after they had financed the setting up of the South-Western SP Co. She made a demonstration trip from Southampton on July 10 1843 and a trial to Le Havre on the 13th and later, on July 26, a voyage to Guernsey. Her first commercial voyage to the Channel Islands arrived on August 1.

During the summer she made two trips a week to Le Havre and one to the Channel Islands, a schedule which was repeated the following year. With the company gaining the Royal Mail contract for the Channel Islands in 1845 the ship remained entirely on this route until the end of 1846. The summer of 1848 saw the ship operate the Poole–Channel Islands–St Malo service and from 1849 to

A sketch of South-Western *(I) as a paddle-steamer, dated September 23 1850 (Author).*

An Ouless sketch of South-Western *(I) ready to sail to Singapore and China, dated August 29 1863 (Société Jersiaise).*

1851 she was based in Jersey during the summer, operating services to France and excursions. At the end of the summer of 1850 the ship had commenced a service between Weymouth and the islands, but this only lasted to the end of the year. From 1852, her only visits to the islands were as relief vessel on the cheap-boat service or on the Weymouth route, which had been reactivated in 1857. Her last service call was on August 25 1860.

She next appeared in Jersey on February 27 1863, having been purchased by Esnouf & Mauger, the local shipowners and shipbuilders, and after a refit and the addition of extra sail, she underwent trials on August 6 1863 when she went to Sark for the day. The paddle floats sponson boxes and funnel were then removed, and the ship sailed from the Channel Islands on August 30 as a barque, bound for Singapore where she arrived on January 12 1864. Her steaming gear was then put back into order, and she traded between Hong Kong and China till September 1865 when she was sold at Shanghai. The only other reference concerning the ship is from a newspaper dated February 17 1869, which states that the *South-Western*, now named *Sud Veste* and now under the Spanish flag, rescued the crew of HMS *Gnat* which was lost on the Balabec Islands in the China Sea on November 15 1868.

South-Western (II)

Owner London & South Western Railway, **Builder** J. & W. Dudgeon, London. **Completed** December 1874. **Yard no** n/a. **Tonnage** 1874 657 g, 364 n (altered to 326 n in 1884); 1887 661 g, 329 n; 1888 639 g, 307 n; 1890 705 g, 290 n (altered to 284 n in 1890); 1903 702 g, 269 n (altered to 295 n in 1914);

1914 674 g, 287 n. **Dimensions** 222.3 (rl) × 27.1 × 13.5 ft. **Propulsion** Single screw, SR, 1874 2 cyl 35" 67"–39" 1,100 ihp, 1888 2 cyl 33¾" 67"–39"; 1890 3 cyl 22" 35½" 60"–39" 1,447 ihp. **Speed** 14 knots.

Built for the St Malo service, this ship was a larger edition of the *Guernsey* and, before her launch, it was said that she would be named *Jersey* though this obviously did not occur. She underwent trials on December 28 1874 and then took up her intended service. Her first visit to the Channel Islands was on March 31 1875, when she arrived on the mail run for a trial period and thereby proved that a screw vessel could maintain the service, which led to the building of the *Diana*.

For all her life she remained linked to the St Malo route, though, when she was replaced later by bigger ships during the summer period, she would work other routes, and return to the St Malo service for the winter. In 1890, the ship was given a major overhaul, during which triple-expansion machinery was installed, together with a new boiler; later, in 1906, electric light was fitted and her deck-house was enlarged to provide four two-berth cabins.

The only time that the ship saw any regular service in the islands was for the summers of 1904 and 1906, when she was stationed in Jersey to operate the French services.

In late 1913 plans were drawn up for a replacement vessel, but the First World War overtook any such new building, and the ship remained in ser-

Passengers crowd the deck of South-Western (II) *as she enters St Helier in 1904 (Author).*

vice. She had the distinction of operating the Channel Islands mail service in November 1915 and again in the same month the following year. Her end came on March 16 1918 when she was torpedoed eleven miles south-west of St Catherine's Point, in the Isle of Wight. Twenty-five of the 31 personnel on board were lost.

Stella steaming away from Guernsey shortly after being built (John Attwood).

Stella

Owner London & South Western Railway. **Builder** J. & G. Thomson Ltd, Clydebank. **Completed** October 1890. **Yard no** 252. **Tonnage** 1,059 g, 193 n. **Dimensions** 253.0 (rl) 259.0 (oa) × 35.1 × 14.8 ft. **Propulsion** Twin screw, SR, 3 cyl 24″ 37″ 56″–33″ 5,700 ihp. **Speed** 19 knots.

The name of this vessel still lives on in shipping circles due to her tragic loss in 1899.

Built in 1890 as the third ship of the *Frederica* class, she reached Southampton on October 24 and, on November 6, arrived in the Channel Islands on her maiden voyage. When leaving Jersey on November 24 1890 in a gale, the cover of the high-pressure

cylinder of the port engine blew off, and the vessel had to remain at the island till December 1.

In late 1896 there were rumours that the ship was to be lengthened, to increase her speed, but this did not take place, though repairs costing £2,300 were carried out.

It was on Maundy Thursday, March 30 1899, that the ship performed a daylight crossing from Southampton, leaving at 11:40 a.m. Fog was encountered during the crossing, and having run her time to the Casquets the order was given to reduce speed, but at the same moment rocks were sighted and the ship struck them at nearly full speed. Of those on board, 112 were saved, but 105 lives were lost. If nothing else, this tragedy brought about the end of the racing between the rival companies' ships and the setting up of the joint service.

Svea Drott
Owner Stockholms Rederi A/B Svea. **Built** 1966. **Tonnage** 4,018 g. **Dimensions** 325′ 5″ (oa) × 59′ 6″.

Svea Drott leaving Jersey on August 21 1974 (Author).

This ship was chartered at short notice to replace the *Falaise*, and sailed from Oskarshamn on August 16 1974, arriving at Weymouth at noon on the 19th and taking that afternoon's sailing, The charter was for 35 days, but this was extended and she left the Channel Islands for the last time as *Svea Drott* on September 26. So pleased were British Rail with the ship, that she was purchased in December 1974 and taken over at Helsingborg on January 10 1975, when she was renamed *Earl Godwin*. (See *Earl Godwin* entry for further information.)

Tonbridge
Owner Southern Railway, Dover. **Built** 1929. **Tonnage** 683 g. **Dimensions** 220.4 (rl) × 33.6 ft.

The *Tonbridge* operated to the Channel Islands in 1932, to help out at the height of the produce season, and also made a couple of trips the following year.

Tonbridge *on the Channel Islands service in 1932 (John Attwood).*

Transit

Owner Commercial Steam Packet Company.
Builder T.E. Snook, Millwall. **Completed** (month n/a) 1836. **Yard no** n/a. **Tonnage** 267 g, 160 n.
Dimensions 126.0 (rl) × 19.6 × 13.0 ft. **Propulsion** Paddle (further details n/a). **Speed** n/a.

Built for the British & Foreign SN Co, the ship was launched in July 1835 and delivered to her owners in January 1836. In January 1837 she passed to the Commercial SP Co and in the September of that year she commenced calling at Southampton on her service between London and the Iberian Peninsular. That service ceased in September 1838 and, the following summer, the ship was placed on the service from Southampton to the Channel Islands. In late August 1839, the ship commenced a service from London to the islands which was not a great success and ceased in February 1841. She then helped out on the Southampton route during the summer.

The ship was one of the vessels which was taken over by the South-Western SP Co when it was formed in 1842. She was the first vessel to carry the official mail when the company gained the contract in 1845, but she was replaced by newer ships after May 10. The following year saw the ship on a direct Portsmouth–Le Havre service and little was seen of the ship in the Channel Islands until February 2

1851, when she commenced a cheap-boat cargo service, which she maintained till October 31 1855. Nothing more was then seen of the ship in the Channel Islands and her register was closed on August 23 1869, as the ship had been converted into a coal hulk. The last mention of the ship was in November 1882 when she sank due to a collision.

Ulrica

Owner Lonon & South Western Railway. **Builder** Ailsa Shipbuilding Co, Troon. **Completed** (month n/a) 1895. **Yard no** 49. **Tonnage** 1916 383 g, 157 n (altered to 151 n in 1916). **Dimensions** 149.9 (rl) 156.0 (oa) × 24.1 × 7.7 ft. **Propulsion** Single screw, SR, 3 cyl 15″ 23″ 39″–24″ 500 ihp. **Speed** 11.5 knots.

This ship was built as the *Granuaile* in 1895 for the Congested Ports of Ireland (sic—her owners) and remained with them until 1915 when she passed to P. Morrison of Glasgow. It was reported that the ship had been arrested for gun-running, but in any case the ship did not remain long with her new owner as she was sold the following year to R.E.V. James Ltd (later to become James Dredging), which in turn leased her to the L & SWR in April 1916 with an option to purchase, this being taken up in July of that year. It was intended to rename the ship *Roxana* but this was not approved, and the ship was renamed *Ulrica* in early September 1916. As a cargo vessel she was an unusual ship in having much accommodation on the upper deck, as well as boasting a very large saloon on the main deck.

Above Ulrica *alongside the jetty in the Outer Dock at Southampton (John Attwood).*

Left Vena, *as* Algeiba, *leaving Hull on June 28 1922, with her funnel painted in L & SWR colours prior to delivery at Southampton (John Attwood).*

Above right Vena *in Southampton Docks in 1923 (Captain R. Large).*

Her first voyage to Guernsey was on April 13 1916. While approaching that port on March 10 1923 she hit the Roustel Rock and barely managed to make harbour, with her holds full of water. 1923 also saw the ship altered for the better conveyance of cattle, and, on this export trade from the islands, the ship visited Plymouth, Southampton and London. She remained in service until June 26 1928, when she was sold to the Dutch ship-breaker, T.C. Pas, together with two paddle steamers for £2,350.

Vena

Owner London & South Western Railway. **Builder** Scott & Sons, Bowling. **Completed** May 1902. **Yard no** 151. **Tonnage** 565 g, 229 n. **Dimensions** 170.4 (rl) × 27.2 × 11.4 ft. **Propulsion** Single screw, SR, 3 cyl 14" 22½" 37"–27" 500 ihp. **Speed** 10.5 knots.

Built in 1902 as the *Clarence* for J. Rank Ltd of Hull, this ship passed in 1907 to R.H. Penny & Sons of Shoreham who renamed the ship *Algeiba*.

By a bill of sale dated June 29 1922 the ship passed to the L & SWR, which in October renamed her *Vena*. At the same time the ship was equipped with electricity, but she did not stay long with the L & SWR, being passed to the SR the following year, and on February 18 1926 she was sold to York Line Ltd. Five days later they resold her to Wilson & Reid Ltd of Belfast and she remained with them

until late 1928, when she passed to V. & S. Castella and was renamed *Rabat*. She remained in Lloyds Register until the 1954–55 edition.

Vera

Owner London & South Western Railway. **Builder** Clydebank Engineering & Shipbuilding Co Ltd, Clydebank. **Completed** September 1898. **Yard no** 330. **Tonnage** 1898 1,136 g, 227 n; 1903 1,178 g, 256 n (altered to 253 n in 1904); 1914 1,178 g, 487 n; 1914 1,088 g, 447 n; 1832 1,063 g, 424 n. **Dimensions** 270.0 (rl) 280.5 (oa) × 35.5 × 14.9 ft. **Propulsion** Twin screw, SR, 4 cyl 19½" 31" 35" 35"–27" 4,500 ihp. **Speed** 18 knots.

Built in 1898 to replace the *Dora* as relief vessel for both the Le Havre and Channel Islands routes, the *Vera* was without doubt one of the finest-looking vessels in the fleet. Her maiden voyage was to the Channel Islands on September 27 1898 and after a short spell there she moved to the Le Havre route. With the loss of the *Stella* early in 1899, the ship spent all of that year on the Channel Islands route and it was not until *Alberta* arrived in mid-1900 that the ship settled to her planned work.

The summer of 1902 saw the ship work the St Malo route and, to fit her better for this crossing, alterations were made early in 1903. A smoke-room was built aft on the boat deck, the latter had rails placed round it so that passengers could use the area and the bridge was moved up one deck. Forced draught was also removed, thus reducing her speed, and the ship was seen little on the islands route for a number of years. Early in 1910, further alterations were made to the ship. The forward end of the promenade deck was plated in, a poop added aft with two lifeboats on it and forced draught was re-introduced, and the ship reached a speed of 18.275 knots on trials held on February 14.

The ship remained with the company during the First World War and, apart from late 1914 and early 1915 when she was loaned to the GWR to relieve the *Ibex* at Weymouth, acted as relief for both the Le Havre and Channel Islands routes.

After the war the *Vera*, like others in the fleet, was given a major overhaul and, leaving the islands on April 5 1920, she proceeded to Birkenhead where new boilers and a 'thermo-tank' ventilation system were installed, and major hull-bottom repairs were carried out. The ship returned to the Channel Islands route on November 11 1920 and, since *Lorina* had replaced her on the St Malo route, she became a permanent ship on the islands station. In 1924, further plating in on the promenade deck took place, the forward end now being total enclosed, and the open rails were also plated in. She remained on the route till March 10 1930 when she sailed for the last time as a regular mail vessel, acting there-

after as extra vessel when required.

In March 1926 the ship had another short spell on the GWR Weymouth–Channel Islands route, due to both the *St Helier* and the *Reindeer* having hit the pierheads at Jersey. The *Vera* arrived 'light' in Jersey on March 13 and took that day's sailing to Weymouth, as well as the service which arrived in the Channel Islands on Sunday the 14th. She took the Tuesday sailing to Weymouth and in the evening returned to Southampton.

When in 1932 the Southern Railway re-opened the Jersey–St Malo route, the *Vera* was the ship selected for the task. The smoke-room on the promenade deck was removed to give more deck space, and she took up service from June 1 and remained on the station till June 17 1933, when she was replaced by the new *Brittany*. She returned to Southampton on June 19 1933, bringing from Jersey the official party who had travelled in the *Brittany*, and was then laid up. She was sold to T.W. Ward for £2,490 and left Southampton on Saturday October 28 1933 towed by the tug *Seaman*, bound for Pembroke where she was broken up.

A newspaper article, dated November 21 1934,

As can be seen from this photograph of her leaving Jersey in 1898, Vera was a most handsome vessel when built (John Attwood).

Twenty-eight years later Vera *still presents a spick and span appearance, albeit with different colours and flying the GWR house flag, as she approaches Weymouth (John Attwood).*

stated that a mast from the ship had been presented by a member of the Hendon Golf Club for use near the clubhouse.

Victoria

Owner London & South Western Railway. **Builder** J. & G. Thomson Ltd, Clydebank. **Completed** July 1896, **Yard no** 297. **Tonnage** 1896 709 g, 157 n; 1904 710 g, 138 n (altered to 302 n in 1914). **Dimensions** 220.5 (rl) × 28.15 × 16.3 ft. **Propulsion** Twin screw, SR, 3 cyl 13½" 24" 33"–24" 1,500 ihp. **Speed** 16 knots.

The *Victoria* was built to replace the two vessels which had hitherto maintained the services from Jersey to Granville and St Malo. Launched on May 15 1896 she arrived at Southampton on July 18, and made a demonstration trip to Jersey and Guernsey between July 25–27 before arriving back in Jersey on July 31, ready to make her maiden voyage to France on August 1 1896.

She remained on the Jersey station until November 24 1903, when she proceeded to Southampton where she was altered for duties as a liner tender at Plymouth. The mainmast was removed, the forward lifeboats moved to a new poop-deck built aft and rails were put around the boat deck so that

passengers could use the whole of the area. She sailed for Plymouth on March 25 1904 and from there, apart from her tender duties, she also operated excursions. In 1907 the purpose-built *Atalanta* took over the duties at Plymouth in May, which allowed the *Victoria* to again take up her position at Jersey, though her mast was replaced and other alterations made before she arrived in the islands on June 29 1907. She relieved the *Atalanta* during the winter months but this ceased after an agreement over services reached between the L & SWR and the GWR in 1910.

The ship stayed on the Jersey station until November 28 1914, when she sailed for Portsmouth where she became a 'Q' ship, despite the local paper claiming that she was to be used as a pilots' home. The ship arrived back in Jersey on January 11 1915 and then remained on the station until September 17 1918, when she was replaced by the *Laura*, and the following month was again taken over for naval duties being renamed *Surf II*. She was in the process of being converted when the Armistice was signed and was then returned to her owners.

With the closing of the Jersey–France service, there was no requirement for the *Victoria* and it was decided to sell her at the Baltic Exchange auction to be held in April 1919, but she was not sold as she did not reach the reserve price. On May 29 1919 she was sold to James Dredging, Towage & Transport Co, which had offered £16,500, but she did not remain long with them, being replaced by the *Lydia*. The ship was sold on the October 20 1920 to J. &

Above Victoria *ready to leave Southampton for tender duties at Plymouth (John Attwood).*

Below Victoria *entering Granville, after 1907 (A.M.S. Russell).*

Above Viking III *moving at speed on May 14 1980 (Author).*

Below *The ungainly bulk of* Viking Trader *approaches St Helier on July 7 1981 (Author).*

M. Constant who operated the ship in Turkish waters and the Black Sea, and she was seen by a Jersey resident in mid-1923 at Constantinople looking very smart and being used, it is stated, as a senior naval officer's despatch boat! On November 11 1926, her register was closed upon being sold to 'The Patriotic' Cie de Nav à Vap et d'Armement of Greece which was managed by K. Kallias & L. Teryazos, and the ship came fully under the Teryazos name before being broken up late in 1937, having retained the name *Victoria* to the end.

Viking III

Owner Thoresen Car Ferries A/S, Oslo. **Built** 1965. **Tonnage** 3,824 g. **Dimensions** 326'5" (oa) × 60' 1".

This ship arrived in the Channel Islands for the first time from Portsmouth on May 13 1980 and maintained the service for a week, her last sailing from the islands being on May 20. She was on service due to the *Earl William* having generator troubles.

Viking Trader

Owner Stena Line A/B, Sweden (chartered to Townsend Thoresen). **Built** 1971. **Tonnage** 1,600 g. **Dimensions** 347' 9" (oa) × 52' 7".

This freight ro/ro vessel was chartered to help cover the Portsmouth–Channel Islands route during the time that the *Earl Granville* and *Earl William* were off service in July 1981. The ship arrived in the Channel Islands for the first time on July 7 and sailed from them for the last time on July 14 1981.

Viking Victory

Owner Thoresen Car Ferries A/S, Oslo. **Built** 1964. **Tonnage** 3,671 g. **Dimensions** 326' 5" (oa) × 60' 1".

This ship was chartered due to the *Earl Godwin* being strike-bound during overhaul. She covered the Weymouth–Channel Islands route for the first time on April 3 1978 and took her last sailing from the islands on April 29.

Vulture

Owner Great Western Railway, Milford. **Built** 1864. **Tonnage** 1873 793 g; 1881 798 g. **Dimensions** 243.2 (rl) × 25.7 ft.

The ship acted at times as relief vessel on the Weymouth–Cherbourg route which operated between August 1878 and June 1885.

Waterford

Owner Great Western Railway. **Built** 1912. **Tonnage** 1,233 g. **Dimensions** 275.2 (rl) × 38.2 ft.

This ship was built for the Fishguard–Waterford service and only had one short period on the Chan-

Above right Waterford *was at Weymouth for a short period in 1920 (John Attwood).*

Right *A dramatically lit Ouless painting of* Waverley, *showing her off Corbières (John Vint).*

Below right Waverley *at the dockside in St Peter Port (John Attwood).*

Below Viking Victory *leaving Jersey on April 22 1978, with the Sealink house flag and funnel emblem (Author).*

nel Islands service. She came to Weymouth in May 1920 to operate on the Guernsey fruit trade and arrived in Jersey on May 22 to operate the potato season but, during the day, orders came for her to return to Fishguard which she did that evening. She made a few trips to Jersey in 1923 to convey cattle which were being exported but, apart from that, she was not seen again in the islands.

Waverley

Owner London & South Western Railway. **Builder** A. & J. Inglis, Glasgow. **Completed** June 1865. **Yard no** n/a. **Tonnage** 1868 593 g, 277 n. **Dimensions** 222.2 (rl) × 26.85 × 13.65 ft. **Propulsion** Paddles, 2 cyl 62″ 62″–72″ 280 hp. **Speed** 13 knots.

Built in 1865 for the Silloth–Dublin route of the North British SP Co, a service which proved unsuccessful, the *Waverley* was acquired in August 1868 by the L & SWR. Following a refit at Southampton, she ran trials on December 18 and sailed for the Channel Islands on the 21st but due to bad weather did not arrive in Jersey until December 23, under the command of Captain Goodridge who made only two further voyages before retiring.

The ship spent most of her time on the Channel Islands route, but did have some spells on the Le Havre service.

The *Waverley* had a short life with the L & SWR as, when approaching Guernsey on June 5 1873, she struck the Platte Boue rock, off the north-east coast of the island, and the ship became a total loss though all the passengers and crew were saved.

Whitstable

Owner Southern Railway. **Builder** D. & W. Henderson & Co Ltd, Glasgow. **Completed** August 1925. **Yard no** 707M. **Tonnage** 1925 687 g, 270 n; 1939 688 g, 270 n; 1941 787 g, 289 n; 1947 858 g, 348 n; 1948 865 g, 310 n. **Dimensions** 220.6 (rl) 229.6 (oa) × 33.6 × 41.1 ft. **Propulsion** Twin screw, SR, 3 cyl 15″ 25″ 14″–24″ 1,850 ihp. **Speed** 15 knots.

Built for the cargo services across the Dover Strait, this ship was used during the evacuation of the Channel Islands and arrived at Southampton on July 14 1945 to help to restore services to the islands. She remained on the station until April 1947, returned in May 1948 and then remained on the Southampton strength, though she spent brief periods on other routes, and from May 1957 relieved at Weymouth during overhauls.

Her last voyage was to Jersey and she returned 'light' back to Southampton on March 25 1959. She did not remain there long, as she was sold for breaking up and arrived at Rotterdam on April 28 1959.

Winchester

Owner Southern Railway. **Builder** Wm Denny & Bros Ltd, Dumbarton. **Completed** November 1947. **Yard no** 1403. **Tonnage** 1,149 g, 424 n.

Whitstable *entering the harbour at Jersey on February 16 1957 (Author).*

Above Winchester *entering Jersey (Dave Hocquard).*

Below Wolf *entering Le Havre (John Atwood).*

Dimensions 230' 0" (bp) 251'6" (oa) × 37' 9" × 12' 9¼" draft. **Propulsion** Twin screw, 5-cyl oil engines 3,000 bhp. **Speed** 15 knots.

Built as a replacement for war losses, the *Winchester* was launched on March 21 1947 and was delivered on November 11. Her maiden voyage was to Jersey, where she arrived on December 2. In September 1949 the ship spent five weeks replacing the *London–Istanbul* on the car-ferry service from Dover/Folkestone.

On December 2 1955, she had a serious collision with the *Haslemere* in the Solent, causing severe damage to her bows. On March 1 1965, the ship was transferred to the Weymouth fleet and, in early September the following year, the ship went to Folkestone for a period to help out. On February 25 1970 the ship hit the Roustel Beacon off the east coast of Guernsey, causing severe damage to the tower.

With the move towards containerisation, she became obsolete and, after having spent the last few years on the Guernsey 'flower specials', the ship made a farewell call to both islands on December 29 1970. She was sold in April 1971 and renamed *Grida* at Weymouth on April 30. On May 5 she was again renamed, this time being called *Exeter* and sailed from Weymouth for Piraeus on May 16. There she was converted into a cruise ship and named *Radiosa* before entering service, being registered to the Allied Finance SA of Greece, and operated in the colours of the Chandis Group.

Wolf

Owner London & South Western Railway. **Builder** Robert Napier & Son, Glasgow. **Completed** (month n/a) 1863. **Yard no** n/a. **Tonnage** 1871 728 g, 420 n; 1873 731 g, 432 n; 1882 767 g, 445 n (altered to 345 n in 1883); 1888 732 g, 309 n; 1889 814 g, 387 n. **Dimensions** 242.7 (rl) × 27.2 × 13.8 ft. **Propulsion** Paddle, 2 cyl (piston size n/a); compounded 1873 2 cyl 33" 60"–72" 310 hp. **Speed** n/a.

Built in 1863 for G. & J. Burns of Glasgow for their service to Belfast, the ship had the misfortune to sink on October 16 1867 but was later raised.

On April 10 1871, it was announced that the L & SWR had purchased the vessel and she arrived at Southampton on May 5. After a short refit, she ran trials on May 23 and made her maiden voyage the next day on the St Malo route. She was sent to Glasgow for alterations in February 1873, which included the compounding of her machinery and she returned to her home port on September 29.

The ship remained on the St Malo route until 1874, when she moved to the Le Havre service where she remained until early 1894. She was then

laid up until July 1896, after which she was used as a hospital ship by the Southampton Corporation and moored in Southampton Docks. In April 1897 she was replaced in this role by the *Alliance* and was sold on the 27th of the month to a Mr J.J. King for £1,200 and was broken up, her register being closed on November 16 1897.

Wonder

Owner South Western Steam Packet Company. **Builder** Ditchburn & Mare, Blackwall. **Completed** September 1844. **Yard no** n/a. **Tonnage** 1844 251 g, 169 n; 1857 218 g, 137 n. **Dimensions** 158.0 (rl) × 20.6 × 13.8 ft. **Propulsion** Paddle, 3 cyl 53" 53" 53"–42" 160 hp. **Speed** n/a.

Wonder was one of the most renowned of vessels on the Channel Islands service due to her speed, which resulted in the ship being involved in trials and races with naval vessels of the day. She arrived at Southampton from her builder on October 4 1844 and, after trial runs to various ports, was placed on the Le Havre service.

The granting of the Channel Islands Royal Mail contract to the owners in 1845 led to the ship being sent to the islands, but her first voyage was dogged by trouble as, during it, she broke her paddle floats. The ship first arrived in Guernsey on May 4 and did not proceed to Jersey until the following day. She then spent most of her time on the Channel Islands route until the end of February 1848 when, relieved by new vessels, she returned to the Le Havre route. After this, she was little seen in the islands until 1856, at which time new tonnage took over the Le Havre route. She then acted as a relief vessel and also had spells on the L & SWR route from Weymouth.

In May 1858 she was collision with the *Havre* and, during the repairs necessitated by this, a new saloon was built on her aft deck. On July 11 1863, the ship arrived in Jersey to take up station in the islands and operate the service to St Malo, which the L & SWR had just taken over from the Jersey SP Co. She remained on these duties until December 8 1873 when she arrived from St Malo and sailed the same day for Southampton, where it was announced on December 29 that she had been sold for breaking up.

Worthing

Operator British Railways. **Built** 1928. **Tonnage** 2,343 g. **Dimensions** 304' 6" (oa) × 38' 7".

This ship came to the Channel Islands in 1949 and operated an excursion from Guernsey to Jersey for the International Road Race on April 28 and then the next day operated a service from the islands to Southampton as a special excursion for the Cup Final.

Above *An Ouless painting 1863, showing* Wonder *against the background of Elizabeth Castle, Jersey (Author).*

Below Worthing *came to the Channel Islands in April 1949 (Author).*

Appendices

1 Titles under which railway company services have operated

1842–1846	South Western Steam Packet Company.
1846–1862	New South Western Steam Navigation Company (leased by L & SWR from January 1 1849).
1862–1922	London & South Western Railway Company.
1889–1947	Great Western Railway.
1923–1947	Southern Railway.
1948–1964	British Railways.
1965–1977	British Rail, Shipping Services ⇌.
1978–	Sealink.

2 Masters of the fleet

Information contained in this list is compiled from the 'daily arrivals' list in the port of St Helier, the Jersey Pilotage lists, the Southampton newspapers and the minute books of the L & SWR held at the Public Record Office at Kew.

For most of the period under review, the masters remained in one ship until appointed to another, while at various levels of seniority some masters did nothing but relief duties.

As the fleet grew and more ships were required for the summer rush, it became customary for senior mates to be made acting masters during this period, reverting to Chief Officer for the winter. The dates given for the first command apply to the first time a master was seen at Jersey in command, the same applying for the first passenger command, though for the latter it is command of what I call a large passenger ship, not a passenger/cargo. Since the Second World War there has been a regular relief roster at Southampton, and that now applies at Weymouth. The former port required 18 masters during the summer while the services from Weymouth/Portsmouth require, at the moment, 16 masters at the peak of the schedule.

3 Southampton masters

Name	First command		Retired/Left	Died
	Cargo	Passenger		
Goodridge, J. (Sen)	—	1842	8.1854	26.2.1855
Goodridge, J. (Jun)	—	1842	12.1868	6.3.1876
Wrightson, P.	—	1842	—	—
Lewis, J.	—	1844	15.9.1873	11.6.1877
Paul, F.W.	—	1846	—	—
Babot, G.	—	1846	31.7.1864	16.5.1887
Priaulx	—	—	—	—
Harvey, H.B.	—	1846	→	Lost 17.3.1870
Smith, W.	—	1847	Ill 30.12.1867	—
Knight, J.	—	1849	12.1874	—
Goodridge, J.W.	—	1849	—	—
Clement, E.B.	1853	9.3.1880	—	—

| Name | First command | | Retired/Left | Died |
	Cargo	Passenger		
Turtle, W.	—	1855	→	28.5.1871
Cooper	—	1.1864	—	—
Mabb, R.C.	29.7.1864	1865	31.12.1894	4.1924
Wright	11.1864	1865	—	24.4.1866
Clement, G.B.	28.4.1865	1865	11.6.1880	—
Cross, A.J.	12.9.1865	1866	28.6.1880	—
Mortimer, H.D.	1.11.1865	—	1.1.1891	3.2.1924
Back, J.	9.9.1867	1867	→	Lost 17.3.1868
Merrells, T.	6.1867	1869	→	15.5.1892
Deal, G.	11.4.1868	—	→	26.9.1868
Le Menu	—	1868	→	19.2.1881
Lewis, G.H.	8.5.1869	1869	Ashore 1892	—
Williams, W.	1.9.1868	1871	4.11.1887	—
Heathcote, I.C.	21.9.1868	1882	31.1.1891	—
Day, G.	3.2.1869	1874	→	30.12.1880
Amy, P.	10.1868	—	—	—
Long, R.	1870	1875	2.1875	3.1876
Wareham, J.	1.1.1871	—	2.6.1874	1874
Stevenson, J.	1.1.1871	—	4.5.1883	—
Harris	1871	—	Last seen 1871	—
Turtle, W.C.	2.6.1874	—	21.8.1883	—
Allix, G.	8.1.1875	1876	Ashore 2.10.1907	11.3.1923
Lainson, T.	16.6.1874	1881	→	19.6.1898
Husher, G.	13.4.1875	—	Last seen 1879	—
Kemp, F.G.	1876	1885	21.6.1895	—
Gregory, W.	1876	1885	→	Lost 18.11.1905
Edom, F.	21.6.1880	—	1901	—
Dyer, J.	31.5.1880	10.1887	1903	—
Nutbeam, G.W.	1880	10.1892	1902	23.12.1913
Barrett, J.D.	1.7.1879	15.3.1880	24.3.1891	13.4.1891
Allix, F.	6.5.1881	—	→	17.1.1894
Vanderplank, C.	28.6.1880	1888	24.3.1905	—
Bishop, W.R.	15.6.1883	1892	10.1901	10.8.1903
Reeks, W.	1887	1893	→	Lost 30.3.1899
Le Bas, E.T.	—	20.4.1891	16.7.1895	—
Butt, J.	19.6.1891	1896	1899	—
Winter, J.	19.6.1891	1894	2.6.1913	—
Heathcote, J.R.	1.7.1895	—	Last seen 1895	—
Jones, A.	25.3.1893	1895	1902	—
Du Feu, P.	20.5.1893	1894	17.12.1914	14.4.1917
Coombs, L.S.	2.5.1893	1899	31.10.1912	—
Carter, R.	25.5.1895	1901	31.10.1911	—
Kernan, W.	23.8.1895	1902	24.12.1907	—
Forrester, H.	25.5.1895	1904	8.2.1910	—
Stride, A.H.	1.7.1896	1902	Ashore 1914 Retired 1926	18.3.1955
Harley, S.	8.6.1897	—	→	2.8.1903
Smith, E.T.	5.6.1900	1904	1.2.1929	—
Howe, A.E.	18.6.1902	1907	Ashore 1927	3.8.1946
Bunce, G.H.	24.6.1902	—	→	4.1909

| Name | First command | | Retired/Left | Died |
	Cargo	Passenger		
Nicholl, H.	1902	—	→	13.2.1907
Moore	1904	—	1904	
Lawry, H.E.	1904 (Plymouth tender)		18.6.1910	—
Popplewell, H.J.	17.4.1905	1908	31.8.1915	—
Pearson, A.E.	1.7.1905	—	→	Lost 18.11.1905
Holt, F.W.	1.6.1905	1908	1.11.1935	—
Kernan, H.E.	20.4.1905	1909	→	12.2.1919
Tubbs, F.E.	1906	30.11.1909	1909	
Large, R.J.	11.1906	1910	15.9.1939	—
Darnell, T.N.	11.1907	1911	31.11.1933	—
Berrows, C.	27.6.1907	—	→	Lost 4.4.1915
Green, E.J.	6.1909	—	31.12.1910	
Swan, J.	2.5.1910	1915	30.11.1934	—
Clark, J.A.	16.6.1910	1920	31.10.1923	—
Green, H.W.	12.10.1910	1923	31.12.1932	30.4.1935
Woods, E.	7.1910	—	1.3.1929	—
Harrison, A.	5.1912	—	28.2.1923	—
Keene, C.D.	27.6.1913	4.6.1927	1.5.1936	—
Smart, J.H.	16.7.1913	22.5.1929	31.12.1938	—
Harms	9.1.1915	—	9.12.1918	—
Turner, H.F.	15.7.1915	1.6.1927	1.12.1935	—
Midgley, W.D.	2.9.1915	5.4.1928	1.11.1934	20.4.1938
Lane, E.F.	9.6.1916	1.7.1931	31.1.1933	—
Pannett, P.H.	26.6.1923	10.3.1930	1.2.1937	—
Franklin, J.P.	8.5.1924	—	30.6.1927	—
Robert, G.E.	27.8.1931	—	4.5.1936	—
Carroll, C.E.	29.5.1925	—	26.11.1929	7.3.1935
Hodges, F.	31.5.1927	18.5.1934	1.6.1941	—
Bennett, H.M	22.6.1925	—	13.12.1928	—
Withers, J.E.	21.5.1929	23.5.1932	1.5.1941	—
Golding, H.H.	21.6.1927	28.7.1933	13.9.1947	—
Lewis, P.	1.7.1931	28.8.1933	11.6.1941	—
Whiting, M.C.	13.5.1929	28.7.1934	9.10.1946	4.1957
Harper, W.A.	1.8.1934	13.8.1935	10.1952	—
Mason, W.F.	11.7.1935	10.6.1936	18.2.1948	—
Trout, F.E.	6.6.1935	8.4.1936	12.8.1962	—
Light, A.	28.5.1936	19.5.1937	5.2.1956	8.1973
Pellow, H.J.	28.5.1936	20.7.1939	4.11.1940	—
Durley, C.E.	3.6.1937	18.8.1946	10.1955	15.5.1980
Pearce, G.	18.5.1937	31.5.1948	4.9.1954	8.12.1972
Breuilly, H.F.	11.7.1939	5.5.1949	→	18.7.1961
Abbey, C.A.	2.8.1939	8.11.1949	27.1.1956	—
Denny, D.R.	28.8.1947	1952	20.4.1956	—
O'Dell, C.	1.2.1948	—	8.7.1954	—
Large, R.A.	1.5.1948	1952	Ashore 21.7.1956	—
Hatchley, C.E.	28.5.1948	1954	12.1965	2.1982
Le Huquet, H.G.	19.8.1949	1956	12.1965	1977
Whitney, J.W.	20.8.1949	—	1949	—
Jones, J.W.	30.8.1949	—	→	27.12.1954

Name	First command		Retired/Left	Died
	Cargo	Passenger		
Dove, P.C.	4.7.1950	1955	Ashore 2.10.1956	—
Cantle, F.J.	16.8.1950	31.5.1956	Ashore 1961	—
Caws, B.A.	4.8.1952	6.11.1956	To Weymouth 1966	—
Hewson, E.F.	26.5.1955	—	1.12.1955	—
Campbell, G.H.	2.7.1955	17.7.1956	To Newhaven 1964	—
Picot, B.A.	21.6.1955	13.6.1959	To Weymouth 1966	—
Wolley, H.L.	23.5.1956	11.9.1957	4.1964	—
Moir, A.B.	8.6.1956	19.9.1957	12.1965	—
Kroon, C.A.	23.6.1956	—	To Dover 1963	—
Watson, L.G.	3.6.1957	—	—	—
Bowen, R.C.	8.6.1957	—	To Newhaven 1964	—
Creed, C.F.	20.7.1957	—	To Weymouth 1966	—
Killinger, N.R.	7.9.1957	—	To Dover 1964	—

4 Weymouth masters from 1889

Name	Cargo	Passenger	Retired/Left	Died
Renouf, F.J.	—	1889	5.1896	19.6.1929
Painter, T.	—	1889	Taken ill 1895	—
Le Feuvre, J.	—	1889	7.1911	28.9.1920
Harley, S.	—	21.2.1895	To L & SWR 7.1896	—
Rumsey, J.	—	3.7.1895	1898	—
Breach, G.W.	—	19.6.1896	Taken ill 1903	23.8.1903
Burnard, J.S.	—	30.6.1896	1902	—
Vine, J.	—	15.6.1897	12.1917	10.1932
Baudains, J.	—	7.1897	1.1900	10.2.1906
Mulhall, W.	—	20.9.1899	→	17.3.1928
Langdon, C.H.	1905	1.6.1910	→	23.9.1927
Iverson	6.1906	—	—	5.4.1920
Imrie, J.R.	1910	—	Ashore 1911	—
Allen	3.9.1914	—	5.1.1927	—
Delanly, R.	1916	—	1920	—
Richardson, L.T.	9.11.1920	9.1927	24.9.1955	—
Bell, C.	1921	1927	12.1927	—
Pitman, R.R.	8.1927	17.11.1927	30.4.1959	—
Joy, C.	12.1927	1933	1936	—
Sanderson, C.W.	1928	1931	5.1940	—
Bond, H.C.	1930	6.6.1937	24.2.1952	—
Halliday	1930	—	1933	—
Larbalestier, W.V.	1933	1939	5.1949	1.10.1952
Freeman	1939	—	4.1948	—
Goodchild, J.P.	17.2.1946	7.1953	1.1962	—
Hawkyard, E.K.	30.10.1947	28.5.1949	Taken ill, 23.6.1953	—
Newton, V.	19.10.1949	30.6.1953	—	—
Cartwright, G.	1.1.1952	11.4.1956	—	—
Walker, H.	16.9.1952	28.9.1958	—	—
Masters, A.W.	10.3.1956	—	4.7.1957	—
Manning, G.	14.8.1958	1.9.1961	—	—
Laity, W.P.	2.5.1960	22.8.1962	—	—
Hurd-Wood, M.	2.8.1961	—	—	—
Rymill, R.	31.5.1962	—	—	—

5 Masters at Southampton and Weymouth stations (amalgamated March 1 1966)

Name	First command		Retired/Left	Died
	Cargo	Passenger		
Newton, V.	19.10.1949	30.6.1953	28.2.1968	7.8.1977
Cartwright, G.	1.1.1952	11.4.1956	2.1.1967	—
Walker, H.	16.9.1952	28.9.1958	Ashore 4.2.1974	—
Caws, B.	4.8.1952	6.11.1956	26.11.1973	2.1982
Picot, B.A.	21.6.1955	13.6.1959	15.9.1974	—
Manning, G.	14.8.1958	1.9.1961	22.8.1968	—
Laity, W.P.	2.5.1960	22.8.1962	17.5.1974	31.7.1981
Creed, F.	20.7.1957	1.7.1969	7.10.1974	—
Hurd-Wood, M.	2.8.1961	23.7.1970	—	—
Rymill, R.	31.5.1962	—	14.5.1971	—
Baker, P.	22.8.1966	6.7.1973	—	—
Escudier, A.J.	19.5.1968	27.7.1973	22.3.1979	—
Barker, C.	10.3.1969	23.7.1973	31.12.1982	—
Atkins, P.	28.5.1969	—	→	5.11.1969
Macmillan, J.	3.7.1970	22.5.1974	—	—
Attwood, J.O.	21.10.1970	26.5.1974	—	—
Leale, M.	7.7.1972	25.7.1974	—	—
Mills, M.	24.5.1974	8.8.1974	—	—
Milward, A.	24.7.1974	17.5.1975	—	—
Hanfield, M.	4.8.1974	2.7.1975	16.11.1976	—
Scott, M.	30.4.1975	11.7.1975	—	—
Davies, J.	19.5.1975	11.8.1975	—	—
Evans, G.	1.7.1975	21.5.1977	—	—
Bill, T.	20.7.1975	3.7.1977	—	—
Craythorne, P.R.	21.7.1975	10.7.1977	—	—
Weston, P.R.	13.6.1976	13.5.1978	—	—
Filor, C.W.	4.7.1977	27.6.1978	12.10.1982	—
Wallbridge, J.	25.7.1977	12.9.1979	—	—
Musset, B.	—	2.8.1979	—	—
Owen, S.J.	—	19.4.1983	—	—
Penson, J.R.	—	18.4.1983	—	—
Williams, J.R.	—	3.7.1983	—	—

Acknowledgements

In researching this work I have visited many establishments and I would like to thank the staffs of the following for their help and kindness during my visits: the City of London, Guildhall Library; the Guille-Allez Library, St Peter Port; the Harbour Office, St Helier; the Harbour Office, St Peter Port; Lloyds Register of Shipping (Information Services); the Public Library (Reference Section), St Helier; the Public Record Office, Kew; the Registrar of Shipping, Southampton; The South-ampton Reference Library, Civic Centre; and the University of Glasgow Archives.

I must also thank the masters who have gone back through their personal records to provide informa-tion. Additionally, I wish to express my gratitude to those who provided me with hospitality, during my many weeks of research in England, and to those who have allowed me the use of their paintings and photographs, and in particular the following for help with information and illustrations: Dave Hocquard; Arthur Russell; Société Jersiaise; Southampton City Museums; John Winser; and Keith Pyman. Finally, I would like to thank the staff of British Rail/Sealink for their courtesy and unfail-ing helpfulness.

No writer achieves anything without the support of his family and, thus, to my wife and children go my thanks for not only keeping quiet at the right times, but also for reading the text and for translating the old French language newspapers that were an information source for the early period of this work.

Lastly, my sincere thanks go to John Attwood who, over the years, has become a close friend, and without whose help and encouragement this book would not be so complete or so richly illustrated.

Index

Note: in this index, page numbers in
bold type denote main ship entries;
numbers in *italics* denote an
illustration.

A moment of history as the first car ferry, Falaise, *passes the passenger ship,* Sarnia, *in St Aubin's Bay, Jersey, on May 25 1973 (Author).*